CONSOLATION IN PHILIPPIANS

Rhetorical criticism seeks to understand and comment on the way texts function in their social and cultural contexts. Paul A. Holloway puts Paul's letter in the context of ancient theories and literary practices of "consolation" and argues that Paul wrote to the Philippians in order to console them. He shows that the letter has a unified overall strategy and provides a convincing account of Paul's argument.

The book falls into two parts. Part I explores the integrity of Philippians, the rhetorical situation of the letter, and ancient consolation as the possible genre of Philippians, while part II examines Philippians 1:3–11; 1:12–2:30; 3:1–4:1, and 4:2–23. The exegetical studies in part II focus on the consolatory *topoi* and arguments of Philippians.

PAUL A. HOLLOWAY is Assistant Professor in the Department of Religion at Samford University. He has published in *Harvard Theological Review*, *Novum Testamentum*, and *Journal of Biblical Literature*.

SOCIETY FOR NEW TESTAMENT STUDIES

MONOGRAPH SERIES

General Editor: Richard Bauchkam

112

CONSOLATION IN PHILIPPIANS

Consolation in Philippians,

Philosophical Sources and Rhetorical Strategy

PAUL A. HOLLOWAY

Samford University
Birmingham, Alabama

CAMBRIDGE
UNIVERSITY PRESS

PUBLISHED BY THE PRESS SYNDICATE OF THE UNIVERSITY OF CAMBRIDGE
The Pitt Building, Trumpington Street, Cambridge, United Kingdom

CAMBRIDGE UNIVERSITY PRESS
The Edinburgh Building, Cambridge CB2 2RU, UK
40 West 20th Street, New York NY 10011–4211, USA
10 Stamford Road, Oakleigh, VIC 3166, Australia
Ruiz de Alarcón 13, 28014 Madrid, Spain
Dock House, The Waterfront, Cape Town 8001, South Africa

http://www.cambridge.org

First published 2001

Printed in the United Kingdom at the University Press, Cambridge

Typeface 10/12pt Times Roman   *System* 3B2   [CE]

A catalogue record for this book is available from the British Library

Library of Congress cataloguing in publication data

Holloway, Paul A.
Consolation in Philippians: philosophical sources and rhetorical strategy /
Paul A. Holloway.
    p.   cm. (Monograph series / Society for New Testament Studies; 112)
Includes bibliographical references and index.
ISBN 0 521 80406 X (hardback)
1. Bible. N.T. Philippians – Socio-rhetorical criticism.
2. Consolation in the Bible.
I. Title.
II. Monograph series (Society for New Testament Studies); 112.
BS2705.6.C584 H65 2001
227′6066–dc21   00–054720 CIP

ISBN 0 521 80406 X hardback

For Melissa

and for Chapney and Abigail and Callie

CONTENTS

ACKNOWLEDGMENTS

This book is a slightly revised version of my University of Chicago dissertation which was accepted in the fall of 1998. I would like to thank again the members of my committee: Professor Adela Yarbro Collins (chair), Professor Elizabeth Asmis, and Professor Arthur Droge. It is difficult to imagine a group of more cordial and talented mentors. I would also like to thank Professor Clark and Nancy Gilpin, former Masters of Burton-Judson Courts, for four happy years in Linn House, and the Delores Liebmann Foundation for a generous dissertation grant. The final preparation of the manuscript was aided by a Faculty Development Grant from Samford University. It is impossible to express adequately the thanks due to my wife Melissa, and to our children, Chapney, Abigail, and Callie – *a quibus didici gaudere*.

ABBREVIATIONS

The following table contains standard references cited only by abbreviation in the notes and those periodicals for which abbreviations are not given in "Instructions for Contributors," *Journal of Biblical Literature* 107 (1988) 579–96. References to papyri should be decipherable on the basis of F. Preisigke and E. Kiessling, *Wörterbuch der griechischen Papyrusurkunden*, 4 vols. (Berlin; Göttingen: Selbstverlag, 1925–44) vol. I:x–xii. and vol. IV:vii–x, and Supplement 1 (Amsterdam: Hakkert, 1971) vii–xii, and Supplement 2 (Wiesbaden: Harrasowitz, 1991) vii–xi.

ABD   *The Anchor Bible Dictionary*, 6 vols., ed. David Noel Freedman (New York: Doubleday, 1992).

AFLA   *Annales de la Faculté des Lettres et Sciences Humaines d'Aix.*

ALCP   *Annali del Liceo classico G. Garibaldi di Palermo.*

ANRW   *Aufstieg und Niedergang der römischen Welt*, ed. H. Temporini and W. Haase (Berlin and New York: De Gruyter, 1972–).

APAW   Abhandlungen. Preussische Akademie der Wissenschaften.

APOT   *Apocrypha and Pseudepigrapha of the Old Testament in English*, 2 vols., ed. R. H. Charles (Oxford: Clarendon, 1913).

BAGD   W. Bauer, *A Greek–English Lexicon of the New Testament and Other Early Christian Literature*, translated, adapted, revised, and augmented by W. F. Arndt, F. W. Gingrich, and F. W. Danker (Chicago: University of Chicago Press, 1979).

BDF   F. Blass and A. Debrunner, *A Greek Grammar of the New Testament and Other Early Christian Literature*,

	translated and revised by R. W. Funk (Chicago: University of Chicago Press, 1961).
BT	Bibliotheca Teubneriana.
C&M	*Classica et Mediaevalia.*
CBull	*Classical Bulletin.*
CCSL	Corpus Christianorum series latina (Turnhout, 1953–).
CP	*Classical Philology.*
CQ	*Classical Quarterly.*
CSEL	Corpus scriptorum ecclesiasticorum latinorum (Vienna, 1866–).
DK	H. Diels and W. Kranz, eds., *Die Fragmente der Vorsokratiker*, 3 vols., 6th edn. (Berlin: Weidmann, 1974–75).
G&R	*Greece and Rome.*
LCL	Loeb Classical Library.
LSJ	H. G. Liddell, R. Scott, and H. S. Jones, *A Greek–English Lexicon*, 9th ed. (Oxford: Clarendon, 1940).
MH	*Museum Helveticum.*
MM	J. H. Moulton, and G. Milligan. *The Vocabulary of the Greek New Testament Illustrated from the Papyri and Other Non-Literary Sources* (London: Hodder, 1930).
NPNF	Nicene and Post-Nicene Fathers.
NTApoc	*New Testament Apocrypha*, 2 vols., ed. E. Hennecke and W. Schneemelcher, trans. R. McL. Wilson (Philadelphia: Westminster, 1992).
OCD	*Oxford Classical Dictionary*, 2nd edn., ed. N. G. L. Hammond and H. H. Scullard (Oxford: Oxford University Press, 1974).
OCT	Bibliotheca Oxoniensis (Oxford Classical Texts).
OSAP	*Oxford Studies in Ancient Philosophy.*
PG	*Patrologia Graeca*, ed. J.-P. Migne (Paris, 1857–66).
PGL	*A Patristic Greek Lexicon*, ed. G. W. H. Lampe (Oxford: Clarendon, 1961).
PhoenSup	Phoenix Supplement.
PL	*Patrologia Latina*, ed. J.-P. Migne (Paris, 1844–64).
PMG	*Poetae Melici Graeci*, ed. D. L. Page (Oxford: Clarendon, 1962).
QJS	*Quarterly Journal of Speech.*
RAC	*Reallexikon für Antike und Christentum*, ed.

	T. Klauser, E. Dassmann, et al. (Stuttgart: Hierse-mann, 1950–).
RE (PW)	*Paulys Realencyclopädie der classischen Altertumswissenschaft*, ed. G. Wissowa, W. Kroll, et al. 24 vols., 19 vols., and supplement (15 vols.) (Stuttgart: Metzler; Munich: Druckenmüller, 1893–1980).
RGG	*Die Religion in Geschichte und Gegenwart*, 3rd edn., ed. K von Galling. 6 vols. (Tübingen: Mohr [Siebeck]) 1957–62.
RThPh	*Revue de Théologie et de Philosophie.*
SVF	*Stoicorum Vetera Fragmenta*, ed. Hans F. A. von Arnim (Leipzig: Teubner, 1905–24).
TDNT	*Theological Dictionary of the New Testament*, ed. G. Kittel, trans. G. Bromiley. 10 vols. (Grand Rapids: Eerdmans, 1964–76).
TrGF	*Tragicorum Graecorum Fragmenta*, ed. B. Snell and S. Radt (Göttingen: Vandenhoeck & Ruprecht, 1971–77).
TWNT	*Theologisches Wörterbuch zum Neuen Testament*, ed. G. Kittel (Stuttgart: Kohlhammer, 1935–79).
YCS	*Yale Classical Studies.*

INTRODUCTION

The following study seeks to understand Paul's letter to the Philippians as an ancient letter of consolation (ἐπιστολὴ παρα-μυθητική). It requires little by way of introduction, except perhaps to alert the reader (1) to the difference between the ancient and modern notions of consolation and (2) to the working definition of genre that has been assumed.

According to modern usage there is little difference, if any, between consolation and sympathy. To console someone is for all practical purposes to sympathize with them in their loss. But the ancient Greeks and Romans carefully distinguished between these terms. Ancient consolers were by no means unsympathetic to those afflicted with grief; however, they understood their primary task to be not one of sharing in the grief of others, but one of removing that grief by rational argument and frank exhortation. Plutarch expresses the typical sentiment:[1]

> For we do not have need of those who, like tragic choruses, weep and wail with us in unwanted circumstances, but of those who will speak to us frankly and instruct us that grief and self-abasement are in every circumstance useless, serving no purpose and showing no sense.

In extreme cases ancient consolation even took the form of open rebuke, as when Seneca upbraids Marullus:[2]

> You are expecting some words of comfort? Receive a scolding instead! You are taking your son's death in a weak and unworthy manner.

[1] *De ex.* 599B: οὐ γὰρ συνδακρυόντων καὶ συνεπιθρηνούντων ὥσπερ χορῶν τραγικῶν ἐν τοῖς ἀβουλήτοις χρείαν ἔχομεν, ἀλλὰ παρρησιαζομένων καὶ διδασ-κόντων ὅτι τὸ λυπεῖσθαι καὶ τὸ ταπεινοῦν ἑαυτὸν ἐπὶ παντὶ μὲν ἄχρηστόν ἐστι καὶ γιγνόμενον κενῶς καὶ ἀνοήτως.
[2] *Ep.* 99.2: *Solacia expectas? Convicia accipe. Molliter tu fers mortem filii.*

We shall discuss the ancient notion of consolation in more detail below in chapter 3. At this point, however, the reader should be aware that this study employs the term consolation throughout in the ancient sense of combating grief through rational means.

In identifying Philippians as an ancient letter of consolation I mean only that Paul wrote to the Philippians in order to console them (in the ancient sense of the term) and that his letter may be compared helpfully with other ancient documents, including but not limited to other letters, composed for similar consolatory purposes. In other words, I have focused on the broader and, at this point in the discussion, more fruitful questions of function and content and have left aside the question of form, which by most accounts, at least in modern biblical studies, is central to the definition of genre. I do not doubt that a fuller description of the genre of Philippians is possible. It also seems reasonable to me that Philippians might be discussed helpfully in terms of other modalities, say, as a "letter of friendship" (ἐπιστολὴ φιλική)[3] – it was certainly the duty of friends to console one another – or as a kind of "Familienbrief."[4] It is my view, however, that Philippians is first and foremost a letter of consolation and that these and any other generic descriptions identify what are at best secondary modes of discourse.

Special mention should be made of two works on ancient consolation upon which I have relied heavily: Rudolf Kassel, *Untersuchungen zur griechishen und römischen Konsolationsliteratur* (Zetemata 18; Munich: Beck, 1958) and J. H. D. Scourfield, *Consoling Heliodorus. A Commentary on Jerome "Letter 60"* (Oxford and New York: Clarendon Press and Oxford University Press, 1993). I have also taken direction on more than a few points

---

[3] For a survey of the scholarship as well as a thoughtful critique of this view, see John Reumann, "Philippians, Especially Chapter 4, as a 'Letter of Friendship': Observations on a Checkered History of Scholarship," in John T. Fitzgerald, ed., *Friendship, Flattery, and Frankness of Speech: Studies on Friendship in the New Testament World* (NovTSup 82; Leiden, Brill, 1996) 83–106. The presence of friendship language, especially friendship clichés, in Philippians is striking and should be addressed in any comprehensive account of the letter. However, it has not always been duly noted that this language often pertains not to Paul's own relationship with the church, which is what we should expect if Philippians were a letter of friendship between Paul and the Philippians, but to relationships within the Philippian community.

[4] Loveday Alexander, "Hellenistic Letter-Forms and the Structure of Philippians," *JSNT* 37 (1989) 87–101. For the category "Familienbrief," cf. Heikki Koskenniemi, *Studien zur Idee und Phraseologie des griechischen Briefes bis 400 n. Chr.* (Helsinki: Kirjakauppa; Wiesbaden: Harrassowitz, 1956) 104–14.

from John Chrysostom's insightful *In Epistolam ad Philippenses commentarius* (*PG* 62.177–298). I regret that Troels Engberg-Pedersen's bold and insightful book, *Paul and the Stoics* (Edinburgh: T. & T. Clark; Louisville: Westminster John Knox Press, 2000), appeared too late to be used in this study.

The following study falls into two parts. Part I is entitled "Literary and rhetorical contexts." It consists of three chapters and treats in order: the integrity of Philippians, the "rhetorical situation" of Philippians, and ancient consolation as the possible genre of Philippians. Part II, which is entitled "Consolation in Philippians," consists of four chapters and is exegetical. It treats in order: Phil. 1:3–11; 1:12–2:30; 3:1–4:1; and 4:2–23. Needless to say, the exegetical studies in part II are selective, focusing on the consolatory *topoi* and arguments of Philippians.

Part I

LITERARY AND RHETORICAL CONTEXTS

1

THE INTEGRITY OF PHILIPPIANS

The literary integrity of Philippians is much debated and must be discussed prior to any study of the letter.[1] It is particularly relevant to our study which argues that the prayer-report of Phil. 1:9–11 is programmatic for the argument of each of the alleged letter-fragments and gives to the canonical letter both a logical and a thematic unity. In this initial chapter we shall examine the case for partitioning. We shall argue that it has not been successfully made and that, on the evidence, it is reasonable to approach Philippians as a unity.

Modern critical reconstructions of Philippians have typically understood it to be a composite of three separate letters,[2] the first two of which at least were written while Paul was in prison. These are, in chronological order: Letter A (4:10–20), a short thank-you

[1] The literary integrity of Philippians was questioned by scholars in the nineteenth and early twentieth centuries, but most dismissed the question as inappropriate given Philippians' casual and letter-like quality. As the image of Paul the letter-writer changed, however, the allegedly disjointed nature of Philippians became a problem. The modern debate over the integrity of the epistle derives from four apparently independent studies published between 1957 and 1960: W. Schmithals, "Die Irrlehrer des Philipperbriefes," *ZTK* 54 (1957) 297–341; revised for *Paulus und die Gnostiker* (TF 35; Hamburg-Bergstedt: Herbert Reich, 1965) 47–87; Eng. trans., "The False Teachers of the Epistle to the Philippians," in *idem, Paul and the Gnostics* (Nashville: Abingdon, 1972) 65–122; J. Müller-Bardorf, "Zur Frage der literarischen Einheit des Philipperbriefes," *WZJena* 7 (1957–58) 591–604; B. D. Rahtjen, "The Three Letters of Paul to the Philippians," *NTS* (1959–60) 167–73; and F. W. Beare, *A Commentary on the Epistle to the Philippians* (London: A. & C. Black, 1959). Subsequent studies have added little to the case for partitioning. On the early debate, see the recent clarifications by David Cook, "Stephanus Le Moyne and the Dissection of Philippians," *JTS* 32 (1981) 138–42; V. Koperski, "The Early History of the Dissection of Philippians," *JTS* 44 (1993) 599–603.

[2] For the two-letter hypothesis, see Joachim Gnilka, *Der Philipperbrief* (HTKNT 10/3; Freiburg: Herder, 1968) 7–10; G. Friedrich, *Der Brief an die Philipper* (NTD 8; 15th edn.; Göttingen: Vandenhoeck & Ruprecht, 1981) 126–8. Gnilka: Letter A: 1:1–3:1a; 4:2–7, 10–23; Letter B: 3:1b–4:1, 8–9. Friedrich: Letter A: 1:1–3:1a; 4:10–23; Letter B: 3:1b–4:9.

note sent immediately after the arrival of Epaphroditus with a gift from the Philippians; Letter B (1:1–3:1), a letter of reassurance sent upon the return of Epaphroditus; and Letter C (3:2–4:3), a polemical letter or *Kampfbrief* sent at some later date (perhaps after his release) when Paul had become more fully apprised of the theological dangers facing the Philippians. The remaining material in 4:4–9 and 4:21–3 is variously assigned, though usually 4:4–7 and 21–3 are assigned to Letter B.[3] Evidence adduced in support of this hypothesis falls into three categories: (1) various pieces of external evidence suggesting either directly or indirectly that Philippians is a composite; (2) internal evidence pointing to 3:2–4:3 as the fragment of a separate letter; and (3) further internal evidence pointing to 4:10–20 as another fragment. We shall consider these in order.

External evidence that Philippians is a composite

The evidence for partitioning Philippians is primarily internal. Nevertheless, four pieces of external evidence have been adduced in support of the theory that Philippians is a composite. Three of these support the more general claim that Paul wrote more than one letter to the church at Philippi.[4] They are: (1) the listing of Philippians twice in the *Catalogus Sinaiticus*;[5] (2) the mention of a "first epistle to the Philippians" in the *Chronographia* of the ninth-century Byzantine historian Georgius Syncellus;[6] and (3) a reference by Polycarp at *Ad Phil.* 3.2 to Paul's "letters" (ἐπιστολάς) to the Philippians.[7] Only the third of these, Polycarp's much-discussed plural, is of any historical value.[8] It is uncertain, however, what

---

[3] See the table in Lukas Bormann, *Philippi. Stadt und Christengemeinde zur Zeit des Paulus* (NovTSup 78; Leiden: Brill, 1995) 110.

[4] Rahtjen, "Three Letters," 167–8. Rahtjen's evidence is typically relegated to the footnotes, even by those who partition the letter: Gnilka, *Philipperbrief*, 11 n. 57; Schmithals, *Paul and the Gnostics*, 81 n. 59.

[5] A. S. Lewis, ed., *Catalogue of the Syriac MSS. in the Convent of S. Catherine on Mount Sinai* (Studia Sinaitica 1; London: C. J. Clay, 1894) 4–16.

[6] W. Dindorf, ed., *Corpus Scriptorum Historiae Byzantinae* (Bonn: Weber, 1828) XII:651 (= 420.14 Mosshammer): Τούτου [Κλήμεντος] καὶ ὁ ἀπόστολος ἐν τῇ πρὸς Φιλιππησίους μέμνηται πρώτῃ ἐπιστολῇ εἰπών, μετὰ καὶ Κλήμεντος καὶ τῶν λοιπῶν συνεργῶν μου. Taken at face value this citation actually counts against the partition theory, since it assigns Phil. 4:3, Letter C according to the critical reconstruction, to ἡ πρὸς Φιλιππησίους πρώτη ἐπιστολή.

[7] *Ad Phil.* 3.2: ὃς [Παῦλος] καὶ ἀπὼν ὑμῖν ἔγραψεν ἐπιστολάς, εἰς ἃς ἐὰν ἐγκύπτητε, δυνηθήσεσθε οἰκοδομεῖσθαι εἰς τὴν δοθεῖσαν ὑμῖν πίστιν.

[8] The double listing of Philippians in the *Catalogus*, which in its first mention is assigned the same number of stichoi (318) as Ephesians which immediately precedes

contribution, if any, such evidence can make to the debate over the integrity of Philippians, since all parties readily admit the likelihood of additional correspondence.[9]

Recently Philip Sellew has introduced a fourth piece of external evidence that speaks more directly to the issue of partitioning.[10] Noting that the pseudepigraphic *Epistle to the Laodiceans*,[11] which draws upon Philippians for both its content and structure,[12] contains no reference either to Letter C (Phil. 3:2–4:3 + 4:7–9) or to Letter A (Phil. 4:10–20) of the critical reconstruction, he concludes that the compiler of *Laodiceans* used a version of Philippians lacking both of these fragments and thus similar to Letter B (Phil. 1:1–3:1 + 4:4–6 + 4:20–3). There are at least two major problems with Sellew's analysis.[13]

---

it, is an obvious case of parablepsis (note also the careless omission of 1 Timothy); B. Metzger, *The Canon of the New Testament* (Oxford: Clarendon, 1987) 221 n. 27; A. Souter, *The Text and Canon of the New Testament*, rev. edn. by C. S. C. Williams (London: Duckworth, 1954) 209 n. 3. Syncellus is unreliable and late; B. S. Mackay "Further Thoughts on Philippians," *NTS* 7 (1961) 162.

[9] Various explanations of Polycarp's plural have been offered. J. B. Lightfoot, ed., *The Apostolic Fathers* (London and New York: Macmillan, 1889) II/3:327, 348, argues that it is a plural used idiomatically for the singular. T. Zahn, *Introduction to the New Testament*, trans. from 3rd German edn., 3 vols. (New York: Scribners, 1909) I:535–6, suggests that it may refer to an early collection of Paul's letters to Macedonia and thus include the Thessalonian correspondence. Walter Bauer, *Die apostolischen Väter*, vol II: *Die Briefe des Ignatius von Antiochien und der Polykarpbrief* (HNT 18; Tübingen: Mohr [Siebeck], 1920) 287, wonders quite plausibly whether Polycarp has simply inferred the presence of additional letters on the basis of 3:1 and Paul's long-standing relationship with the Philippians. Rahtjen, "Three Letters," 167, believes that Polycarp had in his possession several letters from Paul to the Philippians, letters which he contends, on other grounds, were eventually compiled to form the canonical Philippians.

[10] "*Laodiceans* and the Philippians Fragments Hypothesis," *HTR* 87 (1994) 17–28.

[11] A critical text may be found in Rudolf Anger, *Über den Laodicenerbrief. Eine biblisch-kritische Untersuchung* (Leipzig: Gebhardt & Reisland, 1843) 155–65; J. B. Lightfoot, *St. Paul's Epistle to the Colossians and to Philemon* (London: Macmillan, 1892) 281–91; Eng. trans. in Wilhelm Schneemelcher, "The Epistle to the Laodiceans," in *NTApoc* II.42–6 (1992). It is debated whether *Laodiceans*, which survives in Latin and several late vernaculars, was originally composed in Greek or Latin. I agree with Sellew ("*Laodiceans*," 22), who follows Lightfoot (*Colossians*, 289–91), that *Laodiceans* was originally composed in Greek.

[12] Anger, *Laodicenerbrief*, 155–65; Lightfoot, *Colossians*, 293–4; Adolf von Harnack, *Marcion: Das Evangelium von fremden Gott* (Darmstadt: Wissenschaftliche Buchgesellschaft, 1960; reprint of 2nd edn., 1924) Beilage 3, 140; cf. Sellew, "*Laodiceans*," 28.

[13] For a more detailed discussion of these problems, see Paul A. Holloway, "The Apocryphal *Epistle to the Laodiceans* and the Partitioning of Philippians," *HTR* 91 (1998) 321–5, with response by Philip Sellew, "*Laodiceans* and Philippians Revisited: A Response to Paul Holloway," *HTR* 91 (1998) 327–9.

First, it seems that *Laodiceans* does in fact contain a reference to the so-called *Kampfbrief* of Phil. 3:2–4:3. The relevant text is *Laod.* 13, which reads: *Et quod [reliquum]*[14] *est, dilectissimi, gaudete in Christo et praecavete sordidos in lucro*, "And for the rest, beloved, rejoice in Christ and beware of those who are defiled in their pursuit of gain." A number of scholars see here a synthesis of Phil. 3:1 and 2, *gaudete* . . . *praecavete* repeating Paul's troubling χαίρετε . . . βλέπετε.[15] Lightfoot reconstructs the Greek: καὶ τὸ λοιπόν, ἀγαπητοί, χαίρετε ἐν Χριστῷ· βλέπετε δὲ τοὺς αἰσχρο-κερδεῖς.[16] Sellew rejects this interpretation on the grounds that the Vulgate translates the βλέπετε of Phil. 3:2 with *videte* not *praecavete*.[17] But this is beside the point, (1) because the Latin text of *Laodiceans* frequently departs from both the Vulgate and the Old Latin versions of Philippians,[18] and (2) because *Laodiceans* predates the Vulgate translation.[19] To the degree that the Latin translations of Philippians are relevant, a more pertinent question would have been how the Old Latin versions translate βλέπετε. At least one Old Latin version, Frede's Text Type I, derivable from Victorinus' Commentaries on Ephesians, Philippians, and Colossians, translates with the cognate *caveo* (*cavete a canibus*).[20]

---

[14] Mss: *Et quod est.* Anger, *Laodicenerbrief*, 163, supplies *reliquum*, as do Lightfoot, *Colossians*, 286, and Harnack, *Marcion*, Beilage 3, 137–8.

[15] Anger, *Laodicenerbrief*, 162, calls *Laod.* 13b an "Anspielung an Phil. 3, 2, viell. mit Rücksicht auf V. 7 f"; cf. Lightfoot, *Colossians*, 291; Karl Pink, "Die pseudo-paulinischen Briefe II," *Bib* 6 (1925) 190. This kind of synthesis is typical of *Laodiceans* (e.g., *Laod.* 6 [Phil. 1:13 and 8]; *Laod.* 7 [Phil. 1:19–20]; *Laod.* 9 [Phil. 2:1–2]; *Laod.* 15–16 [Phil. 4:8–9]).

[16] *Colossians*, 294; cf. p. 291. Harnack's reconstruction, παραιτεῖσθε τοὺς αἰσχρο-κερδεῖς (*Marcion*, Beilage 3, 139), makes no sense to me, since *praecavete* clearly does not translate παραιτεῖσθε ("decline" or "avoid," typically rendered with some form of *devito* [1 Tim. 4:7; 2 Tim. 2:23] or *recuso* [Acts 15:11]).

[17] "*Laodiceans*," 23 n. 17.

[18] Lightfoot, *Colossians*, 291, has collected the evidence.

[19] By 393 Jerome can report (*De vir. ill.* 5 [*PL* 23.650A]): *Legunt quidam et ad Laodicenses, sed ab omnibus exploditur*; cf. Theodore Mopsuestia, *apud* Rabanus Maurus, *In Epist. ad Col.* (*PL* 112.540B = H. B. Swete, *Theodore of Mopsuestia on the Epistles of Paul* [Cambridge: At the University Press, 1880] I:301): *Unde quidam falsam epistolam ad Laodicenses ex nomine beati Pauli confingendam esse existima-verunt; nec enim erat vera epistola.* Pink, "Die pseudo-paulinischen Briefe II," 192, and Metzger, *Canon*, 183, place the *terminus a quo* at the middle of the third century. Sellew holds a similar view: "[*Laodiceans*] was apparently translated [from Greek into Latin], along with the rest of the Corpus Paulinum, as part of a process not yet completely understood, namely, the production of the pre-Vulgate, Old Latin version or versions" ("*Laodiceans*," 22).

[20] Hermann Josef Frede, *Epistulae ad Philippenses et ad Colossenses*, in *idem*, ed., *Vetus Latina: Die Reste der altlateinischen Bibel* (Freiburg: Herder, 1966–71) XXIV/1:179. Cf. Victorinus, *In Epist. Pauli ad Phil.* (*PL* 8.1217C; Albrecht Locher, ed.,

A similar translation (*cavete canes*) is cited by Ambrose[21] and Augustine.[22]

The second problem with Sellew's analysis is that it fails to consider adequately the kinds of redactional criteria that would have led the compiler of *Laodiceans* to include some and exclude other material from Philippians. So, for instance, Sellew fails to observe: (1) that *Laodiceans*, like its companion Colossians (cf. Col. 4:16), was composed as if written from prison;[23] (2) that Philippians was chosen as a model for *Laodiceans* because it too was a prison letter; (3) that most of the material excerpted from Philippians pertains either directly or indirectly to Paul's imprisonment;[24] and (4) that Phil. 3:2–4:3 (Letter C of the critical reconstruction) contains nothing of Paul's imprisonment and so would naturally have been passed over.[25] Similarly, he fails to observe that everything specific to Paul's relationship with the Philippians has been omitted from *Laodiceans*. Thus the thanksgiving period of 1:3–11, which speaks of the Philippians' long-standing partnership in the gospel, is quickly passed over, as are Timothy's travel plans in 2:19–24 and the report on Epaphroditus in 2:25–30.[26] It is not surprising that the "thank-you note" of 4:10–20, which reiterates the omitted material in 1:3–11, and speaks at length of the gift carried by Epaphroditus, is also omitted on these grounds.

Marius Victorinus. Commentarii in Epistulas Pauli ad Galatas ad Philippenses ad Ephesios [BT; Leipzig: Teubner, 1972] 58.30–1).

[21] *Hexameron* 5.6 (*PL* 14.222A; CSEL 32.1.144.10): *cavete canes, cavete malos operarios.*

[22] *Ep.* 79 (*PL* 33.273.8; CSEL 34.2.346.12): *cavete canes*; *In psalm.* 67.32.4 (*PL* 36.833.18; CCSL 39.892): *cavete canes*; cf. Donatien de Bruyne, *Préfaces de la Bible Latine* (Namur: Godenne, 1920) 240: *admonet etiam ut caveant a pseudoapostolis.* Cf. I. Wordsworth and H. I. White, *Novum Testamentum Latine* (Oxford: Oxford University Press, 1913–41) II:477.

[23] We may set aside the question whether there ever was an epistle to the Laodiceans, which is bound up with the question of the authenticity of Colossians. The compiler of *Laodiceans* simply took Col. 4:16 at face value.

[24] Of the nineteen or so verses excerpted from Philippians (1:2, 3, 12[?], 13, 18–21; 2:2, 12–14; 3:1–2[?]; 4:6, 8–9; 22–3), three of which are taken up with greetings and farewells (1:2; 4:22–3), at least seven directly pertain to Paul's imprisonment (1:12–13, 18–21; 2:12), while six others treat the readers' response to Paul's imprisonment (2:2 [cf. its rendering in *Laod.* 9], 13–14; 4:6, 8–9).

[25] It is also possible that the compiler of *Laodiceans* might have felt that the polemic of Phil. 3 was too pointed for his composition, the purpose of which was simply to fill the gap in the Corpus Paulinum indicated by Col. 4:16.

[26] Sellew, "*Laodiceans*," 26: "The discussion of Epaphroditus's illness at the end of Philippians 2 presumably had no relevance for the fictional audience in Laodicea."

Internal evidence pointing to Phil. 3:2–4:3 as a letter-fragment

The case for partitioning Philippians rests primarily on internal evidence pointing to 3:2–4:3 as a fragment of a separate letter. This evidence may be summarized in three claims: (1) that 3:2–4:3 reflects a different set of circumstances than 1:1–3:1; (2) that an abrupt shift in tone between 3:1 and 3:2 marks a redactional seam; and (3) that various formal elements and verbal clues in 2:14–3:1 signal the end of a Pauline letter. We shall examine each of these in order.

That 3:2–4:3 reflects a different set of circumstances than 1:1–3:1

According to Robert Jewett, the claim that 1:1–3:1 and 3:2–4:3 presuppose different circumstances is the "most powerful argument yet advanced against the literary unity of Philippians."[27] The claim has been formulated in two ways. Schmithals believes that the change lies with Paul, who in writing 3:2–4:3 was much better informed about the problems facing the Philippians than he had earlier been: "Paul could not so cautiously and so generally exhort [the Philippians] to maintain the unity of the faith, as he does in 1:27–2:18, if he had already available to him the information which he uses in passionate agitation in 3:2ff."[28] Müller-Bardorff, on the other hand, feels that changes have also occurred at Philippi: "in Wirklichkeit handelt es sich . . . nicht nur um einen Stimmungsumbruch seitens des Paulus, sondern im Vergleich zum Vorstehenden [= Phil. 1:27–2:16] um eine total veränderte Situation auch in der Adressatgemeinde."[29] In chs. 1–2 Paul is concerned about problems still in the future: a possible schism (*Spaltung*), a dangerous theological tendency (*Richtung*).[30] But in 3:18 the problem is well defined and present: "Das νῦν V. 18 weist auf eine ganz bestimmte, gegenwärtige Situation hin."[31] Bornkamm and Gnilka also point

[27] Robert Jewett, "The Epistolary Thanksgiving and the Integrity of Philippians," *NovT* 12 (1970) 43.
[28] Schmithals, *Paul and the Gnostics*, 74.
[29] Müller-Bardorff, "Frage," 591.
[30] Ibid.
[31] Ibid.

out that in 3:2–4:3 Paul makes no mention of his imprisonment, a dominant motif in chs. 1–2.[32]

Underlying both Schmithals' and Müller-Bardorff's claim that 3:2–4:3 reflects a new set of circumstances is the assumption that the "opponents" (ἀντικείμενοι) casually mentioned in 1:28 are the same as the "dogs" (κύνες) vehemently attacked in 3:2.[33] To establish this connection Schmithals characterizes the ἀντικείμενοι of 1:28 as "false teachers" who like the κύνες of 3:2 are "leading astray the community in its unity of the faith."[34] He adduces in support of this Paul's charge in 1:27 to stand "in one spirit, with one soul struggling together in the faith of the gospel," reasoning that because the ἀντικείμενοι are mentioned immediately after this exhortation they are therefore false teachers controverting the faith. But this inference is contradicted by 1:29–30 where Paul explicitly describes the effects of the ἀντικείμενοι on the Philippians: τὸ ὑπὲρ [Χριστοῦ] πάσχειν, τὸν αὐτὸν ἀγῶνα ἔχοντες, οἷον εἴδετε ἐν ἐμοὶ καὶ νῦν ἀκούετε ἐν ἐμοί.[35] The reference is to Paul's imprisonment, first at Philippi (where he was also beaten) and now at Rome.[36] The ἀντικείμενοι are not, therefore, "false teachers" posing a theological danger to the community, as the argument for partitioning

---

[32] G. Bornkamm, "Der Philipperbrief als paulinische Briefsammlung," *Neotestamentica et Patristica: Eine Freundesgabe Herrn Professor Dr. Oscar Cullmann* (NovTSup 6; Leiden: Brill, 1962) 197; Gnilka, *Philipperbrief*, 9, 13; cf. J.-F. Collange, *L'éptre de Saint Paul aux Philippiens* (CNT; Neuchâtel: Delachaux & Niestlé, 1973) 30.

[33] Schmithals, *Paul and the Gnostics*, 69–70; Müller-Bardorff, "Frage," 592: "Vorstehende Exegese von 3,18 aber verlangt eine akute und konkrete Gefährdung der Gemeinde, die über die latenten Gefahren von 1,27ff. weit hinausgeht"; cf. W. Marxsen, *Introduction to the New Testament: An Approach to Its Problems*, trans. G. Buswell (Oxford: Blackwell, 1968) 61; Collange, *Philippiens*, 27. It goes without saying that the argument disintegrates if the opponents of 1:28 are not the dogs of 3:2, since there is nothing at all inconsistent with Paul having two different opinions about two different groups at the same time. For the sake of completeness, however, I should mention the idiosyncratic view of Rahtjen ("Three Letters," 107) that the dogs of 3:2 may also be in view in 1:15–17 where Paul speaks of those who preach Christ διὰ φθόνον καὶ ἔριν. To my knowledge no one has followed him in this, since the rivals in 1:15–17 are obviously not at Philippi but in the city of Paul's imprisonment, and it is inconceivable that Paul could say of the dogs of 3:2: Τί γάρ; πλὴν ὅτι παντὶ τρόπῳ, εἴτε προφάσει εἴτε ἀληθείᾳ, Χριστὸς καταγγέλλεται, καὶ ἐν τούτῳ χαίρω. The rivals of 1:15–17 err in their motives, but apparently not in their message.

[34] *Paul and the Gnostics*, 69, 74.

[35] So Bormann, *Philippi*, 218.

[36] The provenance of Philippians is not directly relevant to our study of the letter, but I see no problem with the traditional placement of Paul at Rome.

requires, but political oppressors threatening physical punishment and imprisonment.[37]

Müller-Bardorff's further contention that the νῦν of 3:18 indicates the presence of a well-defined problem, and thus that what is simply a tendency in chs. 1–2 has become actual in ch. 3, also falters on an unfounded assumption: namely, that for something to be present and well-defined it must be more than a mere tendency. However, there is nothing self-contradictory in speaking of a present and well-defined tendency – though many would argue that the situation in Philippians 3 is anything but well defined. We shall say more about this later. But here we may point out that despite Paul's heightened language in 3:2, had the situation involved more than a dangerous "Richtung" among the Philippians, as it did in Galatia, that is, if the Philippians had crossed the line from a more or less unconscious tendency to a full-blown theological commitment, Paul presumably would have included them in his verbal scourging (cf. Gal. 3:1, 3). But he does not. Rather, he reserves his harsh words for the false teachers of whom the Philippians are to beware.[38] Furthermore, Paul continues to argue in ch. 3 by way of personal example, which presupposes that Paul's gospel is still authoritative in the church. As for Bornkamm's and Gnilka's observation that Paul may not have written 3:2–4:3 as a prisoner, this is not an argument for partitioning but a consequence of it.[39]

---

[37] On this both Bornkamm ("Der Philipperbrief," 197–8) and Gnilka (*Philipperbrief*, 8, 99–100), who partition Philippians on other grounds, agree; cf. 1 Thess. 2:2; Acts 16:20–1, where Paul is imprisoned as a Jew on charges of disrupting the city and proselytizing Romans: οὗτοι οἱ ἄνθρωποι ἐκταράσσουσιν ἡμῶν τὴν πόλιν, Ἰουδαῖοι ὑπάρχοντες, καὶ καταγγέλλουσιν ἔθη ἃ οὐκ ἔξεστιν ἡμῖν παραδέχεσθαι οὐδὲ ποιεῖν Ῥωμαίοις οὖσιν; cf. Ernst Haenchen, *The Acts of the Apostles: A Commentary* (14th edn.; Philadelphia: Westminster, 1971) 496; Bormann, *Philippi*, 220. That imprisonment is in view is further suggested by Paul's use of σωτηρία in Phil. 1:28 (cf. 1:19) and by the fact that these opponents were "terrifying" (μὴ πτυρόμενοι).

[38] Indeed, the Philippians are so far from crossing such a line that Paul begins his warning with an apology (3:1).

[39] Granted that if 3:2–4:3 is excerpted from its canonical context there is nothing that requires it to have been written from prison; but there is also nothing that requires Paul repeatedly to make explicit mention of his imprisonment. Paul's references to having lost all things in 3:8, to the fellowship of Christ's sufferings in 3:10, to the cross of Christ in 3:18, and his final eschatological appeal in 3:20–1 may all be taken to reflect in some sense his experience as a prisoner.

That an abrupt shift in tone between 3:1 and 3:2 marks a
redactional seam

The second claim advanced in support of excising 3:2–4:3 is that an
abrupt shift in tone between 3:1 and 3:2 indicates a redactional
seam.[40] Goodspeed explains:[41]

> In 3:1 all is serene; [the Philippians] must not mind Paul's
> repeating himself, for it is for their own good. But in the
> next verse he breaks out against the Judaizers with an
> intensity unsurpassed even in Galatians . . . This sharp
> change after 3:1 . . . raises the question whether our
> Philippians does not break at this point into two letters.

Attempts to smooth this break have focused on 3:2 and have
sought by one means or another to qualify its "unsurpassed"
intensity. They have been only marginally successful.[42] However, as
Goodspeed's lucid explanation makes plain, Paul's intensity in 3:2
is problematic only because 3:1 has already been judged "serene."[43]
More attention should be given to 3:1, and in particular to Paul's
command in 3:1a to "rejoice in the Lord" (χαίρετε ἐν κυρίῳ).

Scholars have consistently underestimated the seriousness of
Paul's command to rejoice in the Lord in 3:1a. To some extent
this is a question of translation, for if with Goodspeed we
translate χαίρετε "good bye," then Paul's imperative is reduced
to an epistolary cliché.[44] However, even those scholars who

---

[40] So Schmithals, *Paul and the Gnostics*, 68–72; Beare, *Philippians*, 3–4; Rahtjen,
"Three Letters," 168; Müller-Bardorff, "Frage," 592; Gnilka, *Philipperbrief*, 7;
Collange, *Philippiens*, 21.

[41] *An Introduction to the New Testament* (Chicago, University of Chicago Press,
1937) 90–1.

[42] The intensity of Phil. 3:2 is not to be denied. I do not agree with G. D.
Kilpatrick, "BLEPETE in Phil 3:2," in M. Black and G. Fohrer, eds., *In Memoriam
P. Kahle* (BZAW 103; Berlin: Töpelmann, 1968) 146–8, that βλέπετε in 3.2 is to be
translated "consider" and not "beware"; cf. BDF §149. Even so, Goodspeed's claim
goes beyond the evidence, for the "intensity" of Galatians most certainly surpasses
that of Philippians, if for no other reason than that in Galatians Paul's harsh rhetoric
is extended to include his audience (cf. Gal. 3:1, 3) which is not the case in
Philippians. Furthermore, Mackay ("Further Thoughts," 163) is correct that the
intensity of 3:2, which essentially amounts to name-calling, is short-lived.

[43] This point, which is obvious enough, has to my knowledge been universally
overlooked by commentators. I do not know how to explain this except to say that
the initial formulation of the problem focused attention exclusively on 3:2. At any
rate, regarding the "break" between 3:1 and 3:2, 3:1 is every bit as much a part of the
equation as 3:2.

[44] E. J. Goodspeed, *Problems of New Testament Translation* (Chicago: University

correctly[45] translate χαίρετε "rejoice" typically misunderstand the substantive nature of Paul's charge. Thus Lake asks: "Is it natural to say 'rejoice in the Lord always [sic!]' and then suddenly say 'Beware of the dogs'?"[46] The answer is "Yes," provided we take seriously the command to rejoice in the Lord. But this is not what Lake does. Rather, he trivializes Paul's command, so much so that he inadvertently replaces it with the maxim "Rejoice in the Lord always" from 4:4! Lake's unstated assumption is clear: Paul's command to rejoice in the Lord in 3:1a is general parenesis and belongs with the other pieces of advice collected at the end of the letter. The list of scholars who take 3:1a with the parenesis of ch. 4 is long and includes not only those who partition the letter, but those who do not. Vincent is typical of the latter. After citing for comparison 4:4 and 10, he writes:[47]

> The exhortation [= 3:1a] need not be specifically referred either to what precedes or what follows . . . The summons to rejoice is general, in view of all the trials, past, present, and future, as well as the eternal consolations of the gospel.

The tendency among scholars to trivialize Paul's command to "rejoice in the Lord" in 3:1a is symptomatic of a larger problem: namely, the tendency among scholars to trivialize Paul's use of χαρά and its cognates in Philippians. Müller-Bardorff is typical in his repeated allusions to a characteristic "Grundton der Freude" in the first two chapters of Philippians which is then contrasted with the "Kampfbrief" of 3:2–21.[48] At first glance this is plausible, since there are eleven explicit references to joy in the first two chapters of

of Chicago Press, 1945) 174–5, who renders "Good bye and the Lord be with you"; cf. Beare, *Philippians*, 100, 145–6; Rahtjen, "Three Letters," 171; J. B. Lightfoot, *St. Paul's Epistle to the Philippians* (4th edn.; London: Macmillan, 1903), 125, 159–60, wants it both ways: "neither 'farewell' alone, nor 'rejoice' alone."

[45] Prior to 3:1 Paul has used χαίρω and its cognates a total of eleven times. It is only natural to continue to translate it "rejoice" here. To do otherwise requires that we have *already* decided on other grounds in favor of the partition theory.

[46] "Critical Problems of the Epistle to the Philippians," *The Expositor* 8/7 (1914) 485.

[47] M. R. Vincent, *A Critical and Exegetical Commentary on the Epistles to the Philippians and to Philemon* (ICC; Edinburgh: T. & T. Clark, 1897) 91; cf. H. A. W. Meyer, *Kritisch-exegetisches Handbuch über die Briefe Pauli an die Philipper, Kolosser und Philemon*, 4th edn. (Göttingen: Vandenhoeck & Ruprecht, 1874) 89: "allgemeine Aufmunterung."

[48] "Frage," 591–2; cf. Bornkamm, "Der Philipperbrief," 194; Marxsen, *Introduction*, 63; Collange, *Philippiens*, 21; Rahtjen, "Three Letters," 170, Ulrich B. Müller,

the letter (1:4, 18 [twice], 25; 2:2, 17 [twice], 18 [twice], 28, 29). But
this fails to take into account the purposive way in which Paul uses
"joy" in Philippians, which is not to provide the Philippians with
general encouragement, but to confront them with a moral ideal
and, ultimately, to scold them for not behaving in a manner
"worthy of the gospel" (1:27).[49]

Paul sets the standard himself by his own joyful response to
hardship in 1:18 and again in 2:17–18. Like the philosopher who
remains unmoved by circumstances because he has learned how to
distinguish between the things that matter and the things that do
not (cf. Phil. 1:10) or, as Seneca puts it, who has learned not to
rejoice in unimportant things (*ne gaudeas vanis*),[50] Paul's experience
of joy remains undiminished even though he is in prison awaiting
trial on capital charges. Paul here employs joy – as does Seneca – as
the characteristic emotion or "εὐπάθεια" of the sage, both the
means and the measure of spiritual progress (προκοπή). "He has
made it to the top," Seneca writes, "who understands what should
be the object of his joy (*qui scit, quo gaudeat*), who has not placed
his happiness in the power of externals."[51] Chrysostom's comments
on Phil. 1:18 are worth quoting at length:[52]

> The great and philosophic soul (τὴν μεγάλην καὶ φιλό-
> σοφον ψυχήν) is vexed by none of the grievous things of

Der Brief des Paulus an die Philipper (THKNT 11/1; Leipzig: Evangelische Verlagsanstalt, 1993) 28, 136.

[49] P. F. Aspan, "Toward a New Reading of Paul's Letter to the Philippians in
Light of a Kuhnian Analysis of New Testament Criticism" (Ph.D. diss. Vanderbilt,
1990) 289, writes: "Philippians is not a joyful letter, as is often suggested. Rather, the
'rhetoric of joy' represents a manifestation of the *Vollendungen* towards which
the letter is exhorting the audience." Bengel's familiar summary of the letter makes
the same point: *Gaudeo, gaudete,* "I rejoice, now you do the same!" (*Gnomon Novi
Testamenti*, 3rd edn. [Stuttgart: J. F. Steinkopf, 1860 (1773)] 766).

[50] *Ep.* 23.1: *Huius fundamentum quod sit quaeris? Ne gaudeas vanis. Fundamentum
hoc esse dixit; culmen est.*

[51] *Ep.* 23.2. Two sentences later Seneca exhorts Lucilius: *Hoc ante omnia fac, mi
Lucili: disce gaudere.* Cf. Bengel's summary of Philippians already noted: *Summa
epistolae: gaudeo, gaudete.* For Seneca, of course, the object of joy was to be one's
own virtue (*ad verum bonum specta et de tuo gaude*; *Ep.* 23.6), whereas for Paul it is
the progress of the gospel (1:12–18a), the salvation of the minister of the gospel
(1:18b–21), and ultimately, Christ himself (3:1–4:1). One of Paul's principal concerns
in Philippians is to instruct the Philippians how to rejoice in these truly important
things and not in the things that do not matter.

[52] *In Epist. ad Phil.* 3.1 (*PG* 62.197.37ff.); cf. ibid., praef. 1 (*PG* 62.179.38–40):
"In the beginning of his letter Paul offers the Philippians much consolation (πολλὴν
παράκλησιν) regarding his imprisonment, showing [by his own example] not only
that they should not be grieved, but that they should rejoice (χαίρειν)."

this life: not enmities, not accusations, not slanders, not perils or plots . . . And such was the soul of Paul . . . That blessed man had not only the emperor waging war against him, but many others attempting to grieve him in many ways, even with bitter slander. But what does he say? Not only "I am not hurt or overcome by these things," but "I rejoice and I will rejoice!"

Seneca makes the same argument at *Ad Helv.* 4.2. Writing from exile, he consoles his mother that his deportation is really a matter of indifference and that his "joy" (*gaudium*) remains unaffected by it: "nothing bad has happened to me . . . I am happy in circumstances that usually make others miserable" (*nihil mihi mali esse . . . inter eas res beatus ero, quae miseros solent facere*).[53] For both Paul and Seneca joy is "a matter of the utmost importance" (*res severa*).[54]

The Philippians, on the other hand, have fallen short of Paul's example. Their joy is inexorably linked to such externals as Paul's acquittal and release from prison (cf. 1:25: μενῶ καὶ παραμενῶ πᾶσιν ὑμῖν εἰς τὴν ὑμῶν προκοπὴν καὶ χαρὰν τῆς πίστεως) and the health and safe return of Epaphroditus (cf. 2:28: σπουδαιο-τέρως οὖν ἔπεμψα αὐτόν, ἵνα ἰδόντες αὐτὸν πάλιν χαρῆτε). Paul would have them join him in rejoicing in more substantial things, such as the progress of the gospel (1:12–18a), or even in his own sacrificial death, if that should occur (cf. 2:17–18). As it stands, however, they are unable to look beyond present uncertainties. Ironically, this compromises Paul's own joy, which derives in part from the steadfastness of his converts.[55] Paul is indirect, but more than once he indicates that it is not imprisonment or the possibility of death but the Philippians themselves who are constraining him.[56] Aspan is right to recognize a "rhetoric of joy" in Philippians.[57]

We will discuss the philosophical and consolatory *topos* of joy in more detail in chapter 3 below. However, it should be clear at this point that we need to reassess Paul's use of language expressing joy

---

[53] *Ad Helv.* 4.2; cf. 4.1: *nihil me pati, propter quod ipse dici possim miser;* 5.1 *Leve momentum in adventiciis rebus est et quod in neutram partem magnas vires habeat. Nec secunda sapientem evehunt nec adversa demittunt; laboravit enim semper, ut in se plurimum poneret, ut a se omne gaudium peteret.*

[54] *Ep.* 23.4: *Crede mihi, verum gaudium res severa est.*

[55] 2:1–2: εἴ τις οὖν παράκλησις . . . εἴ τι παραμύθιον . . . πληρώσατέ μου τὴν χαρὰν . . . , i.e., if the Philippians can be consoled Paul's joy will be made complete, but it is currently otherwise. Cf. 4:1: χαρὰ καὶ στέφανός μου.

[56] 1:24: ἀναγκαιότερον δι᾽ ὑμᾶς; 2:25: ἀναγκαῖον; 2:28, κἀγὼ ἀλυπότερος ὦ.

[57] Aspan, "Toward a New Reading of Paul's Letter to the Philippians," 289.

in chs. 1–2 and that we reflect this in our understanding of his command to "rejoice in the Lord" in 3:1a, which in its context is anything but a cliché.[58] Perhaps the best way to avoid reading 3:1a as a cliché is to render it periphrastically: something like "derive your sense of joy from the Lord" or "set your desires on the Lord." When we do this the alleged shift in tone from 3:1 to 3:2 disappears, as the following translation makes plain:

> Finally, my brothers, set your desires on the Lord. You have heard me say this before, but I don't mind repeating myself on such an important matter, and for you it is a wise precaution. Watch out for the dogs, watch out for the evil workers, watch out for the mutilation; for we are the true circumcision who worship by the spirit of God and who set great stock in our relationship with Christ . . .

On this reading 3:1a forms a natural introduction to the rest of ch. 3, where Paul develops at length τὸ ὑπερέχον τῆς γνώσεως Χριστοῦ Ἰησοῦ τοῦ κυρίου μου (3:8).[59] This position was taken by Bernhard Weiss more than a century ago and has much to commend it.[60]

That various formal elements and verbal clues in 2:14–3:1 signal the end of "a Pauline Letter"

The third claim advanced in support of isolating 3:2–4:1 as a separate letter-fragment is that various formal elements and verbal

[58] Peter Wick, *Der Philipperbrief: Der formale Aufbau des Briefs als Schlüssel zum Verständnis seines Inhalts* (BWANT 7/15(=135); Stuttgart: Kohlhammer, 1994) esp. 61–3, 82–5; cf. P. Rolland, "La structure littéraire et l'unité de l'éptre aux Philippiens," *RevSR* 64 (1990) 213–16.

[59] Cf. Phil. 3:3: καυχώμενοι ἐν Χριστῷ Ἰησοῦ; 3:7: διὰ τὸν Χριστόν; 3:8b: ἵνα Χριστὸν κερδήσω; 3:9: καὶ εὑρεθῶ ἐν αὐτῷ; 3:10: τοῦ γνῶναι αὐτὸν καὶ τὴν δύναμιν τῆς ἀναστάσεως αὐτοῦ καὶ τὴν κοινωνίαν τῶν παθημάτων αὐτοῦ, συμμορφιζόμενος τῷ θανάτῳ αὐτοῦ; 3:14: τὸ βραβεῖον τῆς ἄνω κλήσεως τοῦ θεοῦ ἐν Χριστῷ Ἰησοῦ; 3:18: τοὺς ἐχθροὺς τοῦ σταυροῦ τοῦ Χριστοῦ; 4:1: οὕτως στήκετε ἐν κυρίῳ.

[60] *Der Philipper-Brief ausgelegt und die Geschichte seiner Auslegung kritisch dargestellt* (3rd edn.; Berlin: Hertz, 1859) 214–57; cf. Johann Christian Konrad von Hofmann, *Die Heilige Schrift des N. T. zusammenhängend untersucht, 4.3 Der Brief Pauli an die Philipper* (8th edn.; Nördlingen: Beck, 1872); E. Lohmeyer, *Der Brief an die Philippe, an die Kolosser und an Philemon* (MeyerK 9/8; Göttingen: Vandenhoeck & Ruprecht, 1928–30) 123–4. Cf. Wayne A. Meeks, "The Man from Heaven in Philippians," in Birger A. Pearson, ed., *The Future of Early Christianity: Essays in Honor of Helmut Koester* (Minneapolis: Fortress, 1991) 332: "the section as a whole [= chapter 3] is not polemical but hortatory."

clues in 2:14–3:1 signal the end of a Pauline letter. We have already
seen that Goodspeed and others translate 3:1a as a farewell
formula: "Finally, brothers, good bye and the Lord be with you."[61]
But scholars have also pointed out that with the discussion of
logistical matters in 2:18–30 Paul seems to be drawing his letter to
a close.[62] Robert Funk has attempted to support this observation
with a detailed form-critical analysis of the body of the Pauline
letter. He has concluded that the body of the characteristic Pauline
letter ends with a "travelogue" prefaced by an eschatological
climax.[63] Regarding Philippians he writes: "The travel section
occurs in Philippians at 2:18–30, and is preceded, interestingly
enough, by an eschatological conclusion in 2:14–18."[64]

Before turning to the details of Funk's analysis it is important to
observe that Funk brings to his investigation of the body of the
Pauline letter an extreme view of form derived not from earlier
Form Criticism, but from the New Hermeneutic of Ernst Fuchs
and Gerhard Ebeling. Indeed, the first third of Funk's analysis,
over one hundred and twenty pages, is devoted to an exposition of
the philosophy of Heidegger, Fuchs, and Ebeling.[65] Funk's erudi-
tion is impressive, but he clearly imbues Form with a salience that
few NT scholars would accept.[66]

Funk is himself aware of this difference and frequently includes

[61] We must not make too much of τὸ λοιπόν ("finally") in 3:1, as though it signals
the end of the letter. Paul has urged the Philippians to rejoice in the "progress" of
the gospel (1:12–18a), his own assured "salvation" (1:18b–21), his possible death in
the service of the gospel (2:17–18), and the return of Epaphroditus (2:28–9). He
now, finally (τὸ λοιπόν), urges them to "rejoice in the Lord." Indeed, the use of τὸ
λοιπόν in 3:1 ties the exhortation to rejoice in the Lord in 3:1a to these earlier
implicit and explicit exhortations to rejoice in the letter and is a further argument
that 3:1a is not to be trivialized.
[62] See Schmithals, *Paul and the Gnostics*, 70, and the literature cited there; Beare,
Philippians, 95.
[63] Robert Funk, *Language Hermeneutic and Word of God: The Problem of
Language in the New Testament and Contemporary Theology* (New York: Harper &
Row, 1966) 248–9, 257, 263–74. Funk proposes that the eschatological climax at the
end of the body of the letter is analogous to the eschatological climax at the end of
the thanksgiving period described by J. T. Sanders, "The Transition from Opening
Epistolary Thanksgiving to Body in the Letters of the Pauline Corpus," *JBL* 81
(1962) 348–62. Cf. W. G. Doty, *Letters in Primitive Christianity* (Philadelphia:
Fortress, 1973); T. Y. Mullins, "Visit Talk in New Testament Letters," *CBQ* 35
(1973) 350–8.
[64] Funk, *Language*, 265.
[65] Ibid., 1–122. Funk's treatment of parable (124–222) and letter (224–305) is
impossible without his philosophical commitments.
[66] Thus in distinguishing between the *how* and *what* of language, Funk writes that
"the *how* is all-important" (*Language*, 125).

disclaimers in his discussion. But the result is not convincing. Thus, for example, after listing some fourteen features characteristic of the Pauline letter form, Funk writes: "It should be emphasized that these elements are subject to variation in both content and order, and that some items are optional, although the omission of any one calls for explanation." But if these elements can vary in both content and order, and if some are in fact optional, why does the omission of any one of them require explanation?[67] Elsewhere Funk warns that his Pauline letter form is not to be applied too rigidly, quoting with approval Amos Wilder's apt observation that the letter form "is almost as flexible as oral speech itself."[68] But a few pages later, commenting on Paul's request for a room in Philem. 22, Funk remarks: "Paul climaxes his appeal in verses 20f. and then turns abruptly, *as though it were inevitable*, to his anticipated visit (emphasis added)."[69] Paul's request for a room has apparently been rendered "inevitable" by some sort of hard-and-fast letter-recipe that calls for a travelogue to be added at this point.

Funk's use of evidence is also problematic. He selects for study the following "closely argued sections . . . which customarily form the body of the letter": Rom. 1:13–8:39; 1 Cor. 1:10–4:21; 2 Cor. 1:8–2:13 + 7:5–16; 2:14–7:4; 10:1–13:14; Gal. 1:6–5:26 or 6:17; Phil. 1:12–2:30; 1 Thess. 2:1–3:13; Philem. 8–22.[70] But there is much that is questionable in this list. Why, for example, does Funk end the body of Romans at 8:39? He says in a footnote that the "question of the disposition of Rom. 9–11 is left open,"[71] but in fact it is left out. Ending 1 Corinthians at 4:21 is equally odd, though here Funk suggests that chs. 5–15 "be taken as an extended parenesis appended to the body of the letter."[72] As for 1 Thessalonians, the status of chs. 2 and 3 is at best ambiguous, since on an equally compelling form-critical analysis it can be argued that Paul

[67] It is important that we understand clearly what Funk is calling for here. Interpreters are expected to explain the elements present in a text. But what Funk stipulates is that we need to explain not only what is there, but what is not there when the text is measured against some ideal form.

[68] *The Language of the Gospel: Early Christian Rhetoric* (New York: Harper & Row, 1964) 39; quoted with approval in Funk, *Language*, 248.

[69] *Language*, 265.

[70] Ibid., 264.

[71] Ibid., 264 n. 59.

[72] Ibid., 272.

extends his characteristic εὐχαριστῶ up through 3:13.[73] Funk's list, of course, *presupposes* the partitioning of Philippians.

But even given Funk's own selection of texts, it is difficult to see how he comes up with his proposed Pauline letter-form, and in particular how he is able to stipulate that the body of the Pauline letter concludes with an eschatological climax followed by a travelogue.[74] Both Galatians and Philemon, the only two cases in which the limits of the text are undisputed, lack eschatological climaxes,[75] as does 2 Cor. 10–13 and the so-called letter of reconciliation (2 Cor. 1:8–2:13 + 7:5–16).[76] Galatians also lacks a travelogue, though Funk identifies a "travelogue surrogate" in 4:12–20.[77] In Romans, which apparently has two eschatological climaxes (8:31–9; 11:25–36),[78] the travelogue does not occur as part of the body of the letter, but in the epistolary frame: 1:8–17 and 15:14–33.[79] In 1 Thessalonians and 2 Corinthians 10–13 the travel plans are incorporated into the argument of the letter (which seems also to be the case in Philippians),[80] while in 2 Cor. 1:8–2:13 + 7:5–16 the whole letter is taken up with travel plans.[81] Ironically, the only two of Paul's letters that fit Funk's ideal form are his truncated versions of 1 Corinthians and Philippians. Russell has criticized Funk for imposing "an abstract 'Pauline letter structure'" on the evidence.[82]

Paul's inclusion of travel plans in Phil. 2:19–30, assuming the unity of Philippians, is obviously not a severe violation of form.

[73] Paul Schubert, *Form and Function of the Pauline Thanksgivings* (BZNW 20; Berlin: Töpelmann, 1939); Peter T. O'Brien, *Introductory Thanksgivings in the Letters of Paul* (NovTSup 49; Leiden: Brill, 1977). But see H. Boers, "Form-Critical Study of Paul's Letters: I Thessalonians as a Case Study," *NTS* 22 (1976) 140–58.

[74] It is also worth observing that in dismembering Philippians Funk succeeds in coming up with a letter that follows Pauline form (i.e., 1:1–3:1, etc.) only at the expense of producing two letters that do not (4:10–20 and 3:1–4:1)!

[75] Funk, *Language*, 265, 271. Funk allows that Gal. 6:7–10 may be an eschatological climax. He does not explain why it comes so far after the "travelogue surrogate" in 4:12–20.

[76] Ibid., 265.

[77] Ibid., 268, 271.

[78] Ibid., 271.

[79] Ibid., 266.

[80] Ibid., 265.

[81] Ibid.

[82] R. Russell, "Pauline Letter Structure in Philippians," *JETS* 25 (1982) 296; cf. 306. Russell includes in his criticism Doty, *Letters in Primitive Christianity*, 29, and Boers, "Form-Critical Study of Paul's Letters," 151–3. David Garland, "The Composition and Unity of Philippians: Some Neglected Literary Factors," *NovT* 27 (1985) 150, agrees with Russell's assessment.

But the question may still be asked why Paul bothers to mention logistical matters in the middle of his letter. The answer lies in the fact that in 2:19–30 Paul not only explains the movements of Timothy and Epaphroditus, but cites them as additional examples in support of the parenetic material in 2:1–18.[83] Paul's exhortation in 2:1–18 is twofold: in verses 1–4 he exhorts the Philippians to serve one another, not looking out for their own interests (τὰ ἑαυτῶν; 4) but for the interests of others (τὰ ἑτέρων; 4); in verses 12–18 he further exhorts them to accept their current hardship without complaint and thus continue in their obedience (ὑπηκού-σατε; 12) to God. Separating these exhortations is the Christ hymn (vv. 5–11), which Paul cites as an *exemplum*: in his incarnation Christ became a servant to others (μορφὴν δούλου; 7), and in his passion he obeyed God to the point of death (ὑπήκοος μέχρι θανάτου; 8).[84] Timothy, a servant (ἐδούλευσεν; 22) who genuinely cares for the interests of the Philippians (τὰ περὶ ὑμῶν; 19–20 [twice]), supplements Christ's example in regard to the first exhortation, while Epaphroditus, who like Christ was obedient to the point of death (μέχρι θανάτου; 30), supplements Christ's example in regard to the second.[85]

---

[83] A. Culpepper, "Co-Workers In Suffering: Philippians 2:19–30," *RevExp* 72 (1980) 353–7; Duane F. Watson, "A Rhetorical Analysis of Philippians and the Implications for the Unity Question," *NovT* 30 (1988) 71–2; Peter T. O'Brien, *The Epistle to the Philippians: A Commentary on the Greek Text* (NIGTC; Grand Rapids: Eerdmans, 1991), 313–15.

[84] Ernst Käsemann ("Kritische Analyse von Phil. 2,5–11," in *idem*, *Exegetische Versuche und Besinnung* [Göttingen: Vandenhoeck & Ruprecht, 1960] I:51–95; first published *ZThK* 47 [1950] 313–60; ET "A Critical Analysis of Philippians 2:5–11," in Robert Funk, ed., *God and Christ: Existence and Providence* [New York: Harper & Row, 1968] 45–88) and Ralph Martin (*Carmen Christi: Philippians ii.5–11 in Recent Interpretation and in the Setting of Early Christian Worship* [SNTSMS 4; Cambridge: Cambridge University Press, 1967; rev. edn. [with same pagination], Grand Rapids: Eerdmans, 1983] 290) have argued against reading the Christ hymn as an *exemplum*, but their arguments are dogmatically motivated and unconvincing, even to those who share their convictions; cf. Gerald Hawthorne, "The Imitation of Christ: Discipleship in Philippians," in Richard N. Longenecker, ed., *Patterns of Discipleship in the New Testament* (Grand Rapids: Eerdmans, 1996) 163–79. See further, Morna Hooker, "Philippians 2:6–11," in E. E. Ellis and E. Grässer, eds., *Jesus und Paulus, Festschrift für Werner Georg Kümmel zum 70. Geburtstag* (2nd edn.; Göttingen: Vandenhoeck & Ruprecht, 1978) 151–64; Meeks, "Man from Heaven in Philippians," 335.

[85] The mention of Timothy and Epaphroditus in Phil. 2:19–30 is also consolatory. We shall argue below that Paul's principal objective in writing to the Philippians was to console them, and that he pursues this under two headings: 1:12–2:30 and 3:1–4:1. The first heading, to which 2:19–30 forms an apt conclusion, is concerned with Paul's imprisonment and forced separation from the Philippians. Timothy and, to a lesser degree, Epaphroditus are surrogates for Paul (cf. 2:19, 23–4). Cf. *Ad Helv.*

Internal evidence pointing to Phil. 4:10–20 as a separate thank-you note

Most scholars who identify Phil. 3:2–4:1 as a separate letter-fragment also isolate 4:10–20 as a short thank-you note.[86] The evidence for this may be expressed in two claims: (1) that Phil. 2:25–30 presupposes communications between Paul and the Philippians in which Paul must have already thanked the Philippians for their gift, making the thank you of 4:10–20 redundant in its present context,[87] and (2) that 4:10–20, which conveys Paul's formal expression of thanks to the Philippians for their gift, comes unacceptably late in a letter specifically written to acknowledge that gift. To these points may be added a third observation, namely, that 4:10–20 is a self-contained pericope loosely tied to the rest of the letter, and may be read, if there is warrant to do so, as a separate thank-you note.[88]

That Phil. 2:25–30 presupposes communications between Paul and the Philippians in which Paul must have already thanked them for their gift

Regarding the claim that 2:25–30 implies additional correspondence between Paul and the Philippians, Schmithals reconstructs the following scenario:[89] (1) Epaphroditus comes to Paul with a gift from the Philippians and begins his service (λειτουργία) to Paul on behalf of the church; (2) Epaphroditus falls ill and the church at Philippi is informed of this (cf. 2:26); (3) Epaphroditus recovers enough to return to Philippi; and (4) Paul sends the fully recovered Epaphroditus back to Philippi. Schmithals reasons that Paul would not have waited until Epaphroditus' recovery and return to thank

---

18–19 where the exiled Seneca offers his mother a number of surrogates for his presence: *volo interim solacia tibi tua ostendere . . . meos fratres . . . nepotes . . . pronepotes . . . patrem . . . sororem tuam.* In this regard 2:19–30 makes an apt conclusion to 1:12–2:30. It might also be pointed out that 2:19–30 is an apt transition to 3:1–4:1. The Philippians will rejoice to see Epaphroditus, Timothy, and eventually Paul (2:28–9; 2:23–4, cf. 1:25). Ultimately, however, Paul wishes them to rejoice in the Lord (cf. 3:1). See further chapter 5 below.

[86] But see Gnilka, *Philipperbrief*, 9–10; Friedrich, *An die Philipper*, 126–8.

[87] Rahtjen ("Three Letters," 169–70) also argues that the aorists of 2:25 and 28 are historical (not epistolary) aorists; but see Mackay, "Further Thoughts," 165–6; D. Garland, "Composition and Unity," 150, note 34.

[88] Collange, *Philippiens*, 22.

[89] *Paul and the Gnostics*, 78.

the Philippians for their gift, especially since there had always been communications between Paul and the church (cf. 2 in the above scenario). The interval implied on this reading of 2:25–30 is not problematic, since by Paul's own admission he has few trustworthy associates with him at this point in time (cf. 2:19–20).[90] The real difficulty lies in the supposition that correspondence had passed between Paul and the Philippians after Epaphroditus' arrival and before the sending of the letter containing 2:25–30.

But the argument that there had been additional communication from Paul to the Philippians has not yet been successfully made. Schmithals' citation of 1:27 begs the question, since in 1:27 Paul simply mentions the possibility of his hearing about the Philippians in the future (ἵνα εἴτε ἐλθὼν καὶ ἰδὼν ὑμᾶς εἴτε ἀπὼν ἀκούω τὰ περὶ ὑμῶν).[91] Schmithals' appeal to 2:26 also begs the question,[92] since 2:26 says nothing of how the Philippians learned of Epaphroditus' illness nor of how Epaphroditus knew that they had heard. The most reasonable way to read Paul's statement that διὰ τὸ ἔργον Χριστοῦ μέχρι θανάτου ἤγγισεν παραβολευσάμενος τῇ ψυχῇ (2:30) is that in bringing the Philippians' gift to Paul Epaphroditus became sick and, rather than stopping to recover, pressed ahead, so that Paul did not suffer from need in prison.[93] But this means that news could have reached Philippi even before Epaphroditus reached Paul and that Epaphroditus either knew that this had happened (e.g., he had met someone along the way who was traveling to Philippi and he knew that they would report his illness) or, along with Paul, had received a query from Philippi. Paul's report in Phil. 2:27 that Epaphroditus "was indeed ill, even

[90] Mackay, "Further Thoughts," 169, recalls a similar complaint by Cicero, *Ad Att.* 1.13.1: *Quibus epistulis sum equidem abs te lacessitus ad rescribendum; sed idcirco sum tardior quod non invenio fidelem tabellarium.*

[91] *Paul and the Gnostics*, 78.

[92] Ibid.

[93] Schmithals, ibid., assumes without explanation that Epaphroditus fell ill while with Paul. The only possible basis for this is that Epaphroditus' λειτουργία (cf. 2:25 and 30) consisted in ministering to Paul in prison and not in the bringing of the Philippians' gift. But this is unwarranted. At the very least it was both. More likely, however, Epaphroditus' charge lay primarily in the bringing of the gift. In 2:25 Paul refers to him as λειτουργὸς τῆς χρείας μου, but in 4:16 χρεία clearly refers to a monetary gift (and cf. 4:19 where the metaphor is drawn from money, πλοῦτος). Elsewhere (2 Cor. 9:12) λειτουργία itself is used of a monetary gift; and similarly with the verb λειτουργέω (Rom. 15:27). These arguments are made in C. O. Buchanan, "Epaphroditus' Sickness and the Letter to the Philippians," *EvQ* 36 (1964) 158–60; cf. D. Garland, "Composition and Unity," 151, note 36; F. F. Bruce, "St. Paul in Macedonia 3: The Philippian Correspondence," *BJRL* 63 (1981) 274–7.

close to death" (καὶ γὰρ ἠσθένησεν παραπλήσιον θανάτῳ) suggests that the Philippians had in fact received some preliminary report that failed to relate the eventual seriousness of Epaphroditus' illness.[94] At any rate, there is nothing in 2:25–30 that requires a letter from Paul to the Philippians after the arrival of Epaphroditus and prior to the canonical epistle.[95]

That 4:10–20 comes unacceptably late in a letter of thanks

The second claim advanced in support of reading 4:10–20 as a separate thank-you note is that as a formal expression of thanks verses 10–20 come unacceptably late in a letter of which the primary purpose was to acknowledge the receipt of a gift.[96] This assumes, of course, that Paul's overriding purpose in writing to the Philippians was to thank them.[97] But this is by no means obvious. On the contrary, if we accept the commonly held view that Paul communicates his primary concern in writing a given letter in his introductory prayer-report,[98] then the overriding purpose of Paul's letter to the Philippians was to remind them of the things that matter and the things that do not (cf. 1:10; εἰς τὸ δοκιμάζειν ὑμᾶς τὰ διαφέροντα) which, given their present despair over his imprisonment, they had obviously forgotten. Indeed, a major rhetorical hurdle facing Paul in corresponding with the Philippians was how to thank them for their gift while at the same time arguing that such externals do not really matter.[99] This, I would argue, more than accounts for the placement of 4:10–20 after Paul's discussion of the things that matter in the body of the letter, as well as for Paul's insistence on his own self-sufficiency (4:13–14) in the very act of expressing his appreciation.[100] It also explains Paul's brief

---

[94]   Bruce, "St. Paul in Macedonia 3," 276.

[95]   Mackay, "Further Thoughts," 168–9; Buchanan, "Epaphroditus' Sickness."

[96]   Schmithals, *Paul and the Gnostics*, 77, refers to the placement of 4:10–20 as a case of "unbelievable" forgetfulness; cf. Collange, *Philippiens*, 22–3.

[97]   Once we allow that to thank the Philippians was not Paul's primary purpose, then the positioning of 4:10–20 is altogether unproblematic. Indeed, Ign., *Smyrn.* 10.1–2 provides an almost exact parallel. As in Philippians, Ignatius praises the Smyrneans for having done well (καλῶς ἐποιήσατε; the identical expression occurs in Phil. 4:14). Ignatius' closing words also include a εὐχαριστῶ-period: οἳ καὶ εὐχαριστοῦσιν τῷ κυρίῳ ὑπὲρ ὑμῶν ὅτι . . . , "They also thank the Lord for you that . . . " (cf. Phil. 4:10: ἐχάρην δὲ ἐν κυρίῳ μεγάλως ὅτι . . .).

[98]   See chapters 2 and 5 below.

[99]   See chapters 2 and 7 below.

[100]   Paul's so-called "dankloser Dank" (cf. Martin Dibelius, *An die Thessalonischer I–II; An die Philipper* [HNT 2/11; Tübingen: Mohr (Siebeck), 1925] 74) is difficult to

allusion to the gift in 1:3–5; and again in 2:25 and 30, but without dwelling on the subject.[101]

That 4:10–20 is a self-contained pericope loosely tied to the rest of the letter

This leaves us with Collange's contention that 4:10–20 is a self-contained pericope loosely tied to its context and capable of being read as a separate thank-you note.[102] Collange is half right: 4:10–20 is a more or less self-contained pericope. But there is much to link it to the rest of the letter, especially to 1:3–11. Dalton cites the following parallels as evidence of "an inclusion that binds the whole letter into one unit":[103]

1:3–11	4:10–20
μετὰ χαρᾶς (4)	ἐχάρην . . . μεγάλως (10)
κοινωνίᾳ . . . εἰς (5)	ἐκοινώνησεν εἰς (15)
εἰς τὸ εὐαγγέλιον ἀπο τῆς πρώτης ἡμέρας (5)	ἐν ἀρχῇ τοῦ εὐαγγελίου (15)
ἔργον ἀγαθόν (6)	καλῶς ἐποιήσατε (14)
φρονεῖν ὑπέρ (7)	ὑπὲρ . . . φρονεῖν (10)
ἔν τε τοῖς δεσμοῖς μου . . . συγκοινωνούς (7)	συγκοινωνήσαντες μου τῇ θλίψει (14)
πεπληρωμένοι καρπὸν δικαιοσύνης (11)	τὸν καρπὸν τὸν πλεονάζοντα εἰς λόγον ὑμῶν (17)

In addition, Paul's prayer in 1:10 that the Philippians learn to distinguish the things that matter from the things that do not is

---

explain otherwise than in its canonical context. For a different but compatible view, see Abraham Malherbe, "Paul's Self-Sufficiency (Philippians 4:11)," in Fitzgerald, ed., *Friendship*, 125–39; Ken L. Berry, "The Function of Friendship Language in Philippians 4:10–20," in Fitzgerald, ed., *Friendship*, 111–16.

[101] Gnilka, *Philipperbrief*, 9–10.

[102] Collange, *Philippiens*, 22.

[103] W. J. Dalton, "The Integrity of Philippians," *Bib* 60 (1979) 101 (I have slightly augmented Dalton's list). Zahn had already spoken of 4:10–20 as a "doublet" of 1:3–8. Cf. Schubert, *Form and Function*, 76–7; Jewett, "Epistolary Thanksgiving," 53; Rolland, "La structure littéraire," 213; Watson, "Rhetorical Analysis," 77–9; D. A. Black, "The Discourse Structure of Philippians: A Study in Text Linguistics," *NovT* 37 (1995) 24–5.

echoed in his claim to be self-sufficient (αὐτάρκης) in 4:11 and the peristasis catalogue of 4:12.[104]

Here we may also note that to read 4:10–20 as a separate thank-you note – and thus as Paul's first correspondence with the Philippians after his receipt of their gift – only exacerbates the problem of Paul's so-called "thankless thanks." In the context of the canonical letter Paul's indirect expression of thanks coupled with his insistence on self-sufficiency makes good sense. Paul has been exhorting the Philippians not to place too much value in things that do not matter. Removed from this context, however, Paul's extended discussion of how he did not actually need the Philippians' gift is abrupt and unexplained. White's observation that ἐχάρην . . . ὅτι in 4:10 functions as an epistolary introductory formula,[105] only leaves us with the *possibility* that 4:10–20 was a separate letter, since this same formula can occur elsewhere than in an introduction.[106] Against White is the fact that Paul character-istically introduces his letters with the εὐχαριστῶ-period.[107]

---

[104] According to both Cynic and Stoic traditions, one became self-sufficient by learning that the things conventionally understood to be good or evil do not matter. This self-sufficiency was advertised in the peristasis catalogue, where conventional goods and evils are listed as indifferent things. See John T. Fitzgerald, *Cracks in an Earthen Vessel: An Examination of the Catalogues of Hardships in the Corinthian Correspondence* (SBLDS 99; Atlanta: Scholars Press, 1988) 45 and *passim*, and the treatment below in chapter 7.

[105] John L. White, "Introductory Formulae in the Body of the Pauline Letter," *JBL* 90 (1971) 94–5. Cf. PGiss 21.3: λίαν ἐχάρην ἀκούσασα ὅτι; PElephant 13.2 (3rd century BCE); PLond 43.3 (2nd century BCE); PMich 483.3 (Reign of Hadrian); cf. PMert 1.12.4 (Aug. 29, 58 CE); 2 John 4; 3 John 3. Schubert, *Form and Function*, 177. In some cases (e.g., PElephant 13.2), however, the expression of joy seems to be simply an acknowledgment formula (= acknowledgment of a letter received) and not, in addition, as an introductory formula marking the beginning of the letter body; thus Koskenniemi, *Studien*, 75–7.

[106] PYale 42.11 [Jan. 12, 229 BCE]; BGU 2.632.10 [2nd century BCE]). J. White, "Introductory Formulae," 94–5 limits expressions of joy to conventional introduc-tions, but later changes his mind, writing that such phrases are "characteristic of the opening and closing of the letter" (John L. White, *Light from Ancient Letters* [FFNT; Philadelphia: Fortress, 1986] 201); cf. Alexander, "Hellenistic Letter-Forms," 98; esp. Terence Y. Mullins, "Formulas in the New Testament Epistles," *JBL* 91 (1972) 386–8: "expressions of joy . . . might occur anywhere in the letter" (387); "it is not the nature of these forms [e.g., the joy expression, etc.] to introduce, but to punctuate . . . even the thanksgiving cannot be said to introduce the body of the letter apart from Paul's use" (388). For a similar critique of the "introductory" thanksgiving period, see Peter Arzt, "The 'Epistolary Introductory Thanksgiving' in the Papyri and in Paul," *NovT* 36 (1994) 29–46; with response by Jeffrey T. Reed, "Are Paul's Thanksgivings 'Epistolary'?," *JSNT* 61 (1996) 87–99.

[107] *Pace* J. White, "Introductory Formulae," 94, Philem. 7 (χαρὰν γὰρ πολλὴν ἔσχον) does not introduce the body of the letter, which begins in 8 with the request formula (Διὸ . . . παρακαλῶ).

Additional evidence for the integrity of Philippians

The debate over the integrity of Philippians has, understandably, focused on the various arguments for partitioning. However, several positive arguments for the unity of Philippians have been advanced. These are of essentially two types. Recently, a number of studies have appeared in which some new critical methodology (e.g., rhetorical criticism, epistolary criticism, text linguistics) is applied to Philippians in an effort to produce a fresh and coherent analysis of the letter.[108] Naturally, these analyses vary widely in their merit and persuasiveness. More compelling are several older studies that call attention to the many verbal and thematic parallels extending through the various alleged letter-fragments. Here we shall only consider these older studies.[109]

We have already noted the connections between 1:3–11 and 4:10–20. Scholars have long been impressed with the thematic and verbal connections between the Christ hymn of 2:6–11 and Paul's example and exhortation in 3:4–16.[110] But the most striking parallels are between the Christ hymn and 3:20–1.[111] Neal

[108] D. Garland, "Composition and Unity," 141–73; Watson, "Rhetorical Analysis," 57–88; Alexander, "Hellenistic Letter-Forms," 87–101; Stanley Stowers, "Friends and Enemies in the Politics of Heaven: Reading Theology in Philippians," in Jouette M. Bassler, ed., *Pauline Theology*, vol. I: *Thessalonians, Philippians, Galatians, Philemon* (Minneapolis: Augsburg Fortress, 1991) 105–21; Wick, *Der Philipperbrief*; Black, "The Discourse Structure," 16–49; A. B. Luter and M. V. Lee, "Philippians as Chiasmus: Key to the Structure, Unity and Theme Questions," *NTS* 41 (1995) 89–101. Our approach, which argues that 1:10a is programmatic to the argument of the canonical letter, falls somewhat into this category.

[109] We shall have occasion to refer to the more recent studies in the course of our exegesis in part II below.

[110] Maurice Jones, *The Epistle to the Philippians* (Westminster Commentaries; London: Methuen, 1918) xlvii, observes that Paul's "self-emptying" in chapter 3 closely parallels the "self-emptying" of Christ in chapter 2; Pierre Bonnard, *L'épître de Saint Paul aux Philippiens* (CNT 10; Neuchâtel and Paris: Delachaux et Niestlé, 1950) 44, 66, 69, speaks of the "dépouillement" of Christ in 2:7–8 and of Paul in 3:4–11, concluding "que la Philippiens demeurent unis en acceptant le même dépouillement que Paul." T. E. Pollard, "The Integrity of Philippians," *NTS* 13 (1967) 58–9, cites verbal parallels: ἡγεῖσθαι (2:6; 3:7, 8 [twice]), and εὑρίσκω (2:7; 3:9).

[111] If we accept the view that 3:20–1 as well as 2:6–11 are pre-Pauline hymnic material (see especially the judicious analysis by John Reumann, "Philippians 3.20–21 – a Hymnic Fragment?" *NTS* 30 [1984] 593–609), the argument from lexical ties is weakened. Nevertheless the close verbal ties between two independent early Christian hymns is remarkable. The hymns must be linked somehow, which raises again the question of the connection of 3:20–1 with 2:6–11. Cf. Andrew T. Lincoln, *Paradise Now and Not Yet* (SNTSMS 43; Cambridge: Cambridge University Press, 1981) 88; R. H. Gundry, *Sôma in Biblical Theology with Emphasis on Pauline Anthropology* (SNTSMS 29; Cambridge: Cambridge University Press, 1976) 177–83.

Flanagan compiled these in a short note in 1959.[112] William Dalton offered a more extended analysis in 1979.[113] Here is Flanagan's list:

2:5–11	3:20–21
μορφῇ (6); μορφήν (7)	σύμμορφον (21)
ὑπάρχων (6)	ὑπάρχει (20)
σχήματι (7)	μετασχηματίσει (21)
ἐταπείνωσεν (8)	ταπεινώσεως (21)
ἐπουρανίων (10)	οὐρανοῖς (20)
κύριος Ἰησοῦς Χριστός (11)	κύριον Ἰησοῦν Χριστόν (20)
δόξαν (11)	δόξης (21)

To which may be added:

πᾶν ὄνομα . . . πᾶν γόνυ	τὰ πάντα (21)
. . . πᾶσα γλῶσσα (9–11)	

And if we extend the range of comparison to include 3:18–19:

ἐπιγείων (10)	ἐπίγεια (19)
σταυροῦ (10)	σταυροῦ (18)

Not all of these parallels are equally impressive. δόξα, for example, is a common term in Paul and can be found four times elsewhere in Philippians. But as Dalton rightly notes, a number of them are quite remarkable. In all of Paul's letters μορφή is found only in Phil. 2:6 and 7, while σύμμορφος is found only in Phil. 3:21 and Rom. 8:29.[114] Similarly, ταπείνωσις occurs only in Phil. 3:21, while ταπεινόω is found in Phil. 2:9 and 4:12 and in 2 Cor. 11:7 and 12:21.[115] σχῆμα occurs only in Phil. 2:7 and 1 Cor. 7:31, while μετασχηματίζω is found in 1 Cor. 4:6; 2 Cor. 11:13–15 (three times) and Phil. 3:21.[116] Finally, ὑπάρχω occurs a total of twelve times in Paul, but nowhere else in Philippians than in our two texts. It is also commonly noted that Paul typically qualifies κύριος with

---

[112] "A Note on Philippians 3:20–21," *CBQ* 18 (1956) 8–9.
[113] "Integrity," 99–100.
[114] μορφή is found elsewhere in the NT only at Mk. 16:12; σύμμορφος is used only by Paul.
[115] ταπείνωσις is found elsewhere in the NT at Lk. 1:48; Acts 8:33 (citing Isa. 53:8) and Jas. 1:10; ταπεινόω is found at Matt. 18:4; 23:12; Lk. 8:5 (citing Isa. 40:4); 14:11; 18:14; Jas. 4:10; 1 Pet. 5:6.
[116] Both of these terms are used only by Paul in the NT.

the genitive ἡμῶν (e.g., κύριος ἡμῶν Ἰησοῦς Χριστός), but that in both 2:11 and 3:20 κύριος is found without the genitive. Mention should also be made of the exaltation of Christ over "everything" (πᾶν) in heaven, on the earth, and under the earth in 2:9–11 which anticipates Christ's ability to subject "all things" (τὰ πάντα) to himself in 3:21. Dalton is correct to conclude that Paul wrote Phil. 3:20–1 with "the thoughts and phrases of the Christ hymn still fresh in [his] mind."[117]

Other verbal and thematic parallels can also be cited. Garland mentions the following:[118]

πολιτεύεσθε (1:27)	πολίτευμα (3:20)
στήκετε ἐν πνεύματι (1:27)	στήκετε ἐν κυρίῳ (4:1)
συναθλοῦντες τῇ πίστει τοῦ εὐαγγελίου (1:27)	ἐν τῷ εὐαγγελίῳ συνήθλησαν (4:3)
ἀπωλείας, σωτηρίας (1:28)	ἀπώλεια (3:19), σωτῆρα (3:20)
ἐπιποθῶ πάντας ὑμᾶς (1:8)	ἐπιπόθητοι (4:1)

Jewett cites the themes of χαρά and φρονεῖν, as well as the theme of κοινωνία already mentioned, which are introduced in the thanksgiving period and repeated thoughout the letter (χαρά: 1:4, 25; 2:2, 29; 4:1; χαίρω: 1:18 [twice]; 2:17, 18, 28; 3:1; 4:4 [twice], 10; συγχαίρω: 2:17, 18; φρονεῖν: 1:7; 2:2 [twice], 5; 3:15 [twice], 19; 4:2, 10 [twice]).[119] Several scholars have recently pointed to the prominent place given to friendship language in Philippians.[120] Our thesis that the prayer-report of 1:9–11 is programmatic to the argument of each of the alleged letter-fragments is, of course, also further evidence for the integrity of Philippians.

[117] Dalton, "Integrity," 100; Lincoln, *Paradise*, 88. Cf. Dibelius, *An die Philipper*, 72: "was 2.8ff. von Christus erzält wurde, gilt auch von den Christen: erst ταπείνωσις, dann δόξα."
[118] "Composition and Unity," 160–2.
[119] "Epistolary Thanksgiving," 52–3.
[120] L. M. White, "Morality between Two Worlds: A Paradigm of Friendship in Philippians," in D. L. Balch, E. Ferguson, and W. A. Meeks, eds., *Greeks, Romans, and Christians: Essays in Honor of Abraham J. Malherbe* (Minneapolis: Fortress, 1990) 201–15; Stowers, "Friends and Enemies," 105–21; J. T. Fitzgerald, "Philippians, Epistle to the," *ABD* V.218–26 (1992); cf. Detlev Dormeyer, "The Implicit and Explicit Reader and the Genre of Philippians 3:2–4:3, 8–9: Response to the Commentary of Wolfgang Schenk," E. V. McKnight, ed., *Semeia 48: Reader Perspectives on the New Testament* (Atlanta: Scholars Press, 1989) 152–3. The strong form of this argument, that Philippians is a "letter of friendship" (φιλικὴ ἐπιστολή) is rightly criticized by Reumann, "Philippians, Especially Chapter 4."

Conclusion

We have examined the arguments for partitioning individually and have rejected each of them as either unsound or otherwise inconclusive. We have also seen that there are good reasons to accept Philippians as a unity, a point which the following study will attempt to substantiate further. However, it might still be asked whether there is a cumulative argument for the partitioning of Philippians; that is, whether the arguments for partitioning taken together do not make a reasonable case for partitioning. We shall consider this possibility by way of conclusion.

In assessing any cumulative argument for the partitioning of Philippians it is important to distinguish between arguments that fail because they are unsound and arguments that fail because they are inconclusive. Arguments that fail because they are unsound obviously cannot be added up, since unsound arguments do not gain cogency by their number. Arguments that fail because they are inconclusive, however, may in certain cases be added up, but only if they are arguments for the same thing. Of the seven different arguments for partitioning that we have identified, we have argued that five are unsound. They are: (1) that the pseudepigraphic *Epistle to the Laodiceans* passes over Phil. 3:2–4:3; (2) that Phil. 3:2–4:3 reflects a set of circumstances incompatible with Phil. 1:1–3:1; (3) that the abrupt shift in tone between Phil. 3:1 and 3:2 marks a redactional seam; (4) that Phil. 2:25–30 presupposes communications between Paul and the Philippians in which Paul must have already thanked the Philippians for their gift; and (5) that the formal expression of thanks in Phil. 4:10–20 comes unacceptably late in a letter of which the primary purpose was to express that thanks.[121] These arguments may not be added up.

This leaves us with two[122] arguments of the kind that might in theory be added up, provided they are arguments for the same

---

[121] We have argued to the contrary: (1) that *Laodiceans* does contain a reference to Phil. 3:2–4:3; (2) that Phil. 3:2–4:3 and 1:1–3:1 reflect compatible circumstances (since the "opponents" in 1:28 cannot be identified with the "dogs" in 3:2); (3) that there is no harsh break between Phil. 3:1 and 3:2 (provided we take full account of Paul's command to "rejoice in the Lord" in 3:1); (4) that Phil. 2:25–30 does not presuppose additional communication; and (5) that the primary purpose of Philippians is not to express thanks.

[122] A third inconclusive argument might be the fact that Laodiceans makes no reference to 4:10–20. But the likelihood that the compiler of *Laodiceans* would have omitted this material, as I have already argued, is extremely high.

thing: (1) that the logistical information conveyed in Phil. 2:19–30 could come at the end of a Pauline letter; and (2) that, although there is much to tie Phil. 4:10–20 to the rest of the canonical letter, 4:10–20 makes sense as a separate thank-you note. At this point it is important to recognize that the three-letter hypothesis actually argues for two separate conclusions: (1) that Phil. 3:2–4:3 is a letter-fragment; and (2) that Phil. 4:10–20 is also a letter-fragment. Evidence supportive of the partitioning of 4:10–20 cannot, therefore, be indiscriminately added to evidence supportive of partitioning 3:2–4:3. But this is precisely what we would be doing if we were to add these remaining two arguments together. These arguments may not be added up either. At present, there is no cumulative argument for the partitioning of Philippians.

Having made the case that Philippians may be read as a unified letter, we will now consider the rhetorical situation that called it forth.

2

THE RHETORICAL SITUATION OF PHILIPPIANS

Let rhetoric be defined as the art of perceiving the available means of persuasion in any given situation.

Aristotle, *Ars rhet.* 1.2.1

Letters are to be composed from those types that are always fitted to the situation.

Ps.-Demetrius, *Epist. Types*, praef.

To say, as many New Testament scholars now do,[1] that Paul's letters must be studied in light of their respective rhetorical situations is to do more than simply repeat Historical Criticism's familiar creed that documents rooted in a specific historical context can be understood only in reference to that context.[2] It is to say, rather, that Paul's letters were written in response to specific situations (the nature of which I will attempt to define below) and that each letter stands in relation to its situation in much the same

---

[1] Elizabeth Schüssler-Fiorenza, "Rhetorical Situation and Historical Reconstruction in I Corinthians," *NTS* 33 (1987) 386–403; Watson, "Rhetorical Analysis," 57–88, esp 58–9; Andreas H. Snyman, "Style and the Rhetorical Situation of Romans 8.31–39," *NTS* 34 (1988) 218–31; Stephen Mark Pogoloff, *Logos and Sophia: The Rhetorical Situation of I Corinthians* (SBLDS 134; Atlanta: Scholars Press, 1992) 71–95; *idem*, "Isocrates and Contemporary Hermeneutics," in Duane F. Watson, ed., *Persuasive Artistry: Studies in New Testament Rhetoric in Honor of George A. Kennedy* (JSNTSS 50; Sheffield: JSOT Press, 1991) 338–62; Dennis L. Stamps, "Rethinking the Rhetorical Situation: The Entextualization of the Situation in the New Testament Epistles," in Stanley E. Porter and Thomas H. Olbricht, eds., *Rhetoric and the New Testament: Essays from the 1992 Heidelberg Conference* (JSNTSS 90; Sheffield: JSOT Press, 1993) 193–210. Cf. also John T. Kirby, "The Rhetorical Situations of Revelation 1–3," *NTS* 34 (1988) 197–207; Lauri Thurén, *The Rhetorical Strategy of 1 Peter* (Åbo: Åbo Akademis Förlag, 1990) 70–1; Yehoshua Gitay, "Reflections on the Study of the Prophetic Discourse: The Question of Isaiah 1:1–20," *VT* 23 (1983) 206–21.

[2] Herbert A. Wichelns, "Some Differences between Literary Criticism and Rhetorical Criticism," in Raymond F. Howes, ed., *Historical Studies of Rhetoric and Rhetoricians* (Ithaca, New York: Cornell, 1961) 217–24.

way that an answer exists relative to a question or a solution to a problem.[3] Furthermore, it is to say that a fairly detailed description of this generative situation is an early and important step in any critical study of a Pauline letter.[4] In this chapter I will attempt to reconstruct the rhetorical situation of Philippians. Such a reconstruction is, of course, a work of synthesis that can exist only in dialogue with the more detailed exegetical analysis of the letter.[5] As far as possible I will try to indicate the exegetical basis of my reconstruction; at times, however, I will refer to the exegetical chapters in part II below. I begin with a few theoretical considerations.

The rhetorical situation: some theoretical observations

Bitzer's theory of the rhetorical situation

The current emphasis on the rhetorical situation in Pauline studies derives from the theoretical work of Lloyd Bitzer whose programmatic essay, "The Rhetorical Situation," articulates a theory of "rhetoric-as-essentially-related-to-situation."[6] According to Bitzer,

[3] Lloyd Bitzer, "The Rhetorical Situation," *Philosophy and Rhetoric* 1 (1968) 1–14 (reprinted in *Philosophy and Rhetoric*, Supplementary Issue [1992] 1–14); *idem*, "Functional Communication: A Situational Perspective," in Eugene White, ed., *Rhetoric in Transition: Studies in the Nature and Uses of Rhetoric* (University Park and London: Pennsylvania State University, 1980) 21–38.

[4] George Kennedy, *New Testament Interpretation through Rhetorical Criticism* (Chapel Hill: University of North Carolina Press, 1984) 33–8. Kennedy, however, equates the rhetorical situation with Form Criticism's generic *Sitz im Leben* (p. 34); cf. Johannes Schoon-Janßen, *Umstrittene "Apologien" in den Paulusbriefen: Studien zur rhetorischen Situation des 1. Thessalonischerbriefes, des Galaterbriefes und des Philipperbriefes* (GTA 45; Göttingen: Vandenhoeck & Ruprecht, 1991). But see Wilhelm Wuellner, "Where is Rhetorical Criticism Taking Us?," *CBQ* 49 (1987) 456: "the rhetorical situation differs from . . . the generic situation or conventions of the *Sitz im Leben* of forms."

[5] If we allow, as I argue below, that the "rhetorical situation" exists ultimately as a conclusion in the mind of an author, then it will always be the case that the reconstruction of the rhetorical situation will be in part at least a work of synthesis. But this will be particularly the case when we have little or no access to the circumstances giving rise to a document by means other than the document itself, as is the case with Philippians.

[6] "Rhetorical Situation," 3. Situation also played an important role in ancient rhetorical theory, where it was variously conceived. Thus the three rhetorical genres were defined relative to their respective generic situations: judicial rhetoric relative to the courts, deliberative rhetoric relative to the assembly, and epideictic rhetoric relative to the festival. A generic situation is also reflected in the special topics, though here an effort to become more specific is also evident. A more specific situation comes into view in Aristotle's famous definition of rhetoric as the art of

discourse is rhetorical if and only if it is called forth by a particular type of situation, a "rhetorical situation," to which it is offered as a response.[7] Bitzer offers the following definition:[8]

> Rhetorical situation may be defined as a complex of persons, events, objects, and relations presenting an actual or potential exigence which can be completely or partially removed if discourse, introduced into the situation, can so constrain human decision or action as to bring about the significant modification of the exigence.

There are three constituents of any rhetorical situation: (1) an exigence, (2) an audience, and (3) a set of constraints. For a situation to be "rhetorical" the exigence must be capable of positive modification, the audience must be in a position to effect this modification, and there must be a set of constraints (beliefs, attitudes, facts, traditions, images, etc.) accessible to the rhetor by which he or she can move the audience to modify the exigence. Bitzer distinguishes between genuinely rhetorical discourse which stands in relation to an actual exigent situation, and sophistic discourse in which "a contrived exigence is asserted to be real."[9] He also claims that in any truly rhetorical situation there will be "at least one controlling exigence which functions as an organizing principle."[10]

---

discovering the available means of persuasion in a given situation: ἔστω δὴ ῥητορικὴ δύναμις περὶ ἕκαστον τοῦ θεωρῆσαι τὸ ἐνδεχόμενον πίθανον (*Ars rhet.* 1.2.1; cf. 1.2.7; 3.1.3), as well as in the doctrine of τὸ πρέπον (*decorum*; Cic., *Or.* 21.69–70). Ancient epistolary theory was similarly sensitive to the problem of situation. The first-century-BCE handbook attributed to Demetrius of Phalerum (*Epist. Types*) distinguishes twenty-one types of letters based on the different situations that called them forth. The fourth-century-CE handbook ascribed variously to Libanius and Proclus (*Epist. Styles*) distinguishes forty-one types, including one that is "mixed." Both are also explicit that letters should be composed with a specific situation in mind. Thus Ps.-Demetr. (praef.): "letters are to be composed from those types that are always fitted to the situation" ([ἐπιστολοὺς] ἀναβάλλεσθαι ἐκ τῶν ἀεὶ πρὸς τὸ παρὸν ἁρμοζόντων [τύπων]). And Ps.-Lib. (2): "a letter is a kind of written conversation taking place between two people who are separated from each other and fulfilling a useful objective (ἐπιστολὴ μὲν οὖν ἐστι ὁμιλία τις ἐγγράμματος ἀπόντος πρὸς ἀπόντα γινομένη καὶ χρειώδη σκοπὸν ἐκπληροῦσα); cf. Greg. Naz., *Ep.* 51.2: ἔστι δὲ μέτρον τῶν ἐπιστολῶν, ἡ χρεία.

[7] "Rhetorical Situation," 5–6. Bitzer speaks of rhetorical situations "inviting" utterance (p. 4). See further, Alan Brinton, "Situation in the Theory of Rhetoric," *Philosophy and Rhetoric* 14 (1981) 234–48.

[8] "Rhetorical Situation," 6; cf. *idem*, "Functional Communication," 24.

[9] "Rhetorical Situation," 11.

[10] Ibid., 7.

Miller, Vatz, and Consigny on Bitzer

Bitzer's proposal drew a number of responses,[11] not all of which were positive. Most of these focused on Bitzer's more ambitious claim that situation is *sufficient* to define rhetorical discourse, which for our purposes may be set aside. Several scholars, however, have responded to Bitzer's description of the rhetorical situation as such. The earliest response along these lines came from Arthur B. Miller in an essay entitled "Rhetorical Exigence."[12] As the title suggests, Miller focuses on the primary constituent of Bitzer's rhetorical situation, the rhetorical exigence. Miller is troubled by the way exigence seems to function deterministically in Bitzer's model.[13] He agrees with Bitzer that exigencies occur at particular points in time and thus limit when one may speak to an issue. He also agrees that the nature of an exigence serves to limit what one may say about it. But within these limits a speaker has a "creative latitude" to interpret the situation.[14] Miller proposes that a distinction be made between an external exigence existing in the world and that exigence as perceived or interpreted by a rhetor:[15]

> within the limits specified by each exigence, the *ultimate* or *perceived* nature of the exigence depends upon the constraints *of the perceiver*. Thus, the ultimate character of an exigence is a conclusion in the mind of its perceiver (emphases original).

[11] In addition to essays cited below, see K. E. Wilkerson, "On Evaluating Theories of Rhetoric," *Philosophy and Rhetoric* 3 (1970) 82–96; Richard L. Larson, "Lloyd Bitzer's 'Rhetorical Situation' and the Classification of Discourse: Problems and Implications," *Philosophy and Rhetoric* 3 (1970) 165–8; Ralph Pomeroy, "Fitness of Response in Bitzer's Concept of Rhetorical Discourse," *Georgia Speech Communication Journal* 4 (1972) 42–71; Kathleen M. Hall Jamieson, "Generic Constraints and the Rhetorical Situation," *Philosophy and Rhetoric* 6 (1973) 162–70; Barbara A. Biesecker, "Rethinking the Rhetorical Situation from Within the Thematic of *Différance*," *Philosophy and Rhetoric* 22 (1989) 110–30.
[12] *Philosophy and Rhetoric* 5 (1972) 111–18.
[13] Bitzer's alleged determinism is a recurring theme. See especially, J. H. Patton, "Causation and Creativity in Rhetorical Situations: Distinctions and Implications," *QJS* 65 (1979) 36–55; P. K. Tomkins, J. H. Patton, and L. F. Bitzer, "Tomkins on Patton and Bitzer; Patton on Tompkins; Bitzer on Tomkins (and Patton)," *QJS* 66 (1980) 85–93.
[14] Miller, "Rhetorical Exigence," 111. It is not clear, however, how Miller escapes Bitzer's alleged determinism or, for that matter, what is "creative" about the latitude he attributes to the rhetor, since this latitude lies in the perceptions of the rhetor, which are in turn a function of his or her own constraints or judgments (cf. ibid., 118 n. 3).
[15] Ibid., 111–12.

Since audiences also participate in this interpretive process, and since their perceptions will often differ from those of the rhetor, one of the rhetor's first objectives must be "to bring his own constraints and those of his hearers into agreement."[16] We shall return to Miller's suggestion below.

Bitzer's situational model faced its most stringent critique in Richard Vatz's provocative "The Myth of the Rhetorical Situation."[17] Like Miller, Vatz is troubled by what he perceives to be Bitzer's determinism, but his criticism is much more comprehensive. According to Vatz, Bitzer is guilty of a "Platonist" philosophy of meaning that attributes to events in the world "an intrinsic nature . . . from which rhetoric inexorably follows."[18] Vatz could not disagree more:[19]

> Bitzer argues that the nature of the context determines the rhetoric. But one never runs out of context. One never runs out of facts to describe a situation. What was the "situation" during the Vietnam conflict? What was the situation of the 1972 elections? What is any historical situation?

Not surprisingly, Vatz opposes Bitzer point for point:[20]

> I would not say "rhetoric is situational," but situations are rhetorical; not "exigence strongly invites utterance," but utterance strongly invites exigence; not "the situation controls the rhetorical response," but the rhetoric controls the situational response [sic?]; not "rhetorical discourse . . . does obtain its character-as-rhetorical from the situation which generates it," but situations obtain their character from the rhetoric which surrounds them or creates them.

For Vatz, this act of *creating* a rhetorical situation is a radical process in which a rhetor arbitrarily selects from "a scene of inexhaustible events" those which are to be emphasized and then "translates" them so as to construe meaning for his audience.[21] According to Vatz, therefore, meaning does not reside in situations,

---

[16] Ibid., 117.
[17] *Philosophy and Rhetoric* 6 (1973) 154–61.
[18] Ibid., 155.
[19] Ibid., 156.
[20] Ibid., 157, citing Bitzer, "Rhetorical Situation," pp. 3, 5, 6, and 3 respectively.
[21] "Myth," 156; cf. 157: "The very choice of what facts or events are relevant is a matter of pure arbitration"; citing Murray Edelman, *Politics as Symbolic Action: A Treatise on Argumentation* (Chicago: Markham Publishing Co., 1977) 33, and

as Bitzer claims, but exists as a "consequence of rhetorical creation."[22]

Within a year of Vatz's criticism, Scott Consigny, in an article entitled "Rhetoric and Its Situations," modified Bitzer's original account to incorporate Vatz's legitimate, if overstated, objection.[23] Following Vatz, Consigny admits that a rhetor is "thrown" into what might reasonably be described as an indeterminate set of circumstances: "problems do not formulate themselves."[24] But Consigny denies that a rhetorical situation is "created solely through the imagination and discourse of the rhetor."[25] On the contrary, there are certain "facticities" – what Kenneth Burke would call the "recalcitrance" of the situation[26] – that the rhetor must take into account if he is to be persuasive. Consigny writes: "A rhetor speaking in Milwaukee in 1968 to the D.A.R. faces a different task than the rhetor who finds himself in St. Petersburg in 1919 addressing young Bolsheviks."[27] The rhetor's job is thus to uncover and clarify "real issues" in a troubling but otherwise largely unstructured context.[28] He will attempt to do so in a way that ultimately "facilitate[s] their resolution."[29] Consigny theorizes that this uncovering of issues is accomplished by means of the topic or commonplace, "a device which allows the rhetor to discover, through selection and arrangement, that which is relevant and persuasive in a particular situation."[30]

C. Perelman and L. Olbrechts-Tyteca, *The New Rhetoric*, trans. John Wilkinson and Purcel Weaver (Notre Dame and London: University of Notre Dame, 1969) 116–17.

[22] "Myth," 158.

[23] *Philosophy and Rhetoric* 7 (1974) 175–86.

[24] "Rhetoric and Its Situations," 177.

[25] Ibid., 178.

[26] *Permanence and Change* (New York: Bobbs-Merrill, 1965) 255 (cited by Consigny, "Rhetoric and Its Situations," 178).

[27] "Rhetoric and Its Situations," 178.

[28] Ibid., 180.

[29] Ibid., 179.

[30] Ibid., 181. Thus in a political debate one speaker might frame the issue as "freedom vs. safety," emphasizing the need to curtail excessive liberty in the interest of protecting the public, while another might formulate the problem as "freedom vs. slavery," arguing that any curtailing of freedom exposes the citizenry to some form of bondage (183). In focusing on a particular set of issues a rhetor draws from "a repertoire of available topics derived from previous engagements." In novel circumstances it may be necessary to "try several topics before finding those that are fruitful" (183).

"Rhetorical situation" and "Rhetorical problem"

In the following reconstruction of the rhetorical situation of Philippians I shall accept Bitzer's theory of "rhetoric-as-essentially-related-to-situation," but with the provision that Paul's own efforts at formulating the situation be taken into account. I agree with Miller that in its "ultimate" form the rhetorical situation exists as a conclusion in the mind of the rhetor. *Contra* Vatz, however, I do not understand this to be a radical "creation" of the situation but rather, à la Consigny, an attempt to describe a perceptible but still ambiguous situation in familiar categories. What makes these categories persuasive (presumably to both rhetor and audience) is their explanatory power. But they must also admit of solution, and one suspects that familiar categories will give rise to familiar solutions. Consigny is right to speak of these categories as *topoi*, but his stipulative definition of *topos* as "a formal opposition of two (or more) terms"[31] is too narrow, deriving from Aristotle's theory of the "common topics" (*Ars rhet.* 2.19) but neglecting the more fruitful and broadly applicable *loci communes* of the Ciceronean tradition.[32]

In reconstructing the rhetorical situation of Philippians I shall also distinguish between "rhetorical situation" and "rhetorical problem." Every rhetorical situation is in essence a rhetorical "problem" in so far as it revolves around an exigence calling for immediate attention, and some scholars use these terms interchangeably.[33] But in the following analysis I shall reserve the term "rhetorical problem" to refer to some further complication arising

---

[31] Ibid., 182.

[32] *De inv.* bk. 2; cf. Quintilian's distinction between *loci argumentorum* and *loci communes* (Inst. 5.10.20). On the development of the concept of topic, see Perelman and Olbrechts-Tyteca, *The New Rhetoric*, 83–99; cf. William M. A. Grimaldi, SJ, "The Aristotelian *Topics*," *Traditio* 14 (1958) 1–16, reprinted in Keith V. Erickson, ed., *Aristotle: The Classical Heritage of Rhetoric* (Metuchen, NJ: Scarecrow, 1974) 176–93; Joseph Martin, *Antike Rhetorik* (Handbuch der Altertumswissenschaft 2.3; Munich: Beck, 1974) 107–19; cf. Donovan J. Ochs, "Aristotle's Concept of Formal Topics," *Speech Monographs* 36 (1969) 419–25, reprinted in Erickson, ed., *Aristotle*, 194–204. Also Abraham J. Malherbe, "Hellenistic Moralists and the New Testament," *ANRW* II.26.1.320–5 (1992); T. Conley, "Philo's Use of *Topoi*," in David Winston and John Dillon, eds., *Two Treatises of Philo of Alexandria: A Commentary on* De Gigantibus *and* Quod Deus Sit Immutabilis (Brown Judaic Studies 25; Chico, CA: Scholars Press, 1983) 171–8; Richard McKeon, "Creativity and the Commonplace," *Philosophy and Rhetoric* 6 (1973) 199–210.

[33] Stamps, "Rethinking the Rhetorical Situation," 195, 197–8.

from the application of discourse to a situation.[34] I shall argue that Paul confronted at least two "rhetorical problems" in writing the Philippians.

The rhetorical situation of Philippians

Some general observations

We may begin with some basic and generally accepted observations.[35] Paul is writing from prison (1:7, 13–14, 17, 29–30; 4:14) where he is awaiting trial on potentially capital charges (1:21–2; 2:17–18, 23). He has received a gift from the church at Philippi (1:5; 2:25, 30; 4:10, 14, 18) carried by one of its members, Epaphroditus (2:25; 4:18), who tells him of a number of problems in the church. The most glaring of these is a quarrel that has developed between two prominent women, Syntyche and Euodia, whose previous service in Paul's mission is well known (4:2–3); but there is also a more widespread fractiousness in the church (1:27; 2:1–4, 12–16).[36] In addition, there are certain political "opponents" at Philippi who are persecuting the church (1:28–30).[37]

---

[34] Cf. G. Kennedy, *New Testament Interpretation*, 36. A classic example of this type of complication is Seneca's *De clementia*. The occasion is Nero's first murder (i.e., Britannicus) as emperor. Seneca wisely decides not to rebuke his former pupil directly for injustice. Instead he makes the best of a terrible situation by extolling the political virtue of *clementia*. But this creates a problem: for Seneca is a well-known Stoic, and Stoic doctrine calls for *severitas* in the administration of justice (cf. *SVF* 3.637–9; 3.641) which contradicts his call for *clementia*. Seneca attempts to solve this "rhetorical problem" in book 2 where he defines *clementia* as *temperantia* or *moderatio* in the administration of justice (cf. 2.3) and thus consistent with Stoic *severitas*, which contradicts not *clementia* but the vice *misericordia*. Cf. Miriam Griffin, *Seneca. A Philosopher in Politics* (Oxford: Clarendon, 1976) 154–71, who sees in *De clementia* book 2 Seneca's own *ad hoc* development of Stoic doctrine.

[35] See the standard introductions and commentaries.

[36] D. Peterlin, *Paul's Letter to the Philippians in Light of Disunity in the Church* (NovTSup 79; Leiden: Brill, 1995) makes too much of this problem. In particular, I would disagree that internal fighting is the immediate context for all parts of Philippians (note his rather forced readings of 1:12–18 and 3:2–4:1). Significantly, Peterlin omits any discussion of the prayer-report of 1:9–11. Strife in the church may be one obvious occasion of the letter, but it is strife that has been understood in light of its cause, namely, discouragement resulting (ultimately) from a distorted view of what really matters.

[37] Political opponents are clearly in view here. The Philippians are experiencing τὸν αὐτὸν ἀγῶνα . . . οἷον εἴδετε ἐν ἐμοὶ καὶ νῦν ἀκούετε ἐν ἐμοί (1:30). See the discussion of this text above in chapter 1. Some might wish to include at this point the theological opponents ("dogs") of chapter 3. This group has not, however, infiltrated the church at Philippi. They represent a tendency that Paul discerns in the Philippians. Phil. 3:1–4:1 is not in my view polemical, but didactic and hortatory; it

Epaphroditus also tells Paul that his imprisonment, bringing with it
the possibility that the Philippians might never see him again (cf.
1:26–7; 2:12, 24), has been particularly distressing. This, combined
with the Philippians' own hardships, has produced a general
"anxiety" in the church (4:6–9).[38] Epaphroditus is also concerned
that news of his own illness, which will have reached Philippi, will
only further discourage the Philippians (cf. 2:18).

Added to these "facticities" and informing his interpretation of
them is Paul's intimate and long-standing relationship with the
Philippians.[39] He alludes to this relationship at the beginning of his
letter in 1:5 when he speaks of their "partnership in the gospel from
the first day until now," and he returns to it frequently throughout
the rest of the letter.[40] A particularly detailed description comes in
4:15–16:

> οἴδατε δὲ καὶ ὑμεῖς, Φιλιππήσιοι, ὅτι ἐν ἀρχῇ τοῦ
> εὐαγγελίου, ὅτε ἐξῆλθον ἀπὸ Μακεδονίας, οὐδεμία μοι
> ἐκκλησία ἐκοινώνησεν εἰς λόγον δόσεως καὶ λήμψεως εἰ
> μὴ ὑμεῖς μόνοι, ὅτι καὶ ἐν Θεσσαλονίκῃ καὶ ἅπαξ καὶ δὶς
> εἰς τὴν χρείαν μοι ἐπέμψατε.

> Now you yourselves know, Philippians, that in the begin-
> ning of the gospel, when I went out from Macedonia, not

is Paul's consolation of the Philippians taken to its logical conclusion. See chapter 6
below.

[38] Nicholas Walter, "Die Philipper und das Leiden: Aus den Anfängen einer
heidenchristlichen Gemeinde," in Rudolf Schnackenburg et al., eds., *Die Kirche des
Anfangs: Festschrift für Heinz Schürmann zum 65. Geburtstag* (Leipzig: St. Benno, 1977)
417–33: "[Paulus] spricht zu Christen, denen solche Gedanken alles andere als vertraut
sind, denen ein Leiden um Christi, um des Evangeliums willen den Glauben und die
Standfestigkeit, aber auch den Zusammenhalt untereinander zu zerstören droht" (423).

[39] The distinction that I make here between facts and interpretation is obviously
vulnerable to objection on the grounds that everything we know about the immediate
situation at Philippi comes to us by way of Paul's letter and is thus by definition his
interpretation. Nevertheless, it strikes me as excessive to insist that all the background information given to us in Philippians shares the same epistemic status. One
may, of course, wish to maintain *on a priori grounds* that Paul's references to, say,
Epaphroditus or the Philippians' gift or the squabble between Euodia and Syntyche
only exist intentionally as interpretations on the part of Paul. I propose, however,
that we trust Paul on these matters and that we go on to speak of how Paul made
sense of them, that is, how he interpreted them in light of his own philosophical and
religious commitments and beliefs. I concede that it is not always clear where to
place an item along the spectrum that runs from fact to interpretation, and that,
furthermore, at least some of Paul's "facts" came to him second hand by way of
Epaphroditus. Neither of these qualifications, however, nullifies to my mind the
distinction between fact and interpretation in the rhetorical situation of Philippians.

[40] Phil. 1:7–8, 24–6, 27; 2:2, 12, 16, 19, 24, 28; 3:1, 17–18; 4:1, 3, 9, 10–11.

one church shared with me in the matter of giving and receiving except you alone, and that even in Thessalonica you more than once sent to my need.

These verses contain important information about Paul's early relationship with the Philippians.[41] But what makes them especially instructive is that they attempt to relate that information from the perspective of the Philippians themselves ("Now you yourselves know, Philippians . . . "). Here we catch a glimpse of the Philippians' self-understanding which Paul undoubtedly took into account in his assessment of the situation at Philippi.

The Philippians' self-understanding

Three elements of the Philippians' self-understanding may be identified in Phil. 4:15–16. First, the Philippians understood the foundation of their church to mark "the beginning of the gospel" (ἀρχὴ τοῦ εὐαγγελίου).[42] Commentators have interpreted this phrase in one of two ways. Some, such as Meyer, have understood Paul to be speaking "vom Standpunkte der Leser" and thus to be referring to the Philippians' conversion.[43] Others, such as Lohmeyer and Gnilka, understand Paul to be speaking from his own perspective and to have in view the beginning of a new phase in his mission.[44] The text, which continues "when I went out from Macedonia," supports the second reading;[45] however, it is wrong to assign this perspective exclusively to Paul, since 4:15–16 ostensibly relates the Philippians' own understanding of things.[46] Both Paul and the Philippians, therefore, understood the foundation of the church at Philippi to mark a new phase in the Gentile mission. For

---

[41] Peter Pilhofer, *Philippi*, vol. I: *Die erste christliche Gemeinde Europas* (WUNT 87; Tübingen: Mohr [Siebeck], 1995) 245–6.

[42] Cf. 1:5; Polycarp, *Ad Phil.* 1.2; 11.3 (Lightfoot's reconstruction).

[43] Meyer, *An die Philipper*, 144; Dibelius, *An die Philipper*, 163; P. Ewald and E. Wohlenberg, *Der Brief des Paulus an die Philipper* (Leipzig: Deichert, 1919), 231; cited in Pilhofer, *Philippi*, 245 n. 2. Müller, *An die Philipper*, 204, takes a similar view, but broadens it to include happenings in the near vicinity (*Umkreis*) of Philippi.

[44] Lohmeyer, *An die Philipper*, 184–5; Gnilka, *Philipperbrief*, 177; cf. Pilhofer, *Philippi*, 246: "für Paulus die Mission in Philippi einen ganz besonderen Wendepunkt markiert"; G. Bornkamm, *Paul* (New York: Harper & Row, 1971) 60–1.

[45] Gnilka, *Philipperbrief*, 177; cf. Collange, *Philippiens*, 132.

[46] Collange is near the mark when he writes: "Mais sans doute Paul se place-t-il à la fois du point de vue des Philippiens et de celui de son activité [missionnaire] entièrement responsable" (*Philippiens*, 132).

the Philippians this meant that they were in effect founding members of Paul's European mission.[47]

Second, the Philippians also understood themselves to be unique among the Pauline churches in their support of Paul. "No other church," Paul writes," shared with me in the matter of giving and receiving except you alone."[48] The Philippians' financial relationship with Paul has been much discussed. Sampley argues that a formal *societas* or contractual partnership is in view.[49] Malherbe and others understand a less formal friendship (φιλία) relationship.[50] Other possibilities include a kind of patron–client relationship,[51] or the giving and receiving of *beneficia* on analogy with the ideology of gift-giving articulated in Seneca's *De beneficiis*.[52] But whatever model we adopt, if indeed we adopt any, the Philippians had been unique in their support of Paul. This too was part of their self-understanding as a church.

Finally, we may identify in the Philippians' response to Paul an immediacy and enthusiasm that distinguished them even further from other churches. Paul's next stop after Philippi was Thessalonica, where he may have remained only a short while (1 Thess. 2:17; Acts 17:5–10). Yet the Philippians wasted no time in sending support to Paul: "even in Thessalonica you sent more than once to my need."[53] We learn from 2 Cor. 11:8–9 that the Thessalonians

[47] Polycarp, *Ad Phil.* 1.2 and 11.3 suggest that the church at Philippi continued to understand itself in these terms for several generations.

[48] But see 2 Cor. 11:8–9 where Paul refers to the support of "other churches" (plural) while at Corinth. Paul's mission strategy also seems to have developed after Philippi. At Philippi he appears to have accepted the patronage of Lydia (Acts 16:14–15), but at Thessalonica he worked (1 Thess. 2:5, 9; cf. 2 Thess. 3:7–10), and so too at Corinth (1 Cor. 4.12); cf. Gordon D. Fee, *Paul's Letter to the Philippians* (Grand Rapids: Eerdmanns, 1995) 444.

[49] J. P. Sampley, *Pauline Partnership in Christ* (Philadelphia: Fortress, 1980) 51–62; cf. H. A. A. Kennedy, "The Financial Colouring of Phil. iv, 15–18," *ExpT* 12 (1900–01) 43–4.

[50] Malherbe, "Paul's Self-Sufficiency," 129; Berry, "Friendship Language," 118; Fee, *Paul's Letter*, 443–5; Peter Marshall, *Enmity at Corinth: Social Conventions in Paul's Relationship with the Corinthians* (WUNT 2/23; Tübingen: Mohr [Siebeck], 1987) 160–4; criticized by Bormann, *Philippi*, 164–70. Elsewhere in Philippians κοινωνία and its cognates are used not only of partnership in financial matters, but in "partnership" in affliction (4:14), the gospel (1:5), and the grace of suffering (1:7); cf. Bormann, *Philippi*, 181–7.

[51] Bormann, *Philippi*, 187–205.

[52] L. White, "Morality between Two Worlds," and Marshall, *Enmity at Corinth*, treat the conferring of *beneficia* in the context of ancient friendship doctrine, but see Bormann, *Philippi*, 171–81.

[53] Pilhofer, *Philippi*, 246: "engagieren sich die Philipper in bemerkenswerter Weise finanziell für die weitere Missionstätigkeit des Paulus."

eventually joined the Philippians in supporting Paul. But the Philippians, who had supported Paul even during his mission to Thessalonica, would always be first. The church at Philippi thus enjoyed a kind of absolute priority in Paul's mission to Macedonia and Achaia, even among the exemplary churches of Macedonia. Müller is correct to speak of the Philippians' "besondere, ja exklusive Beziehung" with Paul.[54]

Discouragement at Philippi

It is only natural that the Philippians, whose long-standing relationship with Paul contributed significantly to their self-understanding as a church, were disturbed by news of Paul's imprisonment and possible execution. And judging from his response, Paul took Epaphroditus' report of their discouragement seriously. Indeed, Paul's primary purpose in writing to the Philippians seems to have been to console[55] them that things were in fact going much better than they imagined. Paul warms to his subject quickly in 1:6 when he assures the Philippians that it was God who began his mission at Philippi, and that God, regardless of Paul's own fate, would see that mission to completion.[56] His consolation begins in earnest, however, in 1:12–26. Paul here offers a series of three consolatory arguments: (1) that his imprisonment has variously aided "the progress of the gospel" (προκοπὴ τοῦ εὐαγγελίου);[57] (2) that it will also eventually result in his "salvation" (σωτηρία), and (3) that the Philippians will soon see him again (οἶδα ὅτι μενῶ καὶ

[54] Müller, *An die Philipper*, 204.

[55] The ancient notion of consolation will be examined in detail in the next chapter. Here it should be recalled (cf. Introduction above), however, that the ancient notion of consolation differed significantly from the modern notion. When we today speak of consolation, we typically mean a show of sympathy or condolence, an expression of sorrow. But by ancient standards consolation consisted of rational argumentation and exhortation against excessive grief. To say, therefore, that Paul's objective is to console (in the ancient sense) the Philippians, means that he is concerned to correct their distress and restore them to responsible behavior.

[56] ὁ ἐναρξάμενος ἐν ὑμῖν ἔργον ἀγαθόν should be translated "he who began a good work *among* you" and understood to be referring to Paul's mission begun by God at Philippi. See my discussion of this verse below in chapter 4.

[57] The thesis of 1:12 is supported by three arguments. In 1:13 Paul argues that imprisonment has given him something of a reputation with outsiders. In 1:14 he argues that he has become an example and inspiration to other believers. Finally, in 1:15–17, he shows that even his rivals are promoting the gospel more effectively because of his imprisonment. See chapter 5 below.

παραμενῶ πᾶσιν ὑμῖν).[58] "All these things," writes Chrysostom,
"[Paul] says for the consolation (παραμυθίαν) of the Philippians."[59]
Similarly, Jerome: "Here [= Phil. 1:12–18] he consoles (*consolatur*)
them regarding his tribulation, for they have heard that he is being
held in chains in the city of Rome."[60]

Paul returns to the topic of consolation in 2:19–30 when he
repeats his assurance that he will revisit the Philippians in the not
too distant future (2:24), and promises to send Timothy "as soon as
I see more clearly how things will go with me" (2:19, 23).[61] His
decision to return Epaphroditus also seems to have been for the
Philippians' encouragement: σπουδαιοτέρως οὖν ἔπεμψα αὐτόν,
ἵνα ἰδόντες αὐτὸν πάλιν χαρῆτε κἀγὼ ἀλυπότερος ὦ (2:28).
Various other consolatory topics and arguments appear throughout
the letter, including the (Cyrenaic) argument *nihil inopinati accidisse*
("nothing unexpected has happened") in 1:28–30, and the (Epicurean) technique of *avocatio/revocatio* in 4:8–9.[62] We will see
below that Paul's prayer in 1:10a – that the Philippians learn "to

[58] Alexander, "Hellenistic Letter-Forms," 95: "[Philippians] was not written to
inform the church that Paul is in prison (they already know that) but to reassure
them that the situation is 'all right' in three ways: *first*, because 'what has happened
to me has really served to advance the Gospel' (1.12–18); *second*, because death, if it
should come, is not to be feared (1.19–23); and *third*, and slightly contradictorily,
because Paul will probably soon be released anyway (1.24–26)." I disagree with
Collange, *Philippiens*, 26, and Peterlin, *Disunity*, 31–51, that Paul here defends
himself against those critical of his decision not to be come a martyr. Phil. 1:12–26
is not apologetic but consolatory; cf. Pheme Perkins, "Philippians: Theology for the
Heavenly politeuma," in Bassler, ed., *Pauline Theology*, I, 89.
[59] *In Epist. ad Phil.*, hom. 3.3 (*PG* 62.201.36–7): ταῦτα δὴ πάντα πρὸς παραμυθίαν
τῶν Φιλιππησίων λέγει. To my knowledge no modern commentator has argued that
Philippians is consolatory. Alexander comes close to my view when she writes that
Paul's purpose in 1:12–26 is "to reassure" (see the preceding note). But her final
judgment is that Philippians is a "family letter."
[60] *In Epist. ad Phil.* (*PL* 30.842C): *Hic consolatur eos de sua tribulatione: qui
audierant, eum vinctum in urbe Roma custodiri.*
[61] That Phil. 1:12–26 is consolatory is confirmed by 2:19 where Paul writes:
ἐλπίζω δὲ ἐν κυρίῳ Ἰησοῦ Τιμόθεον ταχέως πέμψαι ὑμῖν, ἵνα κἀγὼ εὐψυχῶ γνοὺς
τὰ περὶ ὑμῶν. The implication is that Paul in relating his circumstances (τὰ κατ᾽ ἐμέ
1:12) has sought to comfort the Philippians and that now he wants to hear of their
circumstances (τὰ περὶ ὑμῶν) that he *too* might be consoled (κἀγὼ εὐψυχῶ).
[62] For the association of these and other consolatory methods and arguments
with certain philosophical schools, see Cic., *Tusc.* 3.31.76, and chapter 3 below. On
Cyrenaic theory, see specifically *Tusc.* 3.13.28: *Cyrenaici non omni malo aegritudinem
effici censent, sed insperato et necopinato malo*; 3.22.52: *Cyrenaicorum restat sententia,
qui tum aegritudinem censent exsistere, si necopinato quid evenerit*; on the Epicurean
view, see *Tusc.* 3.15.33: *Levationem autem aegritudinis in duabus rebus ponit,
avocatione a cogitanda molestia et revocatione ad contemplandas voluptates*; cf. Paul
A. Holloway, "*Bona Cogitare*: An Epicurean Consolation in Phil 4:8–9," *HTR* 91
(1998) 89–96. We shall treat these at length in chapters 4–7 below.

discern the things that matter"[63] – and the motif of "joy" that characterizes the letter are also consolatory.[64]

Discouragement as a cause of disunity at Philippi

It is important at this point that we do not overlook a second problem facing Paul at Philippi, namely, the disunity that existed most obviously in the personal rivalry between Euodia and Syntyche (4:2–3), but also more broadly in the church (cf. 1:27; 2:1–4, 12–16). In particular, we should ask how these twin exigencies of discouragement and disunity were related in the mind of Paul. There are good reasons to believe that Paul identified discouragement as the more basic problem in the church at Philippi, and that he understood the various disruptions there as in some sense the result of this.[65] This is implied, for instance, at 1:27 where Paul exhorts the Philippians to "stand in one spirit, in one soul struggling together for the faith of the gospel" whether or not he is returned to them (εἴτε ἐλθὼν . . . εἴτε ἀπών). Similarly, at 2:12–14 he exhorts them to "do all things without murmuring or disputing" despite the fact he is now absent (ἐν τῇ ἀπουσίᾳ μου).[66] Particularly striking is Paul's stated assumption at 1:25 that only his release

[63] For the (Stoic) theory that grief arises when one fails to distinguish between the things that matter and the things that do not, see "Ancient Theories of Consolation" in chapter 3 below (cf. Cic., *Tusc.*, 3.31.76: *Sunt qui unum officium consolantis putent malum illud omnino non esse, ut Cleanthi placet*).

[64] See chapter 3 below. "Joy" (χαρά), the antithesis of "grief" (λύπη; cf. Phil. 2:28), is an important motif in ancient consolation and in Philippians. Paul directly exhorts the Philippians to rejoice 6 times (2:17, 18, 29; 3:1 and 4:4 [twice]); 6 times he exhorts them indirectly (1:18 [twice], 25; 2:17, 18, and 28; cf. 1:4; 2:2).

[65] This is not to say that discouragement was to Paul's mind the sole cause of disunity, or that disunity was not a problem in its own right. Neither is it to say that we must accept Paul's judgment that discouragement actually underlay disunity at Philippi, as long as we understand that Paul composed his letter to the Philippians with just this explanation in mind. However, Paul's assessment does not seem to me to be unreasonable. The Philippians had for a number of years cooperated in a project that allowed them to put aside any personal differences and work together. As that project came into jeopardy and, more importantly, the Philippians began to have doubts about its viability, it would be only natural if personal differences were no longer repressed and interpersonal problems arose. Significantly, Paul's exhortation to the Philippians in 1:27–2:4 is to put aside such personal differences and to work together again.

[66] Ultimately, we must understand the Philippians to be complaining against God for their circumstances. But it is likely that their complaints were more immediately directed toward one another, and especially against those in places of prominence or leadership in the community (cf. 1:1; 2:29–30); cf. Bonnard, *Philippiens*, 49–51. See our discussion of this text below in chapter 5.

from prison and physical return to Philippi will result in their renewed progress in the faith: οἶδα ὅτι μενῶ καὶ παραμενῶ πᾶσιν ὑμῖν εἰς τὴν ὑμῶν προκοπὴν καὶ χαρὰν τῆς πίστεως.

Additional evidence that Paul regarded discouragement to be the more fundamental problem facing him at Philippi lies in the overall progression of thought between chs. 1 and 2. Having reassured the Philippians at some length that the mission is still progressing (1:12–26), and having urged them to embrace their current hardships as an expression of God's purposes for them (1:27–30), Paul exhorts them "therefore" (οὖν) to put aside the selfishness (2:1–4) and complaining (2:12–16) currently characterizing the church and to fill up what is lacking in his joy (2:2, cf. 2:16).[67] The consolation of 1:12–30 is thus the basis for the exhortation to unity in 2:1–16.[68] In this regard, it is not surprising that the two people singled out in 4:2–3 as the most disruptive in the church are Euodia and Syntyche, whose previous support of Paul's mission had set them apart; more than any others they would have been distressed by Paul's circumstances.

Lack of knowledge as the cause of the Philippians' discouragement

If Paul identified discouragement as the more fundamental problem at Philippi, what did he understand to be the cause or causes of that discouragement? Why were the Philippians so distressed by Paul's imprisonment, when Paul himself was not? Paul indicates his answer to this crucial question in the prayer-report of Phil. 1:9–11.[69]

[67] Most commentators take the hortatory material in 1:27–30 with the similar material in 2:1–18 and read the οὖν of 2:1 as resumptive. Even on this account the point holds that Paul's exhortations to unity are based on the consolation of 1:12–26. It is, however, not my view that 1:27–30 should be divided from 1:12–26. (See my discussion of this question below in chapter 5.) To be sure, both 1:27–30 and 2:1–18 are hortatory. But the exhortation of 1:27–30 continues to deal directly with the problem of discouragement, whereas 2:1–18 treats the secondary problem of the various disruptions taking place in the church at Philippi. I understand the οὖν of 2:1 to be *paraeneticum* (cf. Phil. 2:29; Rom. 6:12; 12:1; 1 Cor. 10:31; 2 Cor. 7:1; Gal. 5:1).

[68] The relationship between consolation and exhortation is explicit: εἴ τις οὖν παράκλησις . . . εἴ τι παραμύθιον . . . πληρώσατέ μου τὴν χαρὰν ἵνα τὸ αὐτὸ φρονῆτε . . . See further our discussion of 2:1 below in chapter 5.

[69] For the programmatic nature of Paul's introductory prayer-reports see Schubert, *Form and Function*, 62; Gordon P. Wiles, *Paul's Intercessory Prayers* (SNTSMS 24; Cambridge: Cambridge University Press, 1974) 175–229; cf. O'Brien, *Introduc-*

The substance of Paul's prayer for the Philippians is conveyed in Phil. 1:9–10a, which reads:

καὶ τοῦτο προσεύχομαι, ἵνα ἡ ἀγάπη ὑμῶν ἔτι μᾶλλον καὶ μᾶλλον περισσεύῃ ἐν ἐπιγνώσει καὶ πάσῃ αἰσθήσει εἰς τὸ δοκιμάζειν ὑμᾶς τὰ διαφέροντα.

And this I pray, that your love might increase even more and more in knowledge and all perception, that you might be able to discern the things that matter.

Here we learn that, to Paul's mind at least, the Philippians are deficient in "knowledge and all perception"[70] and that this deficiency has left them unable "to discern the things that matter."[71] The most natural way to understand this is that the Philippians have in some way failed to distinguish the things that matter from the things that do not, and that in so doing they have allowed themselves to be discouraged by the latter, that is, by things that do not matter. The logic of Paul's diagnosis is simple and would have been familiar to most of his contemporaries. It follows closely Stoic consolation theory, according to which grief has its origin in the failure to distinguish accurately between the things that matter and the things that do not, on the assumption that things conventionally believed to be misfortunes fall consistently into the latter category (i.e., things that do not matter) and do not therefore constitute adequate grounds for grief.[72]

tory Thanksgivings, passim; Meeks, "The Man from Heaven in Philippians," 333. See chapter 4 below.

[70] Scholars have generally understood 1:9 to call for an increase in love not knowledge: C. Spicq, *Agapè dans le Nouveau Testament* (Paris: Gabalda, 1959) II.234; cf. Beare, *Philippians*, 55; Gnilka, *Philipperbrief*, 52; Collange, *Philippiens*, 49; O'Brien, *Philippians*, 74; Hawthorne, *Philippians*, 26–7; Vincent, *Philippians*, 13. But the Greek will not bear this interpretation. In the construction τινὰ περισσεύειν ἐν τινί it is not the subject (τινά) that increases but the object of the preposition ἐν (cf. Rom. 15:13; 1 Cor. 15:58). As it stands, therefore, the prayer of 1:9 calls for an increase in knowledge. Cf. Collange, *Philippiens*, 48: "reconnaissant les qualités d'affection de ses lecteurs (ἀγάπη), l'apôtre leur demande de gagner en intelligence et en discernement." See the discussion in chapter 4 below.

[71] Paul implies here the familiar distinction between the "things that matter" (τὰ διαφέροντα) and the things that do not (τὰ ἀδιάφορα). A number of modern commentators now take this view (Lohmeyer, *An die Philipper*, 32–3, Gnilka, *Philipperbrief*, 52; W. Schenk, *Die Philipperbriefe des Paulus: Kommentar* [Stuttgart: Kohlhammer, 1984] 112–13) but fail to make full use of it because of false comparisons with Rom. 2:18 and 12:2. See further the discussion of this text and the Stoic doctrine of indifferent things in chapters 3 and 4 below.

[72] Cf. Cic., *Tusc.* 3.31.76: *Sunt qui unum officium consolantis putent [docere] malum illud omnino non esse, ut Cleanthi placet*; Sen., *Ad Helv.* 4.2: *nihil mihi mali*

50   Literary and rhetorical contexts

A close reading of Paul's efforts to encourage the Philippians in
1:12–26 confirms this interpretation of 1:9–10a. Twice Paul draws
a distinction between things that matter and things that do not. In
1:12–18a it is the "progress" (προκοπή) of the gospel that matters
and Paul's "bonds" (δεσμοί) that do not. In 1:18b–21 it is Paul's
"salvation" (σωτηρία) that matters and his possible execution (εἴτε
διὰ ζωῆς εἴτε διὰ θανάτου) that does not.[73] The Philippians have
obviously failed to make this distinction, and they are thus grieved
by things that do not really matter, namely, Paul's imprisonment
and possible execution. Paul, on the other hand, has carefully
observed this distinction. As a result he rejoices (ἐν τούτῳ χαίρω
ἀλλὰ καὶ χαρήσομαι) in the progress of the gospel and in his own
assured salvation. Chrysostom adroitly summarizes:[74]

> In the beginning of his letter [= 1:12–18] Paul offers the
> Philippians much consolation regarding his imprisonment,
> showing not only that they should not be troubled [by the
> things that do not matter], but that they should rejoice [in
> the things that do].

Paul also employs the *topos* of "things that matter" in the second
part of his letter in 3:1–4:1. Here, however, the distinction is not
drawn relative to the things (plural) that matter, but relative to the
"one thing"[75] that matters most, namely, "the surpassing greatness
of the knowledge of Christ Jesus my lord" (τὸ ὑπερέχον τῆς
γνώσεως Χριστοῦ Ἰησοῦ τοῦ κυρίου μου), against which all else is
"refuse" (σκύβαλα).[76] Paul introduces his subject immediately in

esse. This is not to say, of course, that Paul followed the Stoics point for point in
their doctrine of indifferent things. Most obviously, Paul differed from the Stoa in
his criterion for assigning value (the gospel and, ultimately, Christ). Furthermore,
in the consolation of the Philippians Paul focuses on the things that do matter (τὰ
διαφέροντα) as grounds for rejoicing, whereas Stoic consolers tended to focus on the
things that do not matter (τὰ ἀδιάφορα) as the basis for philosophical indifference or
ἀπάθεια. See further our discussion of these matters in chapters 3 and 4.
[73] Paul uses the correlatives εἴτε . . . εἴτε in 1:18 (εἴτε προφάσει εἴτε ἀληθείᾳ)
and 1:20 (εἴτε διὰ ζωῆς εἴτε διὰ θανάτου) to express his indifference to conventional
evils (cf. 1:27, εἴτε ἐλθών . . . εἴτε ἀπών). For a similar use of εἴτε . . . εἴτε (or *sive
. . . sive*), cf. Epict., *Diss.* 3.22.21; Muson., frag. 38 Hense (= Stob., *Ecl.* 2.8.30; =
Epict., frag. 4 Schenkl); Sen., *Ep.* 36.6; 74.26; 111.4 (see chapter 5 below).
[74] *In Epist. ad Phil.*, praef. 1 (*PG* 62.179.38–40): ἐν τοῖς προοιμίοις τῆς ἐπιστολῆς
πολλὴν προσάγει παράκλησιν ὑπὲρ τῶν δεσμῶν, δεικνὺς ὅτι οὐ μόνον οὐ χρὴ
θορυβεῖσθαι, ἀλλὰ καὶ χαίρειν. Cf. his comments on Paul's treatment of life and
death 1:19–21, *In Epist. ad Phil.*, hom. 3.3 (*PG* 62.202.31–2, 56–7): τὸ γὰρ ζῆν
πάλιν τῶν μέσων ἐστὶ καὶ ἀδιαφόρων . . . καὶ γὰρ ὁ θάνατος τῶν ἀδιαφόρων ἐστίν.
[75] Phil. 3:13: ἓν δέ.
[76] Alexander, "Hellenistic Letter-Forms," 100: "But that simple message of

3:1 when he exhorts the Philippians to "rejoice in the Lord" (χαίρετε ἐν κυρίῳ), "joy" again finding its object in what really matters. Those who do not "boast in Christ Jesus" are "dogs!" and must be avoided at all costs (3:2–3). But even our own accomplishments must be radically revalued (3:4–16). This "revaluation of values"[77] obviously applies to our accomplishments prior to conversion (3:4–11), which are to be considered "loss" (ζημία). But it also encompasses our accomplishments after conversion (3:12–16), which are to be forgotten (ἐπιλανθανόμενος) as we "pursue, as according to a mark, the upward call of God in Christ Jesus." There is really only one things that matters, and that is "to know [Christ], and the power of his resurrection and the fellowship of his sufferings."

In its most fully articulated form, therefore, Paul's thesis in 1:9–10a that the Philippians must learn "to discern the things that matter" extends to the very foundations of Christian existence. Not only have the Philippians failed to distinguish between what does and what does not matter relative to the gospel mission (1:12–26), but they have also failed to perceive that, when measured against the believer's "knowledge of Christ," that mission itself, or at least their ostensible success in it, is a matter of clearly secondary importance (3:1–16).[78] Paul here comes full circle and challenges the Philippians' self-understanding as charter members of his mission into Macedonia and Achaia. He urges them, instead, to view themselves – and this is Paul's own self-understanding – as those who ultimately value but one thing: ἡ γνῶσις Χριστοῦ.[79]

---

reassurance [1:12–26] . . . is developed by Paul at successively deeper levels [referring primarily to chapter 3], not as a logical argument but following a natural train of thought . . ." See further chapter 6 below.

[77] The expression is Gnilka's, *Philipperbrief*, 191: *Umwertung der Werte*. However, he applies it only to Paul's conversion.

[78] Paul has here moved from penultimate to ultimate matters. The implications of this for the Philippians are significant. Whereas in 1:12–26 he relativizes conventional goods to the progress of the gospel, in 3:1–4:1 Paul takes a further step and relativizes all of our accomplishments, including those in the service of the gospel, to "the knowledge of Christ." As a matter of principle, therefore, hardship in the gospel ministry cannot be grounds for discouragement, since it fosters a knowledge of Christ through "the fellowship of his sufferings" (3:10). That to Paul's mind the Philippians were not fully reconciled to suffering in the ministry is suggested also by 1:28–30 where he tells the Philippians that they should not be "surprised" (πτύρομαι) that they have been opposed in the gospel. Paul here treats the Philippians' suffering as a case of unexpected misfortune; cf. Cic., *Tusc.* 3.13.28 (*insperatum et necopinatum malum*). See the discussion in chapter 5 below.

[79] See further our discussion of 3:1–4:1 in chapter 6 below.

Two rhetorical problems

Before concluding our discussion of the rhetorical situation, it will
be helpful to consider how Paul sought to solve the two "rhetorical
problems" arising from his formulation of the rhetorical situation:
namely, (1) how to thank the Philippians for their gift while
counseling indifference to material circumstances, which would
seem to include their gift, and (2) how to rebuke his devoted
supporters for their emotional frailty when what they expect from
him is a letter of thanks for their most recent display of support.

Paul's solution to the first of these problems, how to thank the
Philippians for their gift while at the same time encouraging them
to be indifferent to external things, seems to have been to separate
as much as possible the two issues (i.e., gratitude and indifference).
He accomplishes this in two ways. He first separates them *spatially*.
In 1:1–4:9 he treats at length the more fundamental issue of
indifference, merely alluding to the gift in 1:4–5 and 2:25–30. Only
after this in 4:10–23, a post-scripted thank-you note (in Paul's own
hand?), does he express his appreciation of the Philippians' gift.[80]

Paul also separates the issues *conceptually*. It has often been
noted that the thank-you note of 4:10–20 is uncharacteristically
"thankless" in so far as Paul never explicitly thanks the Philippians
for their gift.[81] Instead of thanking the Philippians Paul commends
them for their mindfulness of him (τὸ ὑπὲρ ἐμοῦ φρονεῖν; 4:10),
their partnership in his suffering (συγκοινωνήσαντές μου τῇ
θλίψει; 4:14),[82] and their historic support of his mission (ἐν ἀρχῇ
τοῦ εὐαγγελίου . . . εἰς τὴν χρείαν μοι ἐπέμψατε; 4:15–16). When
he does finally get around to speaking of the gift (4:18) he describes
it as "a fragrant aroma, an acceptable sacrifice, well pleasing *to*

---

[80] For a somewhat analogous postscript, definitely in Paul's own hand, see the
appended promissory note of Philem. 17–19; cf. A. Deissmann, *Licht vom Osten: das
Neue Testament und die neuendeckten Texte der hellenistisch-römischen Welt* (4th
edn.; Tübingen: Mohr [Siebeck], 1923) 239.

[81] Cf. Dibelius, *An die Philipper*, 74. For the effusive thanks possible in such
letters, see Ps.-Demetr., *Epist. Types* 21: "I hasten to show in my actions how
grateful I am to you for the kindness you showed me in your words. For I know that
what I am doing for you is less than I should, for even if I gave my life for you, I
should still not be giving adequate thanks for the benefits I have received. If you
wish anything that is mine, do not write and request it, but demand a return. For I
am in your debt" (trans Malherbe; *idem*, *Ancient Epistolary Theorists* [SBLSBS 19;
Atlanta: Scholars Press, 1988]; originally in *Ohio Journal of Religious Studies* 5 [1977]
3–77).

[82] Cicero, *Ad fam.* 4.6.1: *societas* [*tua*] *paene aegritudinis . . . consolatur.*

God." Paul thus recasts the Philippians' gift in more abstract terms of friendship and cult, leaving himself free to reassert his independence of material circumstances: οὐχ ὅτι καθ᾽ ὑστέρησιν λέγω, ἐγὼ γὰρ ἔμαθον ἐν οἷ εἰμι αὐτάρκης εἶναι (4:11).[83]

The second "rhetorical problem" confronting Paul as he wrote to the Philippians was how, in a letter expressing his appreciation of their recent gift, to rebuke them for their emotional frailty. Here the rhetoric of Philippians is, in my judgment, the most successful. Two texts call for comment. Both of these will be examined in more detail below.

The first text is Phil. 1:22–6. Whatever we make of Paul's claim in 1:22 that life and death are his to choose (αἱρήσομαι), it is clear that, having introduced the element of choice, Paul unambiguously complains that the Philippians are preventing him from choosing the option he much prefers: "having the desire to depart and be with Christ, which is much better by far (πολλῷ γὰρ μᾶλλον κρεῖσσον), but to remain in the flesh is more necessary on account of you (ἀναγκαιότερον δι᾽ ὑμᾶς)" (1:23–4).[84] Paul immediately follows this complaint with words of reassurance in 1:25a: καὶ τοῦτο πεποιθὼς οἶδα ὅτι μενῶ καὶ παραμενῶ. But these words are not as innocent as they at first appear. For when Paul writes "and being confident of this," the "this" (τοῦτο) of which he is confident is nothing other than the Philippians' need that he be returned. This need is so desperate that Paul is assured (πεποιθώς) that God will meet it, meaning that he will be released.[85] In 1:25b–26 Paul explicitly states that only his "presence" (παρουσία) again at Philippi will result in the Philippians' renewed "progress and joy of faith" (τὴν ὑμῶν προκοπὴν καὶ χαρὰν τῆς πίστεως). This expression brings the Philippians into explicit contrast with the "progress" of the gospel (1:12) and the exemplary "joy" of Paul (1:18). Like the gospel, the Philippians should be making progress despite Paul's imprisonment, and like Paul, they should be rejoicing. But they are not, and their failure to do so works a burden on Paul. Having gone out of his way to suggest this comparison, Paul leaves the Philippians to draw the conclusion for themselves.

[83] We will discuss the rhetoric of 4:10–20 in more detail below in chapter 7.

[84] It will not do to translate αἱρήσομαι "prefer" here. What Paul prefers is not in doubt: he prefers to depart and be with Christ which is much better by far.

[85] Paul uses a similar "confidence formula," but to different effect, in 1:6 and 2:24; cf. 1:14. This formula occurs elsewhere in Paul at Rom. 8:38; 14:14; 15:14; 2 Cor. 2:3; Philem. 21. See also J. White, *Light*, s.v. Conventions (Epistolary Formulas) in Letter Body: Confidence expressions.

The second text is Phil. 2:25–30. Here Paul again complains of
the compulsion he has been placed under because of the Philippians: ἀναγκαῖον δὲ ἡγησάμην Ἐπαφρόδιτον . . . πέμψαι πρὸς
ὑμᾶς.[86] Epaphroditus, who was commissioned by the Philippians to
carry a gift to Paul, has stayed on to care for Paul in his
imprisonment. He has done an admirable job, and Paul praises
him: Ἐπαφρόδιτον τὸν ἀδελφὸν καὶ συνεργὸν καὶ λειτουργὸν τῆς
χρείας μου (2:25; cf. 29–30). Nevertheless Paul is sending him
back. Why? Because the Philippians had heard that Epaphroditus
was ill, and, given the already fragile emotional state of the
congregation, Epaphroditus is worried (ἀδημονῶν) about them
(2:26). It is not, therefore, that Paul wants to send Epaphroditus
back to Philippi, but that he feels compelled (ἀναγκαῖον) to do so,
"in order that seeing him again you might rejoice (χαρῆτε) and I
might also be less grieved (ἀλυπότερος)" (2:28). Again it is a case
of Paul being constrained to act in a way he does not want to
because of the emotional state of the Philippians. This time,
however, Paul is explicit that the Philippians' lack of joy is a source
of additional grief (cf. ἀλυπότερος) for him.[87]

[86] The expression "ἀναγκαῖον ἡγησάμην" is a common epistolary formula. As it
occurs in the papyri the formula explains the compulsion to write that ancient letter-
writers felt when, for example, they learned of the availability of an appropriate
letter carrier (cf. Koskenniemi, *Studien*, 77–87). Paul's point in Phil. 2:25, however,
is not that he considered it necessary to write to the Philippians upon the return of
Epaphroditus, but that he felt it necessary to return Epaphroditus himself. To put
the matter another way, it is not that Epaphroditus' return trip to Philippi was the
occasion for Paul's letter, but that the Philippians themselves were the occasion
(ἀφορμή) for Epaphroditus' return. Here Paul seems to play with an epistolary
formula to make a veiled point.
[87] Cf. Phil. 2:2: πληρώσατέ μου τὴν χαρὰν ἵνα τὸ αὐτὸ φρονῆτε . . .

3

ON THE GENRE OF PHILIPPIANS:
ANCIENT CONSOLATION

For there are specific [remedies] customarily spoken regarding poverty, specific remedies regarding life without
honor or fame; there are separate forms of discourse
respectively for exile, the destruction of one's country,
slavery, illness, blindness, and any other mishap that might
properly be called a calamity.   Cicero, *Tusc.* 3.34.81

If we accept the above reconstruction of the rhetorical situation of
Philippians, and in particular the conclusion that the "controlling
exigence" of the letter was the distress the Philippians felt over
Paul's imprisonment, then Paul's primary objective in writing to
the Philippians will have been to console them[1] or, as Chrysostom
puts it, to "rouse them from their despondency over his bonds."[2]
We will therefore conclude our discussion of preliminary matters
with a brief survey of ancient consolation. We will begin with a few
general comments on the scope and character of ancient consolation. After this we will summarize five theories of consolation
current in Paul's day. We will conclude by examining in more detail

[1] Here and in the following discussion I use the terms "console" and "consolation" in the ancient sense of exhorting someone to rational and responsible
behavior in the face of grief. See the discussion below.
[2] *In Epist. ad Phil.*, praef. 1 (*PG* 62.179.9–10): διανιστῶν αὐτοὺς ἀπὸ τῆς ἀθυμίας
τῆς ἐπὶ τοῖς δεσμοῖς; cf. Theodoret, *Interpr. Epist. ad Phil.* (*PG* 82.564A): ἐπειδὴ
λίαν μεριμνῶντες τὸν μακάριον ἀπέστειλαν Ἐπαφρόδιτον, ψυχαγωγεῖ αὐτοὺς,
διδάσκων ὡς τὰ περιτιθέντα αὐτῷ δεσμὰ πολλοῖς ἐγένετο πρόξενα σωτηρίας; Jer.,
In Epist. ad Phil. (*PL* 30.842C): *Hic* [Phil. 1:12f.] *consolatur eos de sua tribulatione:
qui audierant, eum vinctum in urbe Roma custodiri.* Chrysostom identifies a number of
consolatory arguments throughout Philippians, but especially in chs. 1 and 4 (*PG*
62.179.38–9: πολλὴν προσάγει παράκλησιν, and 180.3–4: πολλὴν τὴν παράκλησιν
προσάγει). For Chrysostom's own efforts at consolation, see Leokadia Malunowicz-
zówna, "Les éléments stoïciens dans la consolation grecque chrétienne," in E. A.
Livingstone, ed., *Studia Patristica, 13. Papers presented to the Sixth International
Conference on Patristic Studies held in Oxford 1971, Part 2* (TU 116; Berlin:
Akademie-Verlag, 1975) 35–45.

two consolatory themes that figure prominently in Paul's consolation of the Philippians.[3]

Ancient consolation: some general observations

The sources

Consolation, the combating of grief through rational argument, was widely practiced in the ancient world and is well attested in both Greek and Latin sources.[4] Its origins predate our earliest evidence, since already in Homer we find the skillful use of consolatory *topoi*.[5] However, judging from extant materials it was not until the late fifth and early fourth centuries that the problem of grief began to be addressed systematically.[6]

Doxographical tradition credits a number of important figures

---

[3] Those *solacia* or "consolatory arguments" not covered in this chapter, but nevertheless relevant to Paul's consolation of the Philippians, will be taken up in our exegesis of the letter in chapters 4–7 below.

[4] The literary sources for the *consolatio mortis* are collected by Carl Buresch, "Consolationum a Graecis Romanisque scriptarum historia critica," *Leipziger Studien zur classischen Philologie* 9 (1886) 1–170; cf. Andreas C. van Heusde, *Diatribe in locum philosophiae moralis qui est de consolatione apud Graecos* (Utrecht, 1840) and Alfred Gercke, "De Consolationibus," *Tirocinium philologum sodalium Regii Seminarii Bonnensis* (Berlin: Weidmann, 1883) 28–70. More recently: Kassel, *Untersuchungen*; H. T. Johann, *Trauer und Trost: Eine quellen- und strukturanalytische Untersuchung der philosophischen Trostschriften über den Tod* (Studia et Testimonia Antiqua 5; Munich: Fink, 1968); J. Hani, "*La consolation antique*," *REA* 75 (1973) 103–10. For the non-literary papyri, see Juan Chapa, *Letters of Condolence in Greek Papyri* (Papyrologica Florentina 29; Florence: Gonnelli, 1998); *idem*, "Consolatory Patterns? 1 Thes 4,13.18; 5,11," in Raymond F. Collins, ed., *The Thessalonian Correspondence* (BETL 87; Leuven: Leuven University Press, 1990) 220–8. Inscriptional evidence can be found in Richmond Lattimore, *Themes in Greek and Latin Epitaphs* (Illinois Studies in Language and Literature 28.1–2; Urbana: University of Illinois, 1942); for Jewish inscriptions, see Pieter W. van der Horst, *Ancient Jewish Epitaphs: An Introductory Survey of a Millennium of Jewish Funerary Epigraphy (300 BCE–700 CE)* (Contributions to Biblical Exegesis and Theology 2; Kampen: Kok Pharos, 1991). For early Christian consolation see note 29 below. Little has been done on Jewish consolation, but see: C. G. Montefiore, *Ancient Jewish and Greek Encouragement and Consolation* (Bridgeport, Connecticut: Hartmore House, 1971) and Otto Schmitz and Gustav Stählin, παρακαλέω, παράκλησις, *TDNT* 788–93 (1967).

[5] As when Achilles reminds Priam of the futility of grief (*Il.* 24.522–51; cited in the pseudo-Plutarchan consolation *Ad Apoll.* 105C), or Hector, in his efforts to comfort Andromache, appeals to the unchangeableness of fate (*Il.* 6.486–9). See also Serapedon's encouragement to Glaucon before the Achaean pallisade at *Il.* 12.322 and Thetis' consolation of Achilles at *Il.* 24.128–32. Later tradition extolled Homer as the model consoler (Quint., *Inst.* 10.1.47; Men. Rh. 2.434.11–18).

[6] Kassel, *Untersuchungen*, 4–48.

from this period with compositions that were either directly or indirectly consolatory. These works, known only by their titles, focused largely on death.[7] But other subjects such as exile, shipwreck, poverty, and old age were not uncommon.[8] Treatises on tranquillity (Περὶ εὐθυμίας) and the passions (Περὶ παθῶν) will also have touched on consolatory themes.[9] The early lyric poets Simonides and Pindar[10] and the dramatic poets, especially Euripides,[11] regularly employed consolatory topics, as did the orators on occasion, if we accept Socrates' parody of contemporary *epitaphioi* in the *Menexenus* (284A–C).[12] Plato treats consolatory themes at *Ap.* 39E–42A, *Phd.* 115D, and in his discussion of

[7] Democritus, Περὶ τῶν ἐν αἴδου (Diog. Laert. 9.46); Antisthenes, Περὶ τῶν ἐν αἴδου, Περὶ τοῦ ἀποθανεῖν, and Περὶ ζωῆς καὶ θανάτου (Diog. Laert. 6.15); Diogenes of Sinope, Περὶ θανάτου (Diog. Laert. 6.80; cf. Jerome, *Ep.* 60.5.2); Xenocrates of Chalcedon, Περὶ θανάτου (Diog. Laert. 4.11); cf. Ps.-Plato, Ἀξίοχος ἢ Περὶ θανάτου; Philodemus, Περὶ θανάτου. At *Tusc.* 1.48.116 Cicero credits the fourth-century sophist and student of Gorgias Alcidamus with a "laudatio mortis." The following excerpt is from Democritus' Περὶ τῶν ἐν αἴδου (Stob., *Flor.* 4.52.40 = E Democritus frag. B 297 Diels and Kranz): "Some people, not knowing the dissolution of mortal nature, and conscious of evil doing in this life, pass through life in misery, agitated and fearful, fabricating myths about the period after death."

[8] Aristippus, Πρὸς τοὺς ναυαγούς, Πρὸς τοὺς φυγάδας, and Πρὸς πτωχόν (Diog. Laert. 2.84); Theophrastus, Περὶ γήρως (Diog. Laert. 5.42); and Demetrius of Phalerum, Περὶ γήρως (Diog. Laert. 9.20); cf. Cicero, *De senectute.* Fragments also survive of a work on exile by the Megarian scholarch Stilpo (c. 380–300 BCE) *apud* Teles, frag. 3 Hense. Cf. Stob., *Flor.* 4.32.1–22 (ΠΕΡΙ ΠΕΝΙΑΣ); 4.50.1–31 (ΠΕΡΙ ΓΗΡΩΣ).

[9] Περὶ εὐθυμίας: Democritus (Diog. Laert. 9.46; cf. Sen., *De tran. an.* 2.3), Hipparchus the Pythagorean (Stob., *Flor.* 4.44.81); cf. Seneca, *De tran. an.*; Plutarch, Περὶ εὐθυμίας. Περὶ παθῶν: Theophrastus (Diog. Laert. 5.42), Xenocrates (Diog. Laert. 4.11), Zeno (Diog. Laert. 7.4), Herillus (Diog. Laert. 7.166), Sphaerus (Diog. Laert. 7.178); Chrysippus (Diog. Laert. 7.111), Hecastus of Rhodes (Diog. Laert. 7.110). The fourth book of Chrysippus' Περὶ παθῶν was apparently entitled τὸ Θεραπευτικόν; Gal., *De plac.* 4.1.1.14 and *passim.* Jerome refers to a consolatory work of Poseidonius at *Ep.* 60.5.2 which may have been a more general treatise on tranquillity or on the passions, though it may also have been a letter; cf. Max Pohlenz, "De Posidonii libris περὶ παθῶν," *Jahrb. für class. Philol.* Suppl 24 (1989) 537–633.

[10] Simonides, frags. 520–31 *PMG* Page; Pindar, frags. 128a-38 Snell–Maehler. Pind., *Pyth.* 3 was composed specifically for the consolation of Hieron on the occasion of his failing health. Buresch, "historia critica," 18–20.

[11] See the texts collected in Constantine C. Grollios, Τέχνη ἀλυπίας: κονοὶ τόποι τοῦ Πρὸς Πολύβιον τοῦ Σενέκα καὶ πηγαὶ αὐτῶν (Ἑλληνικά, παράρτημα 10; Thessaloniki; Athens: Christou & Son, 1956) 49–59; Kassel, *Untersuchungen,* 4–12; cf. W. Schaeffer, "Argumenta consolatoria: quae apud veteres Graecorum scriptores inveniuntur" (Ph.D. diss. Göttingen, 1921 – *non vidi*).

[12] Cf. Lys. 2.80; Ps.-Demosth. 60.33–4; Hyper., *Or.* 6.35ff.; Thuc. (Pericles) 2.44–6. Buresch, "historia critica," 89–91; N. Loraux, *L'invention d'Athènes: histoire de l'oraison funèbre dans la "cité classique"* (Civilisations et sociétés 65; Paris: Mouton, 1981).

tragedy at *Resp.* 10.604B.[13] Particularly striking is the invention ascribed to the fifth-century sophist Antiphon of a τεχνὴ ἀλυπίας or "art for the alleviation of grief."[14] Mention should also be made of Theophrastus' consolatory letter-essay Καλλισθένης ἢ Περὶ πένθους[15] and Epicurus' Ἐπιστολὴ πρὸς Δωσίθεον, written on the death of Dositheus' son Hegesianax.[16] Both of these works, now lost, anticipate the influential Περὶ πένθους of the Academic philosopher Crantor of Soli (*c.* 335–*c.* 275 BCE).

In later tradition, Crantor's Περὶ πένθους, sent to an otherwise unknown Hippocles on the death of his children, attained a kind of paradigmatic status. Panaetius, in his consolatory letter to Tubero, said that it was "to be learned verbatim."[17] Cicero called it "a golden booklet" that everyone reads.[18] Diogenes Laertius, writing after the genre had reached its acme, still referred to it as "especially marvelous."[19] Unfortunately, only fragments of the Περὶ πένθους survive.[20] Of probably equal if not greater influence, especially for the Latin tradition, was Cicero's *Consolatio*, which he composed for his own comfort after the death of his daughter Tullia. A philosophically eclectic piece, the *Consolatio* brought together arguments from Stoic, Epicurean, Cyrenaic, Peripatetic, and Academic sources.[21] It too has been lost, though much of its substance is preserved in books 1 and 3 of the *Tusculan Disputations*.[22]

[13] Buresch, "historia critica," 20–1; *Phaedo* 115D: παραμυθούμενος ἅμα μὲν ὑμᾶς, ἅμα δ᾽ ἐμαυτόν. For consolatory arguments in Xenophon, see Buresch, 21–33. The pseudo-Platonic *Axiochus* (Buresch, 9–18) is an attempt to give Socratic (and Platonic) credence to an eclectic collection of consolatory arguments on death.

[14] Plut., *Vit. X orat.* 833C–D.

[15] Frag. 3 Wimmer; Diog. Laert. 5.44; Ps.-Plut., *Ad Apoll.* 104D; Cic., *Tusc.* 3.10.21; 5.9.25.

[16] Plut., *Adv. Col.* 1101B; probably the Ἡγησίαναξ listed in Diog. Laert. 10.28. Epicurus' consolatory arguments are repeated in Lucr. 3.830–1094. Cf. Metrodorus' consolatory letter to his sister (Sen., *Ep.* 98.9; 99.25).

[17] *Apud* Cic., *Acad. prio.* 2.135: *ad verbum ediscendus.*

[18] Ibid.: *Legimus omnes Crantoris veteris Academici De Luctu, est enim non magnus verum aureolus . . . libellus.*

[19] 4.27: θαυμάζεται δὲ αὐτοῦ μάλιστα βιβλίον τὸ Περὶ πένθους.

[20] F. Kayser, *De Crantore academico dissertatio* (Heidelberg, 1841), F. W. A. Mullach, ed., *Fragmenta philosophorum Graecorum*, 3 vols. (Paris: Didot, 1860–81) III.131–52; K. Kuiper, "De Crantoris fragmentis moralibus," *Mnemosyne* 29 (1901) 341–62. A number of attempts have been made to reconstruct this important source; most recently by Johann, *Trauer und Trost*, 127–36 and *passim.*

[21] *Tusc.* 3.31.76: *ut fere nos in Consolatione omnia in consolationem unam coniecimus.*

[22] Cicero refers to his earlier *Consolatio* at *Tusc.* 1.26.65, 31.76, 34.83; 3.28.70, 31.76; 4.22.63. Cf. K. Kumaniecki, "A propos de la 'Consolatio' perdue de Cicéron," *AFLA* 46 (1969) 369–402.

A large number of consolations survive from the late Republic and early Empire. By far the best attested form is the consolatory letter, examples of which may be found in the letter collections of Cicero, Seneca, and Pliny, and later, in the letters of Fronto, Apollonius of Tyana, Julian, and Libanius.[23] Several much longer letter-essays in the tradition of Crantor's Περὶ πένθους and Cicero's *Consolatio* also survive. Three of these are by Seneca, two are by Plutarch, and one is falsely ascribed to Plutarch.[24] The most substantial verse consolation from this period is the pseudo-Ovidian *Consolatio ad Liviam*, an elegy of almost 475 lines on the death of Drusus.[25] Other consolatory poems include: Catullus 96; Horace, *Carm.* 2.9; Ovid, *Am.* 3.9; *Ex Ponto*, 4.11; Statius, *Silv.* 5.1.[26] Many funerary inscriptions, both Greek and Latin, are also consolatory,[27] as are the private funeral orations of Dio (*Or.* 28

[23] Cic., *Ad fam.* 4.5; (Sulpicius Rufus) 5.16; 5.18; *Ad Att.* 12.10; 15.1; *Ad Brut.* 1.9; Sen., *Ep.* 63; 93; 99; Plin., *Ep.* 1.12; 3.21; 9.9; Fronto, *De nepote amisso*, 1; 2, and *Ad Verum Imp.* 2.9; 10; Apoll. Tyan., *Ep.* 55, 58; Jul., *Ep.* 69; 201; Liban., *Ep.* 344; 1473; cf. Ps.-Phalar., *Ep.* 10; 103; POxy. 1.115; PGrenf. 2.36; PWisc. 84 (letter 1); cf. S. Stowers, *Letter Writing in Greco-Roman Antiquity* (Philadelphia: Westminster, 1986) 145–7, 152. The Lamprias catalogue mentions two consolatory letters of Plutarch (111: Παραμυθητικὸς εἰς Ἀσκληπιάδην; 157: Πρὸς Φηστίαν παραμυθητικός). For early Christian letters, see J. F. Mitchell, "Consolatory Letters in Basil and Gregory Nazianzen," *Hermes* 96 (1968) 299–318. The consolatory letter reached its high point early in Sulpicius Rufus' elegant and still moving letter written to Cicero on the death of Tullia; cf. Kassel, *Untersuchungen*, 98–103.

[24] Seneca: *Ad Polybium de consolatione*, *Ad Marciam de consolatione*, and *Ad Helviam matrem de consolatione*; Plutarch: *De exilio* and *Consolatio ad uxorem*; Ps.-Plutarch: *Consolatio ad Apollonium*. In connection with these longer pieces, often called "consolations proper," mention should be made of Cicero's dialogue *De senectute* and Musonius' diatribe Ὅτι οὐ κακὸν ἡ φυγή (frag. 9 Hense); cf. Teles, frag. 3 Hense (Περὶ φυγῆς) and Dio's thirteenth oration (on his exile). Clitomachus' consolatory letter to the survivors of the destruction of Carthage in 146 (Cic., *Tusc.* 3.22.54; cf. Jer., *Ep.* 60.5.2) may have been of this longer letter-essay type. The Lamprias catalogue (172) attributes a Περὶ ἀλυπίας to Plutarch.

[25] Henk Schoonhoven, *The Pseudo-Ovidian AD LIVIAM DE MORTE DRUSI (Consolatio ad Liviam, Epicedium Drusi). A Critical Text with Introduction and Commentary* (Groningen: Forsten, 1992).

[26] See further: Cat. 3; Ov., *Ex Ponto*, 1.9; Propert., *El.* 2.13; 3.18; Stat., *Silv.* 2.1; 2.4; 2.6; 2.7; 3.3; 5.3; 5.5; Lucr. 3.830–1094; Mart. 1.88; 1.101; 5.34; 5.37; 6.28; 6.29; 6.85; 7.40; 9.74; 10.61; 11.91. José Esteve-Forriol, *Die Trauer- und Trostgedichte in der römischen Literatur* (Munich: Schubert, 1962); M. E. Fern, *The Latin Consolatio Mortis as a Literary Type* (Saint Louis, MO: University of Saint Louis, 1941) 83–169; Traudel Stork, *Nil igitur mors est ad nos: Der Schlussteil des dritten Lukrezbuches und sein Verhältnis zur Konsolationsliteratur* (Bonn: Rudolf Habelt, 1970); Barbara Price Wallach, *Lucretius and the Diatribe against the Fear of Death: De Rerum Natura III 830–1094* (Leiden: Brill, 1976).

[27] Lattimore; *Themes*, 215–65. For consolation in the *laudatio funebris*, see Wilhelm Kierdorf, *Laudatio Funebris: Interpretation und Untersuchungen zur Ent-*

and 29), Aelius Aristides (*Or.* 31), and Libanius (*Or.* 17 and 18).[28]
A large number of early Christian consolations (mostly letters and
sermons) from the third and fourth centuries also survive.[29]

Range of subjects

In principle, consolation could be offered for any misfortune. So,
for instance, Ps.-Demetrius broadly defines the consolatory letter as
one written to those grieving "because something unpleasant has
happened to them" (δυσχεροῦς τινος γεγονότος).[30] We have
already seen the doxographical evidence for consolations on death,
old age, poverty, shipwreck, and exile. Cicero mentions handbook
discussions of these and other misfortunes at *Tusc.* 3.34.81:[31]

> For there are specific [remedies] customarily spoken re-
> garding poverty, specific remedies regarding life without

wicklung der römischen Leichenrede (Beiträge zur klassischen Philologie 106; Meisenheim am Glan: Hain, 1980) 82–90.

[28] Also, Himerius, *Or.* 8 Colonna (on the death of his son Rufinius) and
Themistius, *Or.* 20 (on his father).

[29] The bibliography is extensive. See especially Charles Favez, *La consolation
latine chrétienne* (Paris: J. Vrin, 1937); Robert C. Gregg, *Consolation Philosophy:
Greek and Christian Paideia in Basil and the Two Gregories* (Patristic Monograph
Series 3; Cambridge, MA: Philadelphia Patristic Foundation, 1975); G. Guttilla, "La
fase iniziale della *consolatio* latina cristiana," *ALCP* 21–2 (1985) 108–215; Scourfield, *Consoling Heliodorus*. The primary texts include: (sermons) Cypr., *De mortalitate*; Greg. Nys., *Oratio funebris de Meletio*; *Oratio funebris de Pulcheria*; *Oratio
funebris de Flacio*; Ambr., *De excessu fratris sui Satyri libri duo*; *De obitu Valenti-
niani*; *De obitu Theodosii*; Aug., *Serm.* 172, 173; Greg. Naz., *Or.* 7; 18; (letters) Jer.,
Ep. 23, 39, 60, 66, 75, 77, 79, 108, 118, 127; Aug., *Ep.* 92, 259, 263; Paul. Nol., *Carm.*
31 (cf. also the doubtful Obitus Baebiani [*Carm.* 33]); *Ep.* 13; Bas., *Ep.* 5; 6; 28; 29;
139; 140; 238; 247; 256; 257; 301; 302; Ambr., *Ep.* 15; 39; cf. Chapa, "Consolatory
Patterns?," 220–8.

[30] *Epist. Types*, 5.

[31] Cf. Dio, *Or.* 27.7–9. On the destruction of one's country, see also *Tusc.* 3.22.54
(see Grollios, Τέχνη ἀλυπίας, 29) and Sen., *Ep.* 91.1; for poverty: *Tusc.* 3.24.57; Sen.,
Ad Helv. 10–13; Diog. Laert. 2.84 (which mentions Aristippus' lost Πρὸς πτωχόν);
for illness: Ps.-Jer., *Ep.* 5, Greg. Naz., *Ep.* 31.4; cf. H. Savon, "Une consolation
imitée de Sénèque et de saint Cyprian (Pseudo-Jérôme, epistula 5 ad amicum
aegrotum)," *RecAug* 14 (1979) 153–90; for blindness: Jer., *Ep.* 76.2. Old age was a
common subject: in addition to the two treatises on old age (Περὶ γήρως) attributed
to Theophrastus (Diog. Laert. 5.42) and Demetrius of Phalerum (Diog. Laert. 9.20)
mentioned above, and Cicero's *De senectute*, see the fragments of Favorinus' Περὶ
γήρως (Adelmo Barigazzi, ed., *Favorino di Arelate. Opere: Introduzione, Testo
Critico e Commento* [Florence: Monnier, 1966] frags. 9–17). Cic., *De sen.* 1.3, alludes
to a treatise on old age by Aristo of Chios; cf. Dio, *Or.* 13.3. Basil consoles those
persecuted by Arians in *Ep.* 139, 140, 238, 247, 256, 257; cf. Gregg, *Consolation
Philosophy*, 132; and in general, Scourfield, *Consoling Heliodorus*, 16 n. 70.

honor or fame; there are separate forms of discourse respectively for exile, the destruction of one's country, slavery, illness, blindness, and any other mishap that might properly be called a calamity.

Dio provides a similar list at *Or.* 16.3 (Περὶ λύπης). Other subjects included legal difficulties (Cic., *Ad fam.* 5.18; Sen., *Ep.* 24; cf. *Ep.* 17), political and/or financial setbacks (Cic., *Ad fam.* 5.13; 16; 17; Sen., *Ep.* 21), an ungrateful client (Sen., *Ep.* 81), the flight of a slave (Sen., *Ep.* 107), a forced separation (Cic., *Ad Brut.* 2.2), and fraud (Juv., *Sat.* 13).

The most common type of ancient consolation was, of course, the *consolatio mortis.*[32] It could, if occasion allowed, be offered to someone anticipating his or her own death, as in the pseudo-Platonic *Axiochus* where Socrates consoles Cleinias' father who "is at the end of his life and is distressed at the prospect of death."[33] But more commonly it was extended to bereaved survivors, who were also expected to console themselves.[34] Untimely death (*mors immatura*), especially of young children, was a theme that presented unique problems for consolers.[35] Other typical occasions included the death of a close friend, the death of an immediate family member, death in war, the death of a slave, or, as a literary conceit, the death of a favorite pet.[36]

A significant number of consolations of exile also survive. The oldest of these, Teles' Περὶ φυγῆς,[37] quotes at length an earlier

[32] In addition to Fern, *The Latin* Consolatio Mortis, see Mary Evaristus, *The Consolations of Death in Ancient Greek Literature* (Washington: Catholic University Press, 1917); N. Hultin, "The Rhetoric of Consolation: Studies in the Development of the 'Consolatio Mortis'" (Ph. D. diss. Johns Hopkins, 1965); cf. Stob., *Flor.* 4.51.1–32 (ΠΕΡΙ ΘΑΝΑΤΟΥ).

[33] *Ax.* 365B5–6; Cf. Pind., *Pyth.* 3; Plin., *Ep.* 7.19 (a lament on the imminent death of Fannia). The situation is reversed in the *Phaedo* where Socrates, who is about to die, consoles those who will survive him; cf. *Ap.* 39E–42A.

[34] Cic., *Ad fam.* 4.13.4: *At ea quidem facultas vel tui vel alterius consolandi in te summa est.* The most notable example of this was, of course, Cicero's own *Consolatio.*

[35] Cf. Johann, *Trauer und Trost*, 100–20; Kassel, *Untersuchungen*, 82–4; Lattimore, *Themes*, 172–214; E. Griessmair, *Das Motiv der Mors Immatura in den griechischen metrischen Grabinschriften* (Innsbruck: Universitätsverlag, 1966); A.-M. Vérilhac, Παῖδες ἄωροι. *Poésie funébraire*, 2 vols. (Athens: Athens' Academy Press, 1978–82); R. Garland, *The Greek Way of Death* (London: Duckworth, 1985) 77–88; van der Horst, *Ancient Jewish Epitaphs*, 45–9.

[36] On the death of slaves: Propert., *El.* 2.1; 2.6; 5.5; Pliny, *Ep.* 5.19; 8.1; on the death of pet birds: Cat. 3; Ov., *Am.* 2.6; Stat., *Silv.* 2.4.

[37] Frag. 3 Hense (= Stobaeus, *Flor.* 3.40.8ff.).

treatise on exile by the Megarian scholarch Stilpon (*c.* 380–300 BCE).[38] Unlike the consolation of death, which was offered on the demise of a third party, the consolation of exile was typically offered directly to the person in exile, as in Philiscus' consolation of the exiled Cicero at Cassius Dio 38.18–30. Other examples include: Musonius, frag. 9 Hense (Ὅτι οὐ κακὸν ἡ φυγή), Plutarch, *De exilio*, and Cicero, *Ad fam.* 4.13.[39] One notable exception to this is the *Ad Helviam matrem*, where Seneca consoles his mother on the occasion of his own exile.[40] Dio, *Or.* 13 (Ἐν Ἀθήναις περὶ φυγῆς) and Favorinus, Περὶ φυγῆς (frag. 22 Barigazzi) are autobiographical reflections but draw heavily on various consolatory *topoi*.

Sympathy, consolation, and exhortation

Ancient consolers generally made a sharp distinction between consolation and sympathy or sharing in another's lamentation. We see this distinction already in Thucydides who has Pericles abruptly introduce the peroration to his famous *epitaphios*: "I do not lament; rather, I shall console" (οὐκ ὀλοφύρομαι μᾶλλον ἢ παραμυθήσομαι).[41] Aelianus preserves Aristippus' similar dictum: "I have come not to share your grief but to stop your grief" (ἥκω παρ᾽ ὑμᾶς οὐχ ὡς συλλυπούμενος, ἀλλ᾽ ἵνα παύσω ὑμᾶς λυπουμένους).[42] At *De exilio* 599B, Plutarch contrasts lamentation with consolation, equating the latter with moral instruction:

> For we do not have need of those who, like tragic choruses, weep and wail with us in unwanted circumstances, but of

[38] Cf. Alfred Giesecke, *De philosophorum veterum quae de exilium spectant sententiis.* Leipzig: Teubner, 1891.

[39] The last two of these are letters. Musonius' essay purports to report a conversation Musonius had with an exile. Cora Lutz' contention ("Musonius Rufus: The Roman Socrates," *YCS* 10 [1947] 5 n. 8) that frag. 9 was originally a letter, on the basis of expressions like σὺ δ᾽ εἰπέ μοι, ὦ ἑταῖρε (9.49.3) or πρὸς σὲ λέγω νῦν (9.51.5), cannot be maintained since these are not "epistolary formulas" and the singulars (σύ, σέ) are undoubtedly references to the individual addressed orally at 9.41.5.

[40] In this regard the *Ad Helv.* is similar to Philippians where Paul also consoles a second party regarding his own misfortune. We will return to this important comparison below.

[41] 2.44; cf. Plato, *Men.* 247C–D. More subtle is Epicurus' dictum (*Sent. Vat.* 66) that we should show sympathy to our friends not by lamenting with them but by caring for them in their time of need: συμπαθῶμεν τοῖς φίλοις οὐ θρηνοῦντες ἀλλὰ φροντίζοντες.

[42] *Varia historia* 7.3.

those who will speak to us frankly (παρρησιαζομένων) and instruct us (διδασκόντων) that grief and self-abasement are in every circumstance useless.

Similarly, the pseudo-Plutarchan *Consolatio ad Apollonium* begins with the recommendation that Apollonius not seek out those who will share his grief (μὴ τοῖς συλλυποιμένοις) but those who will remove it by noble encouragement (ἀλλὰ τοῖς ἀφαιρουμένοις τὰς λύπας διὰ τῆς γενναίας καὶ σεμνῆς παρηγορίας).[43]

Even so, it became customary to preface words of consolation with an expression of personal affection and sympathy.[44] Thus a letter of consolation might begin:

> When I heard of the terrible things that you met at the hands of thankless fate, I felt the deepest grief, considering that what had happened had not happened to you more than to me,

followed by various consolatory arguments and exhortations.[45] Similarly, Menander Rhetor specifies that a consolatory speech (λόγος παραμυθητικός) begin with a short monody (μονῳδία) or lament (θρῆνος) followed by "the consolatory part" (μέρος τοῦ λόγου τὸ παραμυθητικόν).[46] Gregory Nazianzen for whom "commiseration counts as a kind of consolation," speaks of the consoler's obligation "to sympathize on some points, exhort on others, and, perhaps, to deliver a rebuke on others" (τὰ μὲν συμπαθεῖν ἔδει, τὰ δὲ παραινέσαι, τὰ δὲ ἴσως ἐπιτιμῆσαι).[47]

---

[43] 117F–118A; cf. Bion's barb in *Tusc.* 3.26.62; Epict., *Ench.* 16.

[44] Kassel, *Untersuchungen*, 51, 98 n. 1; Charles Favez, "Le sentiment dans les consolations de Sénèque," *Mélanges Paul Thomas: recueil de mémoires concernant la philologie classique dédié à Paul Thomas* (Bruges: Sainte Catherine, 1930) 262–70; R. G. M. Nisbet and M. Hubbard, *A Commentary on Horace: Odes, Book I* (Oxford: Clarendon, 1970) 280–1; Stowers, *Letter Writing*, 142–4. Examples include: Cic., *Ad fam.* 4.5.1; 1.18.1; (Sulpicius Rufus) 5.16.1; Sen., *Ep.* 63.1; Ps.-Plut., *Ad Apoll.* 101E; *P.Oxy.* 115 ad init.; Jul., *Ep.* 201 B–C (37 H); Liban., *Ep.* 1473. Scourfield, *Consoling Heliodorus*, 80–1, cites the following early Christian examples: Jer. *Ep.* 39.1.2; 60.1.1; 75.1.1; Ambr., *Ep.* 15.1; *Obit. Valent.* 26; Bas., *Ep.* 29; 301 ad init.; 302 ad init.; cf. Mitchell, "Consolatory Letters," 301–4, who discusses Marcel Guignet, *Les procédés épistolaires de Saint Grégoire de Nazianze* (Paris: Picard, 1911) 80ff.

[45] Ps.-Demetr., *Epist. Typ.*, 5. This is extremely common. Sympathy was an ideal of friendship; Arist., *EN* 9.11.2; Stob., *Flor.* 4.48.16–31 (ΟΤΙ ΟΙ ΑΤΥΧΟΥΝΤΕΣ ΧΡΗΙΖΟΥΣΙ ΤΩΝ ΣΥΜΠΑΣΧΟΝΤΩΝ).

[46] Men. Rh. 2.9. Some of Basil's letters (*Ep.* 5, 6, 28) begin with what is more a monody than a brief expression of sympathy typical of consolatory letters; cf. Mitchell, "Consolatory Letters," 303.

[47] *Ep.* 165.

As a form of moral instruction, ancient consolation consisted primarily of a series of arguments against grief.[48] Like moralists in general, consolers argued from both philosophical precept and the example of others, with example often playing a very prominent role.[49] Many consolatory arguments were ideologically neutral and could be applied to more than one form of suffering.[50] Others were specific to certain misfortunes and/or reflective of a particular philosophical school.[51] In practice, however, consolation tended to be very eclectic and school lines were frequently crossed. Cicero writes: "in my *Consolatio* I threw all types of consolation into one document, for my soul was swollen with pain and I was attempting to cure it by every means."[52]

Exhortation to acceptable and responsible behavior was also an important aspect of consolation.[53] Exhortation could stand by itself as a separate section of a consolation, but more often it was interspersed with argument.[54] Two common exhortations were not

[48] Cicero, following Chrysippus, distinguished two general strategies of consolatory argument: (1) to attack the object of distress or (2) to attack the feeling of distress as such (*Tusc.* 4.27.58–28.61; cf. *Tusc.* 3.32.77). If one chooses the former approach, then one argues that the alleged evil is in fact not so, or at least that it is not great; if the latter, one argues that distress, independent of whether or not it can be justified in terms of its object, is undignified and therefore unworthy of the human soul. On both of these accounts the key to the alleviation of distress is knowledge: *ut constantia scientiae, sic perturbatio erroris est* (*Tusc.* 4.37.80). For the second approach, see especially Kassel, *Untersuchungen*, 54–6; cf. Cic., *Ad fam.* 5.17.3.

[49] Sen., *Ad Marc.* 2–4; *Ad Poly.* 14.1–16.3; 17.3–6. Cf. Cic., *Tusc.* 3.23.56; Ov., *Ex Pont.* 1.3.27, 61.

[50] So, for example, consolers regularly reminded sufferers that their grief would lessen over time and that others had suffered similar or even worse things before them and survived.

[51] Arguments in consolation of death typically differed from arguments offered in consolation of exile; and, of course, an Epicurean would approach death differently than a Platonist. Two ideologically neutral arguments regarding death were: death delivers from all future misfortune and we do not grieve for the dead but for ourselves. These arguments were often combined: death leads either to annihilation (Epicureanism) or to immortality (Platonism), both of which should comfort us.

[52] *Tusc.* 3.31.76: *ut fere nos in Consolatione omnia in consolationem unam coniecimus*; *Ad Att.* 12.14.3; J. E. Atkinson, "Seneca's 'Consolatio ad Polybium,'" *ANRW* II.32.2.860–84 (1985).

[53] Sen., *Ep.* 94.39: *consolationes . . . dissuasionesque et adhortationes et obiurgationes et laudationes . . . omnia ista monitionum genera sunt.*

[54] Ps.-Demetr., *Epist. Typ.* 5 gives the impression that exhortation was a separate section of the consolatory letter (cf. Stowers, *Letter-Writing*, 144; Guignet, *Saint Grégoire*, 80 ff.), and some have seen a separate hortatory conclusion in Menander Rhetor's prescription for the consolatory speech (2.9.25): "Let us, therefore, sing his [the deceased's] praises as a hero, or rather as a god let us count him blessed . . . " (ὑμνῶμεν οὖν αὐτὸν ὡς ἥρωα, μᾶλλον δὲ ὡς θεὸν αὐτὸν μακαρίσωμεν . . .). But a quick survey of the evidence indicates that while exhortation was an important

to neglect one's duties (*officia*)[55] and not to complain against God or Fate.[56] If a consoler decided that a mourner was indulging excessively in grief, exhortation changed to rebuke. This was typically indirect, as when Seneca, who is convinced that Marcia is being self-indulgent, rails not against her but against Octavia who had notoriously clung to grief after the death of Marcellus.[57] But in extreme cases the rebuke could be very direct, as when Seneca writes to Marullus: "You are expecting some words of comfort? Take a scolding instead! You are taking your son's death in a weak and unworthy manner."[58]

Ancient theories of consolation

Despite its intensely practical objective and characteristic eclecticism, ancient consolation contained a significant theoretical component. Each major philosophical school developed its own approach based on such things as its view of the soul, its doctrine of good and evil, and its theory of the passions. Cicero identifies five major theories of consolation at *Tusc.* 3.31.76.[59]

aspect of ancient consolation, it did not necessarily form a distinct section of consolatory letters and speeches. Cf. Mitchell, "Consolatory Letters," 303: "The division [into sympathy, consolation, and exhortation] appears to be one of subject matter rather than of form. Although all three elements find a place in consolations, Christian and pagan, of all periods, their separation into three distinct sections is by no means generally observed." It is probably better to describe consolation as a form of "rational exhortation" that contains both arguments and directives, the former offered in support of the latter.

[55] Sen., *Ad Helv.* 18.7–8: "this sacred duty (*officium*) will bring you relief"; *Ad Poly.* 5.4: "Nothing will so effectively restrain your devotion from such useless tears as the thought that you ought to give your brothers an example by bearing this injustice of Fortune bravely."

[56] Sen., *Ad Marc.* 10.2 (*sine querella*); *Ad Poly.* 2.2 (*facere litem*) 4.1 (*accusare fata*); *Ep.* 107.9 (*sine murmuratione*; *gemens*); Plut., *Ad ux.* 610E–F, 611B. Lattimore, *Themes*, 147–58, and esp. 183–4 has collected the epigraphic evidence; cf. Albert B. Purdie, ed., *Some Observations on Latin Verse Inscriptions* (London: Christophers, 1935) 44–8.

[57] *Ad Marc.* 2–3.

[58] *Ep.* 99.2: *Solacia expectas? Convicia accipe. Molliter tu fers mortem filii.* Cf. 99.32 (*castigarem*); Cic., *Ad Brut.* 1.9.1; Greg. Naz., *Ep.* 165: τὰ δὲ ἴσως ἐπιτιμῆσαι; Jer., *Ep.* 39.3–4; Ambr., *Ep.* 39; Chrys., *Ep. ad Olymp.* 8.3.11–13 Malingrey: εἰ δὲ πάλιν μοι τὰ αὐτὰ λέγεις ὅτι "βούλομαι μέν, οὐκ ἰσχύω δέ," πάλιν σοι καὶ ἐγὼ τὰ αὐτὰ ἐρῶ "σκήψις ταῦτα καὶ πρόφασις" cf. 17.4.32–43.

[59] *Sunt qui unum officium consolantis putent malum illud omnino non esse, ut Cleanthi placet. Sunt qui non magnum malum, ut Peripatetici. Sunt qui abducant a malis ad bona, ut Epicurus. Sunt qui satis putent ostendere nihil inopinati accidisse, [ut Cyrenaici]. Chrysippus autem caput esse censet in consolando detrahere illam opinionem maerenti, si se officio fungi putet iusto atque debito.*

Some, like Cleanthes, believe that the consoler's only task is to convince the person afflicted with grief that the alleged "evil" is not an evil at all. Others, like the Peripatetics, argue that the evil in question is not great. Others, like the Epicureans, try to avert our attention away from evil things to good things. Others, like the Cyrenaics, think that it is sufficient to show that nothing unexpected has happened. Chrysippus, however, believes that the most important thing in consoling another is to disabuse the mourner of his opinion, lest he imagine that he is fulfilling a just and obligatory duty.

Cleanthes' theory

The first view Cicero lists is that of the Stoic scholarch Cleanthes, according to which "the consoler's only task is to convince the person afflicted with grief that the alleged 'evil' is not an evil at all" and that grief is therefore unwarranted. This is the Stoic ideal of ἀπάθεια ("apathy") applied to the πάθος of grief.[60] Three suppositions underlie the Stoic theory of the passions in general and Cleanthes' theory of grief in particular: (1) that the soul is unitary and is therefore wholly rational;[61] (2) that the only real good is virtue, the only real evil is vice, and that everything else is morally indifferent (ἀδιάφορον),[62] and (3) that the passions, deriving as they do from conventional judgments of good and evil, are always irrational and excessive and thus have no place in the rational

---

[60] The Stoics recognized four principal πάθη: ἐπιθυμία (desire), ἡδονή (pleasure), φόβος (fear), and λύπη (mental pain). Various species of these were distinguished, but the lists were by no means standardized. Cicero distinguishes fourteen species of "pain" (*Tusc.* 4.7.16), Ps-Andronicus twenty-five (Περὶ παθῶν 2 = *SVF* 3.414); Diogenes Laertius nine (7.11 = *SVF* 3.412); Nemesius four (*De nat. hom.* 19 = *SVF* 3.416). In the consolatory tradition λύπη (*aegritudo*) was broadly conceived of as any form of grief or distress. For a general discussion of the passions, cf. Maximilian Forschner, *Die stoische Ethik: Über den Zusammenhang von Natur-, Sprach- und Moralphilosophie im altstoischen System* (Stuttgart: Klett-Cotta, 1981) 114–41; Brad Inwood, *Ethics and Human Action in Early Stoicism* (Oxford: Clarendon, 1985) 127–81.

[61] Chrysippus *apud* Gal., *De plac.* 4.4 = *SVF* 3.462 (p. 115.22–5): μηδὲ γὰρ εἶναί τινα τοιαύτην . . . ἐπιθυμητικήν τε καὶ θυμοειδῆ προσαγορεύοντες, τὸ ὅλον γὰρ εἶναι τὸ τῶν ἀνθρώπων ἡγεμονικὸν λογικόν, "there is no such thing as the appetitive and the spirited elements, for the whole of the human governing principle is rational."

[62] Forschner, *Die stoische Ethik*, 160–82; cf. Sen., *Ep.* 13.4.

soul.[63] On this account grief always originates in a false judgment of the form:

X is an evil (where "X" stands for some present state of affairs),

when the correct judgment would have been:

X is neither good nor evil but a matter of indifference.

Cleanthes' method was regularly employed in consolations treating lesser forms of misfortune such as poverty and exile.[64] However, since it stipulated that grief in any measure was excessive, it was rarely used in consolations of death, where it was criticized as harsh and unrealistic.[65]

Peripatetic theory

Cicero next mentions Peripatetic theory, according to which the consoler's task is to convince the person afflicted with grief that "the evil in question is not great" and that they should therefore show moderation in their grief.[66] Like the Stoics, the Peripatetics

---

[63] Stob., *Ecl.* 2.88.10 (= *SVF* 3.378): Πάθος δ' εἶναι φασιν ὁρμὴν πλεονάζουσαν καὶ ἀπειθῆ τῷ αἱροῦντι λόγῳ ἢ κίνησιν ψυχῆς ἄλογον παρὰ φύσιν. On the relationship of the passions and false judgments, see Cic., *Tusc.* 3.11.24; 4.7.14: *Sed omnes perturbationes iudicio censent [Stoici] fieri et opinione* (cf. 4.38.82); Epict., *Ench.* 5; Gal., *De plac.* 4.3.2. For the view of Chrysippus, see Gal., *De plac.* 4.7.12–17 (= *SVF* 3.466). Cf. Marc. Aur., *Med.* 8.47: Εἰ μὲν διά τι τῶν ἐκτὸς λυπῇ, οὐκ ἐκεῖνό σοι ἐνοχλεῖ, ἀλλὰ τὸ σὸν περὶ αὐτοῦ κρῖμα.

[64] Cf. Sen., *Ad Helv.* 5.1; Peter Meinel, *Seneca über seine Verbannung. Trostschrift an die Mutter Helvia* (Bonn: Habelt, 1972) 56–72; Karlhans Abel, *Bauformen in Senecas Dialogen. Fünf Strukturanalysen: dial. 6, 11, 12, 1 und 2* (Bibliothek der klassischen Altertumswissenschaften n.F., 2. Reihe, Bd. 18; Heidelberg: Winter, 1967) 58; Charles Favez, *L. Annaei Senecae Dialogorum liber XII Ad Helviam matrem de consolatione, texte latin publié avec une introduction et un commentaire explicatif* (Lausanne and Paris: Payot, 1918) xlii–xliii, 10. Other examples include: Teles, frag 3 (Περὶ φυγῆς) 22.1f. Hense (citing Stilpo); 29.2f. Hense; Muson. frag. 9 ("Ότι οὐ κακὸν ἡ φυγή) 42.6 Hense, cf. 50.9f. Hense; Plut., *De ex.* 599D; Philiscus *apud* Cass. Dio 38.26.2; Dio Chrys., *Or.* 13.8; Favorin., frag. 22.22.44–8 Barigazzi; cf. Malunowiczówna, "Les éléments stociens," 35; A. C. van Geytenbeck, *Musonius Rufus and the Greek Diatribe*, rev. edn., trans. B. L. Hijmans (Assen: Van Gorcum, 1962).

[65] Crantor *apud* Cic., *Tusc.* 3.6.12–13; Sen., *Ad Marc.* 6.1–2; *Ad Poly.* 2.1; 4.1; 18.5; *Ep.* 63.1; 77.12; but see Teles, frag. 7 (Περὶ ἀπαθείας) 56–7 Hense; Epict., *Ench.* 16.

[66] Middle Platonism never developed its own theory of consolation. Thus Antiochus of Ascalon sided with the Peripatetics, while Eudorus of Alexandria sided with the Stoics. Plutarch and Calvenus Taurus agreed with Antiochus; Albinus and Atticus with Eudorus. Philo preferred the Stoic line, but did not stick to it all the time. See John M. Dillon, *The Middle Platonists: A Study in Platonism, 80 B.C. to A.D. 220* (London: Duckworth, 1977), 44, 123–4, 146–8, 251–2, 299.

derived their theory of consolation from their doctrines of the soul, good and evil, and the passions. However, they differed from the Stoics in their interpretation of each of these central doctrines.[67] First, they held that the soul was not unitary and rational, but partite with both rational and irrational elements.[68] Second, they did not limit good and evil to virtue and vice but in general accepted conventional notions of good and evil, provided that the objects thus encompassed were not overvalued. And third, they held that passion, when based on an accurate assessment of value, was a proper and reasonable expression of the irrational part of the soul. Thus Peripatetic consolation had as its goal not the complete erasure of grief (ἀπάθεια) but its moderation (μετριοπάθεια).[69] It is understandable that in treating death consolers almost without exception judged Peripatetic μετριοπάθεια better suited to their task than Stoic ἀπάθεια.[70]

[67] John M. Dillon, "*Metriopatheia* and *Apatheia*: Some Reflections on a Controversy in Later Greek Ethics," in John P. Anton and Anthony Preus, eds., *Essays in Ancient Philosophy II* (Albany: SUNY, 1983), 508–17; Gregg, *Consolation Philosophy*, 81–123; Johann, *Trauer und Trost*, 41–50.

[68] Arist., *EN* 1.13.9: τὸ ἄλογον and τὸ λόγον ἔχον; see the discussion in Forschner, *Die stoische Ethik*, 124–34. Plato's theory of the soul is much less straightforward, wavering between a trichotomist scheme (τὸ ἐπιθυμητικόν, τὸ θυμοειδές, and τὸ λογικόν), as at *Tim.* 69Cff., and simple dichotomism (ἀλογίστικον and λογιστικόν), as at *Resp.* 4.434Dff. At *Phd.* 78C he states that the soul is uncompounded (ἀσύνθετος). See further, T. M. Robinson, *Plato's Psychology* (PhoenSup 8; Toronto: University of Toronto, 1970).

[69] The Peripatetic mean lay between ἀπάθεια, the *inhumana duritia* of the Stoics, and δυσπάθεια, the *infinitus dolor* of the unphilosophical masses (Ps.-Plut., *Ad Apoll.* 102C–E; cf. Sen., *Ad Helv.* 16.1). For the excesses of ancient ritual lament, see M. Alexiou, *The Ritual Lament in Greek Tradition* (Cambridge: Cambridge University Press, 1974) 27–9; cf. Stat., *Silv.* 2.6.1–2 and Hor., *Carm.* 1.24.1–2. According to Cicero, *Tusc.* 3.23.56, Peripatetic theory recognized two general means of arguing for moderation: (1) to examine the nature and magnitude of the evil itself (*ipsius rei natura qualis et quanta sit*), and (2) to cite the examples of others (*exempla*) who have endured similar misfortune; cf. *Tusc.* 3.24.58.

[70] The metriopathic ideal is articulated, among other places, at Pl., *Men.* 247C–248C; Cic., *Ad Att.* 12.10; *Ad fam.* 5.18.2; Ps.-Plut., *Ad Apoll.* 102C–E; Sen., *Ad. Marc.* 7.1f.; *Ad Poly.* 18.5f.; *Ep.* 63.1; 99.14–16. For the motif in Christian consolations, see the following texts collected by Scourfield, *Consoling Heliodorus*, 130–2: Ambr., *Ep.* 39.8; *Exc. Sat.* 2.11; Paul. Nol., *Ep.* 13.10; Aug., *Ep.* 263.3; Bas., *Ep.* 28.1, 62; Greg. Naz., *Ep.* 165.2; John Chrys., *Ep.* 197; Jer., *Ep.* 39.5.2, 6.4; 60.7.3. Cicero, however, rejects Peripatetic moderation as indulgent (*Tusc.* 3.10.22). To be sure, Stoic indifference is to be shunned as inhuman; but to pursue the mean is no solution either. Instead we must strive for the barest possible minimum of grief: a soul where only the tips of the roots (*fibrae radicum*; 3.6.13) of grief still cling, but nothing more.

Epicurean theory

The third view Cicero mentions is that of Epicurus. Unlike Stoic
and Peripatetic theorists, Epicurus was constrained by his hedonism
to take most conventional forms of evil at face value.[71] Epicurus
did, of course, insist that death, being the cessation of all sensation,
was not an evil, pain being the only evil.[72] And he also distinguished between natural and unnatural desires, of which the latter
should not be cultivated.[73] But in general he could not deny that
experiences traditionally judged to be painful were indeed painful
and grievous. For Epicurus, therefore, the consoler's task was to
direct the grieving person's mind away from his or her current
misfortune to other more pleasurable experiences (*a malis ad bona*).
Cicero explains:[74]

[71] He could not appeal to virtue as a supervening good, as did both the Stoics and
the Peripatetics, since on his theory the virtues were of purely instrumental value;
Cic., *Tusc.* 3.18.42 (= Usener 69); *De fin.* 2.69; Athen., *Deip.* 546F (= Usener 70); cf.
Plut., *Adv. Col.* 1125B. In general see J. C. B. Gosling and C. C. W. Taylor, *The
Greeks on Pleasure* (Oxford: Clarendon, 1982) 345–413, esp. 362–4; John M. Rist,
"Pleasure: 360–300 B.C.," *Phoenix* 28 (1974) 167–79; M. Hosenfelder, "Epicurus:
Hedonist malgré lui," in M. Schofield and G. Striker, eds., *The Norms of Nature:
Studies in Hellenistic Ethics* (Cambridge: Cambridge University Press, 1986) 245–63.
The texts are collected in Anthony A. Long and David N. Sedley, *The Hellenistic
Philosophers* (Cambridge: Cambridge University Press, 1987) I:112–25 and
II:114–29.

[72] *KD* 2: ὁ θάνατος οὐδὲν πρὸς ἡμᾶς· τὸ γὰρ διαλυθὲν ἀναισθητεῖ· τὸ δ᾽
ἀναισθητοῦν οὐδὲν πρὸς ἡμᾶς; cf. *Ep. Men.* 124: συνέθιζε δὲ ἐν τῷ νομίζειν
μηδὲν πρὸς ἡμᾶς εἶναι τὸν θάνατον ἐπεὶ πᾶν ἀγαθὸν καὶ κακὸν ἐν αἰσθήσει·
στέρησις δέ ἐστιν αἰσθήσεως ὁ θάνατος; Philod., *Adv. sophist.* 4.7–14: καὶ διὰ
παντὸς ἔστω καὶ πανταχῆι παρεπόμενον ἡ τετραφάρμακος "ἄφοβον ὁ θεός, ἀνύ-
ποπτον ὁ θάνατος· καὶ τἀγαθὸν μὲν εὔκτητον, τὸ δὲ δεινὸν εὐεκκαρτέρητον";
Lucr. 3.830–1: *nil igitur mors est ad nos neque pertinet hilum,* | *quandoquidem natura
animi mortalis habetur.* See Stork, *Nil igitur mors est ad nos,* 25–42; David Furley,
"Nothing to us?," in Schofield and Striker, eds., *The Norms of Nature,* 75–91.

[73] Epicurus actually distinguished three types of desires: (1) those that were both
natural and necessary (φυσικαὶ καὶ ἀναγκαῖαι); (2) those that were simply natural
(φυσικαὶ καὶ οὐκ ἀναγκαῖαι); and (3) those that were neither natural nor necessary
but the product of empty opinion (οὔτε φυσικαὶ οὔτ᾽ ἀνακαῖαι ἀλλὰ παρὰ κενὴν
δόξαν γινόμεναι); *KD* 29; *Schol. KD* 29; *KD* 30; *Ep. Men.* 127; *Sent. Vat.* 59.
Epicurus also held that certain pleasures which were productive of pain were to be
avoided while certain pains which were ultimately productive of a lasting pleasure
were to be accepted (*Ep. Men.* 129; *KD* 8; cf. Cic., *De fin.* 1.32). Another relevant
distinction was between mental and bodily pain, the former of which (e.g., the fear of
death) could be dispensed with by knowledge (e.g., of death, the gods, etc.).

[74] *Tusc.* 3.15.33 (= 444 Usener); cf. 3.31.76: *Sunt qui abducant a malis ad bona, ut
Epicurus*; 5.26.73–4: *se dicit* [*Epicurus*] *recordatione acquiescere praeteritarum voluptatum*; *De fin.* 1.57 (Torquatus speaking): *Est autem situm in nobis ut et adversa quasi
perpetua oblivione abruamus et secunda iucunde ac suaviter meminerimus*; Epicur.,
Sent. Vat. 55: θεραπευτέον τὰς συμφορὰς τῇ τῶν ἀπολλυμένων χάριτι καὶ τῷ

He [Epicurus] places the alleviation of distress in two activities: calling the mind away from thinking about things that disturb us (*avocatione a cogitanda molestia*) and calling the mind back to the contemplation of pleasure (*et revocatione ad contemplandas voluptates*).

Epicurus himself offers two striking examples of this technique (*avocatio-revocatio*) in his letters to Idomeneus[75] and Hermarchus.[76] Writing from his death bed and suffering from "urinary blockages" and intense "dysenteric pain" he fills his mind with thoughts of his disciples and philosophy.[77] Epicurus' method was popular with consolers who, as we have already noted, typically drew from many sources.[78] Cicero proposed a modified version of the method that called for the contemplation of virtue and not

---

γινώσκειν, ὅτι οὐκ ἔστιν ἄπρακτον ποιῆσαι τὸ γεγονός; *Incert. Epist. Frag.* 50: ἡδὺ ἡ φίλου μνήμη τεθνηκότος; Philodem., Περὶ θεῶν 3 col. d (2) 23: τὴν συνεχεστάτην ἐπιβολὴν ἐπὶ τὰ γεγονότα καὶ παρόντα καὶ μέλλοντα; Περὶ θανάτου 38.21. A slightly different view is espoused by Metrodorus in his consolatory letter to his sister (*apud* Sen., *Ep.* 99.25).

[75] Diog. Laert. 10.22 = Epicur., frag. 138 Usener (cf. frag. 52 Arrighetti).

[76] Cic., *De fin.* 2.20.96 = Epicur., frag. 122 Usener.

[77] To Idomeneus he writes: "But over against all these discomforts are placed (ἀντιπαρετάττετο) the joy in my soul produced by the recollection of the discussions we have had." Similarly to Hermarchus: "All my sufferings are counterbalanced (*compensabatur*) by the joy of soul that I lay hold of by recalling my [our?] theories and discoveries." Cf. *Ep. Pyth.* 84: μνημονεύειν τῶν εἰς μακάριον βίον συντεινόντων διαλογισμῶν. These letters, which gave concrete expression to Epicurus' recollections, were no doubt an integral part of his distraction; cf. Cic., *Ad Att.* 8.14.1: *crede mihi, requiesco paulum in his miseriis, cum quasi tecum loquor, cum vero tuas epistulas lego, multo etiam magis*; 9.4.1: *Ego . . . tam diu requiesco, quam diu aut ad te scribo aut tuas litteras lego*; cf. 9.10.1: *in quo uno* (= *scribere*) *acquiesco.*

[78] Ps.-Ov., *Cons. ad Liv.* 377–92; Sen., *Ad Poly.* 5–8 and 12–13; *Ad Helv.* 18–19; *Ad Marc.* 2.3–4; 4.3–5.6; 24.1–4; *Ep.* 63.4; 99.3–5; cf. *De ira,* 3.39.4; *De brev. vit.* 10.2ff.; *De vit. beat.* 6.1–2; *De benef.* 3.4.1. Cf. Johann, *Trauer und Trost,* 150–5; Constantine C. Grollios, *Seneca's Ad Marciam: Tradition and Originality* (Athens: Christou, 1956) 52–4; Abel, *Bauformen,* 26; Schoonhoven, *AD LIVIAM,* 178–82; C. E. Manning, *On Seneca's "Ad Marciam"* (Mnemosyne Supplement 69; Leiden: Brill, 1981) 47–8; *idem,* "The Consolatory Tradition and Seneca's Attitude to the Emotions," *G&R* 21 (1974) 71–81, esp. Appendix, 79–81. Seneca criticizes the method in its grosser forms at *Ad Helv.* 17.2; *Ad Marc.* 1.5, 8; cf. *Ad Helv.* 2.4–4.1; *Ad Marc.* 1.2–5. Plutarch also makes repeated use of the method: cf. *De tran. an.* 468F–469D; *De ex.* 600D; *Ad ux.* 608A-B; 610E. Elsewhere the technique occurs in Ps.-Ovid, *Cons. ad Liv.* 377–400 and 411–16; Ps.-Plut., *Ad Apoll.* 116A–B; Plin., *Ep.* 8.5.2; Julian, *Or.* 8.246C–E; and in early Christian literature, in Ambr., *Exc. Sat.* 1.3; Jer. *Ep.* 60.7.3; 108.1.2; 118.4.2; Bas., *Ep.* 5.2; 269.2; and Paul. Nol., *Ep.* 13.6. The so-called "apocalyptic cure" of 4 Ezra 7:16; 2 *Apoc. Bar.* 81.4 also resembles this technique.

pleasure.[79] Seneca makes use of this modified version in both the *Ad Polybium* and the *Ad Marciam*.[80]

Cyrenaic theory

Cicero next mentions Cyrenaic theory, according to which grief is caused not by misfortune as such but by misfortune that is unanticipated.[81] Like the surprise attack of an enemy or a sudden storm at sea – two popular Cyrenaic analogies[82] – misfortune overwhelms us when it catches us off guard, but not when we are prepared for it.[83] To lessen the shock of misfortune Cyrenaics advocated the contemplation of future evils (*praemeditatio futurorum malorum*).[84] For those already afflicted with grief, consolation lay in the knowledge that "nothing unexpected has happened" (*nihil inopinati accidisse*).[85] Cicero does not find in Cyrenaic theory

---

[79] *Tusc.* 3.16.34–3.21.51; cf. *De fin.* 2.30.96–8. "You bid me to reflect on good things (*bona cogitare*) and to forget evil things . . . But you are turning my thoughts towards pleasures . . . However, Epicurus, if you call me back (*revocas*) to these goods (sc. courage, self-control, justice, prudence), I obey, I follow, I make you my leader, I shall even forget evil, as you urge" (*Tusc.* 3.16.35–3.17.37).

[80] *Ad Poly.* 18.8: *Cogita modestiam eius, cogita . . . sollertiam . . . industriam . . . constantiam*; *Ad Marc.* 24.1–4: *Incipe virtutibus illum non annis aestimare . . . Harum contemplatione virtutum filium gere quasi sinu!* Cf. Jerome, *Ep.* 60.7.3: *ita in parvo isto volumine cernas adumbrata, non expressa, signa virtutum*; J. C. Logemann, "De defunctorum virtut. in carm. sepulcr. lat. laudatis" (Ph.D. diss. Amsterdam, Rotterdam, 1916); Favez, *La consolation*, 106–26. Manning, *On Seneca's "Ad Marciam,"* 47–8, 71–2, sees in the Seneca passages, in which he would include *Ad Marc.* 12.1–2, the combination of the Epicurean *avocatio* with the theme of *laus mortui*.

[81] *Tusc.* 3.13.28: *insperato et necopinato malo*; Grollios, *Ad Marciam*, 44–51.

[82] *Tusc.* 3.22.52; cf. Ps.-Plut., *Ad Apoll.* 112D; Sen., *Ad Helv.* 5.3; *Ep*, 47.4; *De prov.* 4.6, 13; *De clem.* 1.7.3; Chrys., *Ep. ad Olymp.* 15.1 Malingrey. Cf. Malunowiczówna, "Les éléments stoïciens," 39.

[83] The connection between the Cyrenaic philosophy and consolation is not to my knowledge expressly stated in the sources. Presumably, however, since the Cyrenaics equated pleasure and pain with movements of the soul, unexpected misfortune produced a more violent motion and thus greater pain.

[84] As a practical technique the *praemeditatio futuri mali* extended well beyond Cyrenaic consolation theory. Diogenes of Sinope taught it (Diog. Laert. 6.63); as did Chrysippus (Cic., *Tusc.* 3.22.52); Panaetius (Plut., *De coh. ir.* 463D); Posidonius (Gal., *De plac.* 4.5.34), Carneades (Plut., *De tran. an.* 474E), Epictetus (*Diss.* 3.10.1ff.; *Ench.* 21), Seneca (*Ad Helv.* 5.3; *De tran. an.* 11.6); Plutarch (*De tran. an.* 465B); cf. Virg., *Aen.* 6.103–5. Grollios, *Ad Marciam*, 48–9; Kassel, *Untersuchungen*, 66; Johann, *Trauer und Trost*, 63–84; Rabbow, *Seelenführung: Methodik der Exerzitien in der Antike* (Munich: Kösel-Verlag, 1954) 160–79; Abel, *Bauformen*, 37–8; Manning, *On Seneca's "Ad Marciam,"* 60.

[85] *Tusc.* 3.23.55; 3.31.76.

a complete account of grief, but he does agree that the element of surprise intensifies anguish, "for all sudden occurrences seem more serious."[86] Cyrenaic theory was obviously better suited to preventing grief than alleviating it.[87] Nevertheless, the assumption that grief is due, at least in part, to the element of surprise is found in a number of consolations.[88]

Chrysippus' theory

The fifth theory Cicero identifies is that of Cleanthes' successor Chrysippus. Chrysippus agreed with Cleanthes that grief is traceable to false conventional judgments regarding the nature of evil, and that as such it has no place in the rational soul.[89] However, he located the proximate or immediate cause of grief in the additional judgment that, given a particular misfortune, grief is an obligatory response (τὸ καθῆκον): "grief is an opinion about some present misfortune in which is contained the [further judgment] that it is right to feel grief."[90] Grief thus has its origin in a kind of double

[86] *Tusc.* 3.13.28; cf. 3.22.52ff.

[87] Kassel, *Untersuchungen*, 66–7; cf. Epict., *Diss.* 3.24.115: ταῦτα ἔχων ἀεὶ ἐν χερσὶ καὶ τρίβων αὐτὸς παρὰ σαυτῷ καὶ πρόχειρα ποιῶν οὐδέποτε δεήσῃ τοῦ παραμυθουμένου, τοῦ ἐπιρρωννύντος.

[88] Ps.-Pl., *Ax.* 370A (cf. 364B); Ps.-Ov., *Cons. ad Liv.*, 397–400; Sen., *Ad Marc.* 9.2; *Ad Helv.* 5.3; *Ad Poly.* 11.1; *Ep.* 63.14; 107.4; cf. *De vit. beat.* 8.6; *De brev. vit.* 9.4; Ps.-Plut., *Ad Apoll.* 112D; cf. Plut., *De vir. mor.* 449E; *De tran. an.* 476A, D.

[89] Chrysippus treated the passions in his Περὶ παθῶν in four books, the last of which was "therapeutic" (known to Galen variously as τὸ Θεραπευτικόν or τὸ Ἠθικόν) and dealt with the treatment of the passions (cf. Gal., *De plac.* 4.1.14 p. 238 De Lacy and *passim*). The fragments of the Περὶ παθῶν, most of which are from books 4 and 5 of *De plac. Hip. et Pl.*, are collected by von Arnim at *SVF* 3.456–90; cf. Phillip De Lacy, *Galen. On the Doctrines of Hippocrates and Plato. Third Part: Commentary and Indexes* (Corpus Medicorum Graecorum V 4,1,2; Berlin: Akademie-Verlag, 1984) s.v. θεραπευτικός, ἠθικός; Max Polhenz, "Das Dritte und Vierte Buch der Tusculanen," *Hermes* 41 (1906) 332, 347–55; *idem*, "De Posidonii libris," 572–4; Kassel, *Untersuchungen*, 19, 23–4; cf. Peter Steinmetz, "Die Stoa" in Hellmut Flashar, ed., *Grundriss der Geschichte der Philosophie*, vol. IV/2: *Die Philosophie der Antike: Die hellenistische Philosophie* (Basel: Schwabe, 1994) 591; Abel, *Bauformen*, 86.

[90] *Tusc.* 3.31.74: *aegritudinem esse opinionem mali praesentis, in qua opinione illud insit, ut aegritudinem suscipere oporteat*; cf. Stob., *Ecl.* 2.90.14–16 W: λύπην δ᾽ εἶναι συστολὴν ψυχῆς ἀπειθῆ λόγῳ, αἴτιον δ᾽ αὐτῆς τὸ δοξάζειν πρόσφατον κακὸν παρεῖναι, ἐφ᾽ ᾧ καθήκει συστέλλεσθαι; *SVF* 3.391 (= Ps.-Andronicus, Περὶ παθῶν 1): λύπη μὲν οὖν ἐστιν ἄλογος συστολή. ἢ δόξα πρόσφατος κακοῦ παρουσίας, ἐφ᾽ ᾧ οἴονται δεῖν συστέλλεσθαι; Cic., *Tusc.* 3.11.25: *aegritudo est opinio magni mali praesentis et quidem recens opinio talis malis, ut in eo rectum videatur esse angi; id autem est, ut is, qui doleat, oportere opinetur se dolere*; *Tusc.* 4.7.14: *est ergo aegritudo opinio recens mali praesentis, in quo demitti contrahique animo rectum esse videatur.*

judgment: 1) that a misfortune has indeed occurred, and 2) that grief is the correct response. Only when one holds the second opinion as well as the first does grief occur (*Tusc.* 3.26.61):[91]

> But when, to the opinion that some great evil has occurred, the further opinion is added that it is appropriate, that it is right, that it is a matter of duty to be distressed at what has happened, then, and only then, does the passion of deep distress occur.

On this account grief is open to attack in two ways. On the one hand, one may challenge (à la Cleanthes) the root assumption that what has occurred is a genuine misfortune, arguing to the contrary that what has been lost is in reality a matter of indifference. But one may also simply argue that grief, independent of the perceived misfortune, is an unfitting response (παρὰ τὸ καθῆκον), on the theory that even if we mistakenly believe that a particular state of affairs, say, poverty, is a misfortune, we will still not grieve unless we also judge that grief is appropriate.[92] Consolers argued the inappropriateness of grief in at least three ways:[93] (1) that it is useless;[94] (2) that it causes us to act irresponsibly, that is, that grief

---

Inwood, *Ethics and Human Action*, 148–51; Adolf F. Bonhöffer, *Epictet und die Stoa: Untersuchungen zur stoischen Philosophie* (Stuttgart: Enke, 1890) 281–2. The judgment that grief is a duty was conventionalized in conventional rites of mourning.

[91] *Sed ad hanc opinionem magni mali cum illa etiam opinio accessit, oportere, rectum esse, ad officium pertinere ferre illud aegre, quod acciderit, tum denique efficitur illa gravis aegritudinis perturbatio*; cf. *Tusc.* 3.11.25; 3.27.64; cf. Posidonius' criticism *apud* Gal., *De plac.*: 4.5.27; εἰ γὰρ τὸ μέγεθος τῶν φαινομένων ἀγαθῶν ἢ κακῶν κινεῖ τὸ νομίζειν καθῆκον καὶ κατὰ ἀξίαν εἶναι παρόντων αὐτῶν ἢ παραγινομένων, μηδένα λόγον προσίεσθαι περὶ τοῦ ἄλλως δεῖν ὑπ' αὐτῶν κινεῖσθαι, τοὺς ἀνυπέρβλητα νομίζοντας εἶναι τὰ περὶ αὐτοὺς τοῦτ' ἔδει πάσχειν.

[92] There is reason to believe that Chrysippus favored the second approach, and that he postponed the first until the intense irrationality of grief had subsided. Cf. Inwood, *Ethics and Human Action*, 152–3; Cic., *Tusc.* 4.27.59ff.: *Nimirum hoc melius, ne, si forte de paupertate non persuaseris, sit aegritudini concedendum*; Gal., *De plac.* 4.7.25–7 p. 286 De Lacy = *SVF* 3.467.

[93] Cic., *Tusc.* 3.26.61ff.; Pohlenz, "Das Dritte und Vierte Buch der Tusculanen," 326–7.

[94] This argument is well attested. For the inscriptional evidence, see Lattimore, *Themes*, 217–19; for the literary evidence see, Johann, *Trauer und Trost*, 56–7; Kassel, *Untersuchungen*, 70; cf. Hom., *Il.* 24.522–51. Cicero attests to its popularity at *Tusc.* 3.28.66 when he asks, *Quid est autem quod plus valeat ad ponendum dolorem, quam cum est intellectum nihil profici et frustra esse susceptum?* Cf. *Ad Att.* 12.10: *consolationum autem multae viae, sed illa rectissima*; Sen., *Ad Marc.* 6.1–2; *Ad Poly.* 2.1: *nihil profuturum dolorem tuum nec illi, quem desideras, nec tibi.*

contradicts other outstanding obligations;[95] and (3) that grief, an inherently irrational act, is always beneath our dignity as human beings.[96]

Two important consolatory *topoi*

Before turning to the second, exegetical part of our study, it will be helpful to examine in more detail two important consolatory *topoi* that figure prominently in the argument of Philippians. The first of these is the familiar distinction between things that matter and things that do not. We have already seen this distinction in Cleanthes' theory of consolation. Paul introduces it in Phil. 1:10a in his introductory prayer-report: εἰς τὸ δοκιμάζειν ὑμᾶς τὰ δια-φέροντα.[97] The second consolatory *topos* we will consider is the

---

[95] This argument is also well-documented. At *Ad Brut.* 1.9.2 Cicero reminds Brutus of his *officia* both as a military and political leader, and at *Ad fam.* 4.6.2 he complains that he himself has no compelling duties to claim his thoughts in his grief over the death of Tullia (*non amicorum negotiis, non reipublicae procuratione impediebantur cogitationes meae*). Similarly, Seneca reminds Polybius (*Ad Poly.* 5.4–6.5) that he must be an example for his brothers and that he must not neglect his office nor his service to Caesar; Abel, *Bauformen*, 86; Kurth, *Senecas Trostschrift an Polybius. Dialogue 11: Ein Kommentar* (Beiträge zur Altertumskunde 59; Stuttgart: Teubner, 1994) 71–89. Cf. Sen., *Ad Marc.* 4.3–4; Cic., *Tusc.* 3.27.65–6: *Ergo in potestate est adiicere dolorem, cum velis, tempori servientem*; *Ad Att.* 12.10; 12.11; Pind., *Pyth.* 1.86–8; Jer., *Ep.* 60.14.5; cf. Ennius frag. 158 Vahlen (= frag. 215 in H. D. Jocelyn, *The Tragedies of Ennius* [Cambridge Classical Texts and Commentaries 10; London: Cambridge University Press, 1967]; Esteve-Forriol, *Trauer- und Trostgedichte*, 153; Ps.-Ov.,*Cons. ad Liv.* 355–6: *an melius per te virtutum exempla petemus quam si Romanae principis edis opus?*

[96] *Tusc.* 4.27.59: *hominem aegre ferre nihil oportere.* The argument that grief is unworthy of us as rational beings is scattered throughout the tradition, often in the form of short asides that one should bear misfortune with manly courage; cf. Sen., *Ad Marc.* 1.1; 7.3; *Ad Poly.* 6.2. Cic., *Ad Brut.* 1.9.1 (*ferre . . . quam deceret virum*). In the Latin tradition the more typical exhortation is to patience (*patientia*). Hor., *Carm.* 1.24.19–20; Ov., *Met.* 8.633; Sen., *Ad Marc.* 13; cf. Fern, *The Latin Consolatio Mortis*, s.v. *patientia* and *patientia et constantia*; Judson Tolman, *A Study of the Sepulchral Inscriptions in Buecheler's Carmina Epigraphica Latina* (Chicago: University of Chicago Press, 1910) 76. The status and/or philosophical attainments of the mourner were also often taken into account, as when Seneca exhorts Polybius not to behave in a manner unworthy (*indignum*) of his philosophy. Cf. Cic., *Ad Brut.* 1.9.1: *alienum tanto viro, quantus es tu.* Mourners were often exhorted not to complain against God or Fate. Cf. Sen., *Ad Marc.* 10.2 (*sine querella*); *Ad Poly.* 2.2 (*facere litem*) 4.1 (*accusare fata*); Purdie, ed., *Latin Verse Inscriptions*, 44–8; Lattimore, *Themes*, 183–4.

[97] For the *adiaphora topos* in Paul, cf. H. D. Betz, *Galatians: A Commentary on Paul's Letter to the Churches in Galatia* (Hermeneia; Philadelphia: Fortress Press, 1979) 94; J. Paul Sampley, *Walking Between the Times: Paul's Moral Reasoning* (Minneapolis: Fortress, 1991) 77–83; James L. Jaquette, "Paul, Epictetus and Others on Indifference to Status," *CBQ* 56 (1994) 68–80; *idem, Discerning What Counts:*

disposition of "joy" (χαρά, *gaudium*) which characterized the true philosopher in both good times and bad. Paul uses χαρά and its cognates sixteen times in Philippians.[98] The *topos* of "joy" will be particularly important for our interpretation of 3:1–4:1.

The *adiaphora topos* in ancient consolation

According to Cleanthes, grief originates in a failure to distinguish between things that matter and things that do not, on the assumption that things conventionally thought to be misfortunes fall consistently into the latter category. Cleanthes' theory was rarely used in consolations of death. However, it was frequently employed in consolations treating lesser misfortunes. It was particularly popular in consolations of exile, which were regularly organized around the thesis that exile is not an evil and should therefore be endured with philosophical indifference.[99]

The oldest surviving consolation of exile, Teles frag. 3 Hense (Περὶ φυγῆς), takes just this approach. The fragment falls into two parts. In the first part Teles argues that exile is not an evil because it does not deprive us of anything that is truly good: neither the goods of the soul (τὰ περὶ ψυχὴν ἀγαθά), nor goods of the body (τὰ περὶ τὸ σῶμα), nor any other external goods (τὰ ἐκτός).[100] In the second part Teles anticipates objections. His characteristic response is "What does it matter?" To the objection that exile deprives us of political involvement, he responds: "What does it matter (τί διαφέρει) whether we exercise authority in our own country or live a private life in another?"[101] To the objection that an exile is deprived of burial in his homeland, he responds: "What is the

---

The Function of the Adiaphora Topos in Paul's Letters (SBLDS 146; Atlanta: Scholars Press, 1995).

[98] 1:4, 18 (twice), 25; 2:2, 17 (twice), 18 (twice), 28, 29; 3:1; 4:1, 4 (twice), 10.

[99] In addition to the texts cited below, cf. Plut., *De ex.* 599D; Favorin., frag. 22.22.44–8 Barigazzi: ὥστε οὔτε φυγὴ οὔτε πάλιν αὖ μονή, οὔτε ἀτιμία οὔτε τιμή, οὔτε ἀδικία οὔτε . . . , οὔτε ἐλευθερία οὔτε δουλεία, οὔτε πλοῦτος ἢ πενία ἀγαθὰ ἢ κακά, ἀλλὰ ἡ μὲν τούτων εἰς τὸ δέον χρῆσις ἀγαθή, ἡ δὲ εἰς τὸ μὴ δέον κακή. For the *topos* in later Christian consolation, cf. Malunowiczowna, "Les éléments stoïciens," 35 who cites: Chrys., *Ep. ad Olymp.* 7.1; 9.4 Malingrey; *Ad Theod. laps.* 2.4 (*PG* 47.314); *De stat.*, hom. 5.2 (*PG* 49.70); *Ep.* 102 (*PG* 52.662); *Ad Stag.* 3.14 (*PG* 47.492).

[100] Teles here quotes an earlier treatise on exile by the Megarian scholarch Stilpon.

[101] Frag. 3.24 Hense.

difference (τί γὰρ τὸ διάφορον)? Isn't the road to Hades equal and
alike from every direction?"[102] He concludes:[103]

> Now if it happens that you are not buried at all but are
> tossed out unburied, what is hateful in that (τί τὸ
> δυσχερές)? Indeed, what does it matter (τί διαφέρει)
> whether we are consumed by fire, or are eaten by a dog, or
> are devoured by ravens above the ground or by worms
> below?

Musonius takes the same approach in frag. 9 Hense (Ὅτι οὐ
κακὸν ἡ φυγή), asserting that the wise man remains unmoved by
exile since he "does not value or despise any place as the cause of
his happiness or unhappiness, but he makes the whole matter
depend upon himself."[104] He is more realistic than Teles, allowing
that exile may deprive us of certain conventional goods, "things the
masses consider to be goods" (ὧν οἱ πολλοὶ νομίζουσιν
ἀγαθῶν).[105] But exile cannot deprive us of "things that are truly
good" (τῶν γὲ ἀληθῶν ἀγαθῶν).[106] If anything, exile aids us in our
pursuit of that which is truly good "since it furnishes men leisure
and a greater opportunity for learning the good and practicing it
than they formerly enjoyed."[107]

Dio Chrysostom uses the *topos* of indifferent things to similar
effect in *Or.* 13 (Ἐν Ἀθήναις περὶ φυγῆς). Strictly speaking, *Or.* 13
is not consolatory but autobiographical. Nevertheless, it begins
with an account of Dio's exile and subsequent conversion to
philosophy in which Dio consoles himself along the lines of

[102] Frag. 3.29 Hense.
[103] Frag. 3.29 Hense; E. N. O'Neil, ed., *Teles (The Cynic Teacher)* (SBLTT 11;
Missoula, MT: Scholars Press, 1977) 83 n. 44, cites Epict., *Diss.* 4.7.31.
[104] Frag. 9.42.6–7 Hense: ὁ γὰρ τοιοῦτος χωρίον μὲν οὐδὲν οὔτε τιμᾷ οὔτ᾽
ἀτιμάζει οὕτως ὡς εὐδαιμονίας ἢ κακοδαιμονίας· αὐτὸς δὲ ἐν αὑτῷ τίθεται τὸ πᾶν.
The test for whether something was a matter of indifference was whether it
contributed anything to one's happiness or unhappiness; cf. Diog. Laert. 7.104 (=
SVF 3.119): ἀδιάφορα . . . τὰ μήτε πρὸς εὐδαιμονίαν μήτε πρὸς κακοδαιμονίαν
συνεργοῦντα; Sext., *Adv math.* 9.59 (*SVF* 3.122): τὸ ἀδιάφορον τὸ μήτε πρὸς
εὐδαιμονίαν μήτε πρὸς κακοδαιμονίαν συλλαμβανόμενον.
[105] Frag. 9.50.7 Hense. Here we may infer Teles' goods of the body and external
goods.
[106] Frag. 9.50.9 Hense; cf. Teles' "goods of the soul" (τὰ περὶ ψυχὴν ἀγαθά).
[107] Frag. 9.43.10–11 Hense. He cites the example of Diogenes who was led to the
life of philosophy because of his exile; cf. Epict., *Diss.* 4.11.23; Diog. Laert. 6.49;
Plut., *De tran. an.* 467C; Dio, *Or.* 13 (discussed below); Favorin., frag. 22.1.30
Barigazzi.

Cleanthes' theory.[108] Banished by Domitian, Dio is forced "to consider whether exile is truly a difficult and unfortunate thing, as most people think (πότερον ὄντως χαλεπόν τι καὶ δυστυχὲς εἴη τὸ τῆς φυγῆς ὡς κατὰ τὴν τῶν πολλῶν δόξαν)," or whether it is something that can easily be endured, if approached "according to the importance (διαφοράν) of the matter."[109] He concludes that exile is a matter of indifference (οὐ πάντως ἡ φυγὴ βλαβερὸν . . . οὐδὲ τὸ μένειν ἀγαθὸν).[110] This earns him the reputation of a philosopher, and people begin to seek him out to hear his opinion about what really matters (ὅ τι μοι φαίνοιτο ἀγαθὸν ἢ κακόν).[111]

According to Cassius Dio, Cicero was consoled during his brief exile to Macedonia in 58 BCE by a certain Philiscus. He reports Philiscus' speech at *Hist.* 38.18, which turns on the question whether Cicero's circumstances are truly evil (εἰ κακὰ ὡς ἀληθῶς ἐστι ταῦτα τὰ περιεστηκότα σε).[112] He concludes that they are not evil and that exile "is shameful and evil only by convention and a certain popular opinion" (νόμῳ τε καὶ δοκήσει τινὶ καὶ αἰσχρὰ καὶ κακά ἐστι).[113] Philiscus is sure that Cicero, an educated man, is above such opinion, and suggests that had his exile not taken him by surprise (αὐτὸς ἑαυτοῦ ἐκπλαγείς),[114] he would have risen above his circumstances as matters of indifference.

Seneca appeals to the distinction between things that matter and things that do not in his *Ad Helviam matrem de consolatione*.[115] The *Ad Helviam* is particularly instructive for our understanding of Philippians, for, like Paul who writes from prison to console his supporters at Philippi, Seneca composed the *Ad Helviam* while in exile for the consolation of his mother.[116] He calls attention to the uniqueness of his situation at 1.3:

[108] An autobiographical piece, *Or.* 13 nonetheless draws on the consolatory tradition as Dio reports how he consoled himself when faced with exile. Cf. J. L. Moles, "The Career and Conversion of Dio Chrysostom," *JHS* (1978) 79–100.
[109] *Or.* 13.2.
[110] *Or.* 13.8.
[111] *Or.* 13.12.
[112] 38.19.2.
[113] 38.24.3.
[114] 38.22.4; another theme we meet in Philippians: μὴ πτυρόμενοι ἐν μηδενὶ ὑπὸ τῶν ἀντικειμένων (1:28); cf. 1 Thess. 3:3–4, 1 Pet. 4:12 (μὴ ξενίζεσθε . . . ὡς ξένου ὑμῖν συμβαίνοντος); John 16:1, 33. See our discussion of Phil. 1:28 below.
[115] A second extremely relevant text is *Ep.* 107. We will examine this text below in our exegesis of Phil. 1:9–10a. The relevant passage is §1 which reads: *Ubi illa prudentia tua? Ubi in dispiciendis rebus subtilitas? Ubi magnitudo? Tam pusilla te res tangit?*
[116] John Chrysostom faced a similar rhetorical situation in his *Epistolae ad*

Although I unrolled all the works that the most famous writers had composed for the purpose of repressing and controlling sorrow, not one instance did I find of a man who had offered consolation to his dear ones when he himself was bewailed by them.

Like Paul, Seneca argues that his circumstances offer no occasion for grief since they have not affected the things that really matter. He states his theme in a formal *propositio* at 4.2:[117]

I have determined to conquer your grief, not to dupe it. And indeed I shall conquer it, I think, if, in the first place, I show that I have suffered nothing on account of which I may be called miserable (*si ostendero nihil me pati, propter quod ipse dici possim miser*) . . . and, secondly, if I turn next to you and prove that your fortune is also not severe (*probavero ne tuam quidem gravem esse fortunam*).

Seneca insists that exile is not an evil: *nihil mihi mali esse*.[118] He is the victim of only "so-called evils" (*quae mala vocantur*) and has lost "no truly good thing" (*nihil veri boni*). He knows that external things like exile are matters of indifference and neither add to nor detract from our happiness.[119] As a result he is even now full of joy (*gaudium*) in circumstances that would make others miserable.[120] He develops his thesis in chs. 6–13 in an extended exposé on the so-called evils of exile where he "puts aside the judgment of the many who are carried away by first appearances."[121]

"Joy" in ancient consolation

Through the specialized vocabulary of Stoicism,[122] χαρά and its cognate χαίρω (Lat. *gaudium, gaudeo*) became important terms in

---

Olympiadem. Cf. Malunowiczówna, "Les éléments stoïciens," 35–45; Anne-Marie Malingrey, *Jean Chrysostome. Lettres à Olympias: seconde édition augmentée de la Vie d'Olympias* (Sources Chrétiennes 13; Paris: Les Editions du Cerf, 1968) 53–64.

[117] Paul states his similar theme in the "propositio" (the introductory prayer report) of 1:9–11.

[118] Cf. Phil. 1:12.

[119] *Ad Helv.* 5.1: *Leve momentum in adventiciis rebus est et quod in neutram partem magnas vires habeat*. Cf. Meinel, *Seneca über seine Verbannung*, 56–72; Abel, *Bauformen*, 58; Charles Favez, *L. Annaei Senecae Dialogorum liber XII*, xlii–xliii, 10.

[120] Cf. Phil. 1:18.

[121] Paul offers a similar "exposé" on his imprisonment in Phil. 1:12–26.

[122] The Stoics were well known for their technical terminology and often criticized for it; cf. Cic., *De fin.* 3.1.2–2.5.

the moral discourse of the Hellenistic and Roman periods.[123] In contrast to the Academic/Peripatetic ideal of μετριοπάθεια (measured emotion) which called for the control of appetite by reason,[124] Stoicism advocated ἀπάθεια (apathy), the complete eradication of the always irrational and excessive πάθη and their replacement with the εὐπάθειαι (rational emotions) of the sage.[125] Stoicism recognized four primary πάθη: ἐπιθυμία (desire) and its opposite φόβος (fear), and ἡδονή (pleasure) and its opposite λύπη (mental pain).[126] Corresponding to the first three of these were the εὐπάθειαι of βούλησις (wishing), εὐλάβεια (caution), and χαρά (joy).[127] The last of these, χαρά, which replaced the Epicurean ἡδονή, became the characteristic emotion of the wise man.[128] As the antithesis of "grief" (λύπη), for which there was no corresponding εὐπάθεια,[129] χαρά was also an important concept in consolation.[130]

Despite some ambiguity in the sources,[131] Stoicism seems to have

[123] For the influence of Stoic ethics, and in particular the Stoic theory of the passions, on Middle Platonism, see Dillon, *The Middle Platonists*, 43–5, 77–8, 146–52.

[124] Diog. Laert. 5.31; Alcinous, *Didask.* 62.20–35 Whittaker (= 184.18–24 C. F. Hermann's Teubner edn. of Plato); Ps.-Plut., *Ad Apoll.* 102D; Plut., *De virt. mor.* 444D; Alex. Aphr., *In Top.* 239.6 Wallies; cf. Dillon, *Middle Platonists*, 301–2; idem, *Alcinous. The Handbook of Platonism* (Oxford: Clarendon, 1993) 186–9.

[125] The Stoic doctrine of the passions has been treated most recently by Forschner, *Die stoische Ethik*, 114–41. In a word, Stoic ἀπάθεια is εὐπάθεια; cf. Inwood, *Ethics and Human Action*, 173.

[126] ἐπιθυμία is an irrational impulse (ἄλογος ὄρεξις) for a perceived good.

[127] Joy, however, is a form of pleasure and thus a vice in 4 Macc. 1:22.

[128] Philo, *Abr.* 156 (= *SVF* 3.436): ἡ εὐπαθειῶν ἀρίστη χαρά; *Her.* 315: τέλος; *Praem.*, 32; Sen., *Ep.* 66.5 (= *SVF* 3.115): *primum bonum*; cf. Philo, *Det.* 135; *Plant.* 138.

[129] The rational counterpart of λύπη would be the correct response to the presence of something bad, but nothing bad ever happens to the sage, who on the one hand understands that conventional evils are really indifferent, and who furthermore accepts his circumstances as providentially given (cf. *Tusc.* 4.6.12–7.14 = *SVF* 3.438; Sen., *De prov.* 6.1–5). But see Philo, *QGen.*, 2.57, who adds δηγμός (a biting) as the rational analog to λύπη (cf. Plut., *De vir. mor.* 449A). For the translation of this difficult text, which survives only in a faulty Armenian translation, see Dillon, *The Middle Platonists*, 151 n. 2.

[130] Sen., *Ep.* 99.4: *Sed plerique non computant, quanta perceperint, quantum gavisi sint.* For the language of "joy" in the context of the *avocatio-revocatio*, see: Sen., *Ad. Marc.* 3.4 (*laetam*); *Ad Poly.* 10.6 (*gaude . . . gaudere*), 11.2–4; *Ep.* 99.3 (*gauderes*); Plut., *De tran. an.* 469D (χαίρειν); Ambr., *Exc. Sat.* 1.3 (*laetandum . . . est*); Jer., *Ep.* 60.7.3 (*gaudeas*). Cf. Apoll. Tyan., *Ep.* 93 Hersh; Teles 7.59 says that we should rejoice at the deaths of those who have died well. This is a common theme in funeral orations.

[131] F. H. Sandbach, *The Stoics* (New York: Norton, 1975) 67; Inwood; *Ethics and Human Action*, 174–5; T. H. Irwin seems to take εὐπάθεια exclusively in terms of

allowed for two varieties of joy distinguished by their objects. According to Stoic doctrine, the passions are irrational because they express false judgments about apparent good or evil (φαινό-μενον ἀγαθὸν ἢ κακόν). Thus the person driven by passion always commits the mental error of assigning excessive value (ἀξία) or disvalue (ἀπαξία) to something that is in reality morally indifferent (ἀδιάφορον).[132] This error is corrected in the rational εὐπάθειαι of the sage, but in two possible ways. On the one hand, the sage may continue to pay attention to indifferent things, but in so doing assign them only the relative value or disvalue they actually merit.[133] Here the sage's εὐπάθεια retains the same object as the corresponding πάθος, but not its intensity. Epictetus has this scheme in mind at *Diss.* 3.24.11 when, after instructing his students "in the nature of good and evil" (τὴν δ᾽ οὐσίαν τοῦ ἀγαθοῦ καὶ τοῦ κακοῦ; 3.24.3), he exhorts them to enjoy their friends, but with restraint, so as not to be grieved when they are taken away (τοῖς μὲν συνοῦσι χαίροντας, τοῖς δ᾽ ἀπαλλαττομένοις μὴ ἀχθο-μένους).[134] To be surrounded by one's friends, while an occasion for joy, is ultimately a matter of indifference and must be responded to as such.

But the sage may also redirect his attention away from indifferent things to real goods or evils where the assigning of "excessive" value or disvalue is by definition ruled out.[135] Here the εὐπάθεια has the same intensity as the corresponding πάθος, but not its object. Cicero has this scheme in mind at *Tusc.* 5.25.72 when he speaks of the sage "rejoicing in the goods of the soul, that is, in the virtues" (*gaudere . . . bonis animi, id est, virtutibus*).[136] Seneca takes a similar approach in *Ep.* 59 when he claims that joy arises from

indifferents ("Conceptions of Happiness," in Schofield and Striker, eds., *The Norms of Nature*, 240 n. 38); cf. Michael Frede, " The Stoic Doctrine of the Affections of the Soul," in Schofield and Striker, eds., *The Norms of Nature*, 95.

[132] Sen., *Ep.* 59.4: *voluptatem voco, opinione falsi boni motam, inmoderatam et inmodicam.*

[133] The Stoics conceived of this relative value as a kind of "preference." Though lacking value in any absolute or moral sense, these objects might nevertheless, all things being equal, be preferred (προηγμένα) or "dispreferred" (ἀποπροηγμένα).

[134] Cf. Cic., *Tusc.* 4.6.13–7.14, Plut., *De vir. mor.* 449A; Lact., *Div. inst.* 6.15; Sen., *Ep.* 99.21. This scheme also seems to be presupposed by Diogenes Laertius when he says that unlike virtue, joy is a good not always present in the sage (7.98 = *SVF* 3.102); cf. Stobaeus, *Ecl.* 2.68 (= *SVF* 3.103): χαράν . . . οὔτε πᾶσι τοῖς φρονίμοις ὑπάρχειν οὔτε αἰεί; *Ecl.* 2.77 (= *SVF* 3.113) ἀγαθὸν οὐκ ἀναγκαῖον πρὸς εὐδαιμονίαν.

[135] Cf. Sen., *Ep.* 23.7: *Veri boni aviditas tuta est.*

[136] Cf. Epict., *Ench.* 6.

one's awareness of virtue[137] and defines joy as "the elation of a spirit that trusts in its own goods and truths."[138] Epictetus extends this type of joy to include the philosopher (the example is Socrates) rejoicing in his own progress.[139]

In both of these instances joy is a "causal by-product" (ἐπι-γέννημα)[140] of virtue, and thus may be experienced in its fullest sense only by the sage.[141] However, in the first instance it is occasioned by indifferent things and is therefore contingent on external circumstances. Joy in this sense is not always experienced by the sage.[142] But in the second instance joy derives directly from the sage's virtue and is therefore independent of circumstances. This type of joy is the sage's constant companion.[143] In the first sense joy is obviously not necessary for happiness.[144] In the second sense, however, it is almost the equivalent of happiness, being the sage's enjoyment of his own virtue. Joy in this second sense became the characteristic emotion of the sage. Paul uses joy in the second sense in Philippians when he directs the Philippians away from the things that do not matter to the things that do (τὰ διαφέροντα).[145]

Seneca discusses joy (*gaudium*) as the characteristic emotion of the sage in *Ep.* 23 and again in *Ep.* 59.[146] Both of these letters are instructive for our understanding of Philippians because of the seriousness with which they treat joy: "Believe me," Seneca writes,

[137] *Ep.* 59.16: *Gaudium hoc non nascitur nisi ex virtutum conscientia.*

[138] *Ep.* 59.2: *animi elatio suis bonis verisque fidentis.*

[139] *Diss.* 4.8.23; cf. 3.5.14; *Ench.* 34, where it is contrasted with ἡδονή.

[140] Diog. Laert. 7.94 = *SVF* 3.76.

[141] Glenn Lesses, "Virtue and the Goods of Fortune in Stoic Moral Theory," *Oxford Studies in Ancient Philosophy* 7 (1989) 106.

[142] Diog. Laert. 7.98 = *SVF* 3.102; Stob., *Ecl.* 2.68; see note 134 above.

[143] Sen., *Ep.* 59.2, 16.

[144] Stob., *Ecl.* 2.77 = *SVF* 3.113.

[145] "Joy" does not, of course, have the same *content* for Paul the Christian as it does for Seneca the Stoic. According to Seneca, Lucilius is to rejoice "in what is his own", that is in the goods of his own soul. For Paul, on the other hand, joy is to be in the progress of the gospel (1:12), in his continued bold confession (1:20), and, ultimately, in the Lord (3:1) At least the first and third of these Seneca would reject as proper objects for joy since, among other things, they are external to oneself and therefore uncertain. Paul can accept them, however, because although external they are not uncertain because of the providence of God, a point he is at pains to make in his letter. For consolation as joy elsewhere in Paul, see 2 Cor. 7:4: πεπλήρωμαι τῇ παρακλήσει, ὑπερπερισσεύομαι τῇ χαρᾷ ἐπὶ πάσῃ τῇ θλίψει ὑμῶν; 2 Cor. 7:13: διὰ τοῦτο παρακεκλήμεθα. ἐπὶ δὲ τῇ παρακλήσει ἡμῶν περισσοτέρως μᾶλλον ἐχάρημεν ἐπὶ τῇ χαρᾷ. For joy in the face of affliction (θλίψις), cf. 2 Cor. 6:10; 8:2; 1 Thess. 1:6; Philem. 7; Rom. 12:15 (opposite of κλαίω).

[146] For unbroken joy in suffering, see also Epicurus' Letter to Idomeneus (Diog. Laert. 10.22 = 138 Usener; 52 Arrighetti).

"true joy (*verum gaudium*) is a matter of the utmost importance (*res severa*)."[147] The opening words of *Ep.* 23 bear quoting at length:

> Do you want to know what is the foundation of a sound mind? It is that you do not take joy from things that do not matter (*ne gaudeas vanis*). Did I say "foundation"? It is the pinnacle! He has made it to the very top who understands what should be the object of his joy (*qui scit, quo gaudeat*), who has not placed his happiness in the power of things that do not belong to him.

Seneca concludes: "This you must do before all else, my dear Lucilius, learn how to rejoice (*disce gaudere*)."[148]

To experience this kind of joy Lucilius must learn to distinguish between the things that matter and the things that do not and limit his desires to the former: *ne gaudeas vanis*. If he will do this he will be lifted above even the most severe calamities of life (*super omnia erectus*)[149] and experience a joy that never fails (*numquam deficiet*). Like the sage he will live "full of joy" (*plenus gaudio*). In the meantime he can measure what is still lacking in his pursuit of wisdom by what is still lacking in his experience of joy: *tantum tibi ex sapientia, quantum ex gaudio deesse*.

It is easy to see how joy, the characteristic disposition of the sage who is always victorious over grief (λύπη, *dolor*), became a *topos* in ancient consolation, first, in direct exhortations to those afflicted with grief that they should rejoice,[150] but also, when the one offering consolation has also suffered loss, in reports that the consoler is himself joyful, as when the exiled Seneca assures his mother that he is himself happy (*beatus*), full of joy (*gaudium*) in circumstances that would make others miserable (*miser*).[151] We shall see that Paul employs the *topos* of joy in precisely both of these manners in Philippians. He expresses concern for the Philippians' joy in 1:25–6 and 2:28, and exhorts them to rejoice in

[147] *Ep.* 23.4.
[148] *Ep.* 23.3. Paul offers a similar summary of the Christian life in Phil. 3:1: χαίρετε ἐν κυρίῳ. Cf. Sen., *Ep.* 23.6: *Fac, oro te, Lucili carissime, quod unum potest praestare felicem: dissice et conculca ista, quae extrinsecus splendent . . . ad verum bonum specta et de tuo gaude.*
[149] Such as death (*mors*), poverty (*paupertas*), pain (*dolor*).
[150] Sen., *Ad. Marc.* 3.4 (*laetam*); *Ad Poly.* 10.6 (*gaude . . . gaudere*); *Ep.* 99.3 (*gauderes*); Plut., *De tran. an.* 469D (χαίρειν); Ambr., *Exc. Sat.* 1.3 (*laetandum . . . est*); Jer., *Ep.* 60.7 (*gaudeas*).
[151] *Ad Helv.* 4.2–5.1; cf. Chrys., *Ep. ad Olymp.* 9.3.60–7; 12.1.44, 136; 16.1.12 Malingrey.

2:17–18, 28; 3:1; and 4:4. He proclaims his own joy in 1:18 and again in 2:17–18. We have already noted Chrysostom's insightful comments on 1:18:[152]

> The great and philosophic soul is vexed by none of the grievous things in the present life: not enmities, not accusations, not slanders, not perils or plots . . . And such was the soul of Paul; it had taken possession of a place higher than any fortress, the seat of spiritual philosophy, true philosophy . . . That blessed man had not only the emperor waging war against him, but many others attempting to grieve him in many ways, even with bitter slander. But what does he say? Not only "I am not hurt or overcome by these things," but "I rejoice and I will rejoice!"

[152] *In Epist. ad Phil.*, hom. 3.1 (*PG* 62.197.37–51): τὴν μεγάλαν καὶ φιλόσοφον ψυχὴν οὐδὲν τῶν ἐν τῷ παρόντι βίῳ λυπηρῶν δύναται δακεῖν, οὐκ ἔχθραι, οὐ κατηγορίαι, οὐ διαβολαί, οὐ κίνδυνοι, οὐκ ἐπιβουλαί . . . τοιαύτη ἦν ἡ τοῦ Παύλου ψυχή, πάσης ἀκρωρείας ὑψηλότερον τόπον τὸν τῆς φιλοσοφίας καταλαβοῦσα τῆς πνευματικῆς, τῆς ὄντως φιλοσοφίας . . . ὁ μακάριος ἐκεῖνος καὶ τὸν βασιλέα ἔχων πολεμοῦντα αὐτῷ, πρὸς τούτῳ εἶχε καὶ ἑτέρους ἐχθροὺς διαφόρως αὐτὸν λυποῦντας, καὶ μετὰ πικρᾶς διαβολῆς· καὶ τί φησιν; οὐ μόνον οὐκ ἀλγῶ τούτοις οὐδὲ καταπίπτω, ἀλλὰ καὶ χαίρω καὶ χαρήσομαι.

Part II

CONSOLATION IN PHILIPPIANS

4

PAUL'S CONSOLATORY STRATEGY: DISCERNING THE THINGS THAT MATTER (PHIL. 1:3–11)

> Where is that prudence of yours? Where is that skill in making the necessary distinctions? Where is that ability to rise above circumstance? Does a matter of such insignificance affect you so much?
> Seneca, *Ep.* 107.1

> For our aim is not simply to rid you of depression, but to fill you with a great and lasting joy.
> Chrysostom, *Ep. ad Olymp.* 10.1.21–23 Malingrey

We begin the exegetical part of our study with the εὐχαριστῶ-period of Phil. 1:3–11.[1] Our exegesis of 1:3–11 will be selective, focusing on the way in which Paul uses this material to introduce the consolation of the letter.[2] We are primarily interested in the intercessory prayer-report that comes at the end of this period (1:9–11),[3] and even more specifically in the initial purpose clause of verse 10a, in which Paul states his thesis that the Philippians need to learn how to identify "the things that matter" so as not to be discouraged by the things that do not. Phil. 1:3–11 may be divided into the following three parts: (1) the thanksgiving prayer proper (vv. 3–6); (2) a digression in which Paul offers "personal assur-

---

[1] It is conventional to refer to all of Phil. 1:3–11 as a period even though there is a new syntactical unit beginning at 1:9 after the digression of 1:7–8.

[2] The form and epistolary function of Paul's εὐχαριστῶ-periods were first studied in detail by Paul Schubert, *Form and Function*. Subsequent studies, following James M. Robinson, "Die Hodajot-Formel in Gebet und Hymnus des Frühchristentums," in W. Eltester and F. H. Kettler, eds., *Apophoreta: Festschrift für Ernst Haenchen* (BZNW 30; Berlin: Töpelmann, 1964) 201–2, have also called attention to the εὐχαριστῶ-period's liturgical backgound; cf. O'Brien, *Introductory Thanksgivings*. For a recent reassessment of the evidence, see Arzt, "The 'Epistolary Introductory Thanksgiving' in the Papyri and in Paul," 29–46 and the response by Reed, "Are Paul's Thanksgivings 'Epistolary'?," 87–99.

[3] Paul's prayer-reports have been studied by Wiles, *Intercessory Prayers*; cf. O'Brien, *Introductory Thanksgivings*.

ance" (Gnilka) that his expressed appreciation of the Philippians is sincere (vv. 7–8); and (3) the intercessory prayer-report (vv. 9–11).

The thanksgiving prayer proper: Paul's appreciation of the Philippians (Phil. 1:3–6)

Schubert has correctly identified the basic syntax of 1:3–6.[4] Paul begins with a characteristic expression of thanks to God for the Philippians (εὐχαριστῶ τῷ θεῷ μου ἐπὶ πάσῃ τῇ μνείᾳ ὑμῶν) which he then develops in two circumstantial participle clauses.[5] The first of these locates Paul's thanksgiving in the context of his intercessory prayer: πάντοτε ἐν πάσῃ δεήσει μου ὑπὲρ πάντων ὑμῶν, μετὰ χαρᾶς τὴν δέησιν ποιούμενος (vv. 4–5). The second is more loosely related to the main clause.[6] It indicates the ultimate basis for Paul's thankfulness, namely, his confidence in God: πεποιθὼς αὐτὸ τοῦτο, ὅτι ὁ ἐναρξάμενος ἐν ὑμῖν ἔργον ἀγαθὸν ἐπιτελέσει ἄχρι ἡμέρας Χριστοῦ Ἰησοῦ (v. 6).

There is disagreement among commentators on how best to translate the prepositional phrase ἐπὶ πάσῃ τῇ μνείᾳ ὑμῶν in 1:3. It has traditionally been understood in a temporal sense: "in all my remembrance of you" (RSV), "whenever I pray for you" (NEB), "whenever I think of you" (JB). More recently, O'Brien, following Schubert, has argued that ἐπί is causal and introduces the object of εὐχαριστῶ.[7] He translates: "because of your every remembrance [of me]," taking ὑμῶν as a subjective genitive.[8] This preserves the natural sense of εὐχαριστῶ ἐπί τινι which typically means "I am thankful because of something."[9] Here, however, the temporal sense is required, since the epistolary idiom μνείαν ποιεῖσθαί τινος ("to make mention of someone") is in view, as the next verse makes plain (τὴν δέησιν ποιούμενος).[10] Bauer, Arndt, and Gingrich translate correctly: "as often as I make mention of you [in

---

[4] Form and Function, 13.
[5] Cf. Philem. 4–5; 1 Thess. 3:9–10; Col. 1:3–4.
[6] Some translators therefore place a full stop after verse 5.
[7] O'Brien, Introductory Thanksgivings, 41–6; Schubert, Form and Function, 71–82.
[8] Introductory Thanksgivings, 44; cf. Epist. Bar. 5:5 for μνεία with a subjective genitive.
[9] 1:5 (ἐπὶ τῇ κοινωνίᾳ ὑμῶν) would thus be translated "because of your partnership"; cf. 1 Cor. 1:4.
[10] Cf. Rom. 1:9; 1 Thess. 1:2; Philem. 4; Koskenniemi, Studien, 146–8.

prayer]."[11] The point of 1:3, then, is that each of Paul's prayers for the Philippians is also an occasion for thanksgiving.

The next two verses (1:4–5) are epexegetical and explain more fully the nature and cause of Paul's thanksgiving.[12] Paul thanks God every time he mentions the Philippians in prayer inasmuch as whenever he prays for them (ἐν πάσῃ δεήσει μου ὑπὲρ πάντων ὑμῶν), and that is often (πάντοτε), he does so with joy (μετὰ χαρᾶς τὴν δέησιν ποιούμενος). Paul here recasts his customary εὐχαριστῶ-formula in terms of χαρά,[13] the dominant motif of the letter.[14] The object of Paul's joy, and thus the cause of his thanksgiving,[15] is the Philippians' long-standing partnership in the gospel ministry: ἐπὶ τῇ κοινωνίᾳ ὑμῶν εἰς τὸ εὐαγγέλιον ἀπὸ τῆς πρώτης ἡμέρας ἄχρι τοῦ νῦν (1:5).[16] Paul will report his current prayer for the Philippians in 1:9–11.

Underwriting Paul's appreciation of the Philippians' partnership is his confidence (πεποιθώς) that God will see to completion the "good work" (ἔργον ἀγαθόν) that he has begun at Philippi (ἐν ὑμῖν).[17] The immediate context allows for two possible interpretations of ἔργον ἀγαθόν, each of which requires a different sense of ἐν ὑμῖν. On the one hand, Paul may have in view the Philippians' "partnership" (κοινωνία) in the gospel ministry mentioned in verse 5. On this interpretation ἐν ὑμῖν would be rendered "in you," the Philippians' partnership being an expression of an inner work of

[11] S.v. μνεία.

[12] The ἐν πάσῃ δεήσει μου ὑπὲρ πάντων ὑμῶν of verse 4a explains the ἐπὶ πάσῃ τῇ μνείᾳ ὑμῶν of verse 3b, while the μετὰ χαρᾶς τὴν δέησιν ποιούμενος of verse 4b explains the εὐχαριστῶ τῷ θεῷ μου of verse 3a.

[13] Paul combines these motifs again in 4:4–6: χαίρετε ἐν κυρίῳ πάντοτε· πάλιν ἐρῶ, χαίρετε . . . ἐν παντὶ τῇ προσευχῇ καὶ τῇ δεήσει μετὰ εὐχαριστίας τὰ αἰτήματα ὑμῶν γνωριζέσθω πρὸς τὸν θεόν; cf. 1 Thess. 3:9: τίνα γὰρ εὐχαριστίαν δυνάμεθα τῷ θεῷ ἀνταποδοῦναι περὶ ὑμῶν ἐπὶ πάσῃ τῇ χαρᾷ ᾗ χαίρομεν δι' ὑμᾶς ἔμπροσθεν τοῦ θεοῦ ἡμῶν; 1 Thess. 5:17: πάντοτε χαίρετε, ἀδιαλείπτως προσεύχεσθε, ἐν παντὶ εὐχαριστεῖτε; Col. 1:12: μετὰ χαρᾶς εὐχαριστοῦντες. Cf. Sen., *Ep.* 99.4.

[14] Elsewhere: 1:18, 25; 2:2, 17, 18, 28, 29; 3:1; 4:1, 4, 10.

[15] Grammatically ἐπὶ τῇ κοινωνίᾳ ὑμῶν is the object of χαρά, but *ad sensum* it is also the object of εὐχαριστῶ (1:3). For the expression χαρὰ ἐπί τινι, cf. Lk. 15:7, 10; Jos., *Ant.* 7.252.

[16] Some scholars have read κοινωνία in a passive sense of "sharing in," while understanding εὐαγγέλιον to mean the gospel message not the gospel ministry. The result is that Paul is joyful over the Philippians' conversion, the fact that they have accepted the gospel message. But this is completely out of step with the rest of the letter where the Philippians' active support of the gospel ministry is in view; cf. esp. 4:14–16. Paul here touches on a key element of the Philippians' self-understanding. See our discussion of 4:15–16 in chapter 2 above.

[17] The Philippians, who did not share Paul's confidence, had begun to question the value of their contribution.

divine grace. But "good work" may also refer to the gospel mission itself (τὸ εὐαγγέλιον) which took a fresh point of departure at Philippi.[18] In this case ἐν ὑμῖν would more naturally be rendered "among you."[19] Both interpretations make excellent sense and build organically on the ideas of 1:4–5. However, the latter interpretation is to be preferred, since it expresses Paul's concern, evident in 1:12–18a, to reassure the Philippians that his mission continues to succeed despite current hardship. Paul's appreciation of the Philippians' partnership in his mission (1:3–5) is based on his confidence that that mission is guaranteed to succeed by God (1:6). The Philippians, who have supported Paul "from the first day until now" (ἀπὸ τῆς πρώτης ἡμέρας ἄχρι τοῦ νῦν), should therefore rest assured that God will see the work to completion "until the day of Jesus Christ" (ἄχρι ἡμέρας Χριστοῦ Ἰησοῦ).

A digression: Paul's appreciation of the Philippians is justified (Phil. 1:7–8)

Paul cannot take it for granted that the Philippians, who do not share his optimism regarding the mission (1:6), will find his unflagging appreciation of their contribution credible. He therefore pauses in 1:7–8 to further justify his claim: ἐστιν δίκαιον[20] ἐμοὶ τοῦτο φρονεῖν ὑπὲρ πάντων ὑμῶν ὅτι . . .[21] He assures the Philip-

[18] For "work" in this sense, see Phil. 1:22: τοῦτό μοι καρπὸς ἔργου; 2:30: ἔργον Χριστοῦ; cf. Gnilka, Philipperbrief, 72. Stowers, "Friends and Enemies," 117, comes close to this idea: "The fundamental theological tactic of the letter's discourse interprets the Philippians' experience by means of a larger narrative about God, Christ, and Paul . . . God began the good work of creating the Philippian community and he will bring it to completion (1:6)."

[19] Gnilka, Philipperbrief, 46: "Gott hat ein gutes Werk begonnen ἐν ὑμῖν, nicht 'in euch', als sei auf die in jedem einzelnen wirkende Gnade hingewiesen, sondern 'bei euch', in dem er 'euch' als lebendige Gemeinde schuf"; Bonnard, Philippiens, 16: "parmi vous." Cf. 2:13: θεὸς γάρ ἐστιν ὁ ἐνεργῶν ἐν ὑμῖν, "for God is the one producing among you . . ."

[20] Cf. PCairo Zen. 1.59076.3: ὑγίαιον σοῦ διὰ π[αντὸς μνείαν ποι]ούμενος . . . ὥσπερ δίκαιον ἦν (Koskenniemi, Studien, 146); cf. BAGD, s.v. δίκαιος. Meyer, An die Philipper, 14, cites similar expressions: δίκαιον ἐμὲ τοῦτο φρονεῖν (Herod. 1.39; Dem. 198.8; Pl., Symp. 224C); δίκαιός εἰμι τοῦτο φρονεῖν (Herod. 1.32; Dem. 1469.18; Thuc. 1.40.3).

[21] How we understand Paul's digression in 1:7–8 depends in large part on what we take to be the antecedent of τοῦτο in 1:7. Some commentators (Weiss, Philipper-Brief, 54; Vincent, Philippians, 8; Dibelius, An die Philipper, 53) understand the reference to be to the immediately preceding expression of confidence in 1:6; others (Lightfoot, Philippians, 84; Gnilka, Philipperbrief, 48; Collange, Philippiens, 47) see a reference to all of 1:3–6; yet others (e. g., Bonnard, Philippiens, 17) take only 1:3–5 to be in view. Given our interpretation of 1:6 as referring not to the inner working of

pians that they have won a permanent place in his heart (ἐν τῇ καρδίᾳ) as those who have joined in partnership with him not only materially (cf. 1:5) but existentially in suffering for the gospel: ἔν τε τοῖς δεσμοῖς μου καὶ ἐν τῇ ἀπολογίᾳ καὶ βεβαιώσει τοῦ εὐαγγελίου συγκοινωνούς μου τῆς χάριτος. He expresses his affection for them in the strongest possible terms: μάρτυς γάρ μου ὁ θεὸς ὡς ἐπιποθῶ πάντας ὑμᾶς ἐν σπλάγχνοις Χριστοῦ Ἰησοῦ.

Paul's unequivocal expression of affection in 1:7–8 and his acknowledgment of the Philippians as his "mutual partners" (συγκοινωνούς) in suffering and grace are well suited to the overall consolatory function of the Philippians.[22] We have already seen that consolation typically began with some expression of sympathy or fellow-suffering.[23] Expressions of affection, though not as common,[24] can also be found. So, for example, Julian at *Ep.* 69.412B bemoans the fact that Himerius, "who of all my friends is undoubtedly the most beloved" (ἡμῖν εἰς τὰ μάλιστα τῶν φίλων ὁ ποθεινότατος), has lost his young wife.[25] Similarly, Marcus Aurelius, who is always affectionate in his letters to his teacher Fronto, is particularly affectionate when he writes to console him on the death of his grandson, addressing him first as "sweetest master" (*dulcissime magister*) and then as "most delightful master" (*iucundissime magister*).[26] That Paul intended his expressions of

God in the Philippians but to Paul's European mission, the last view seems best for two reasons. First, Paul's primary purpose in 1:7–8 is to state his affection for the Philippians. It is easy to see how this justifies Paul's appreciation of the Philippians (1:3–5), but it is not clear how this justifies his confidence in the success of the mission (1:6). Second, in 1:7 Paul bases his affection on the fact that the Philippians are "mutual partners" (συγκοινωνούς) with him in suffering. This recalls their "partnership in the gospel" (τῇ κοινωνίᾳ ὑμῶν εἰς τὸ εὐαγγέλιον), the focal point of 1:3–5. Paul thus offers two bases for his appreciation of the Philippians' partnership in the gospel. First, because he knows that their work will last, being guaranteed in providence of God (1:6), and second, because their financial partnership is part of a more thoroughgoing partnership in grace, the thought of which evokes his strongest feelings (1:7–8). The second of these forms a separate syntactical unit (1:7–8) that necessitates a new beginning in 1:9–11: καὶ τοῦτο προσεύχομαι, ἵνα . . .

[22] In addition to Phil. 1:5, 7–8, see: 2:1, 12; 3:1; 4:1, 14–16; cf. 2:19: ἵνα κἀγὼ εὐψυχῶ γνοὺς τὰ περὶ ὑμῶν; 2:28: ἵνα ἰδόντες αὐτὸν πάλιν χαρῆτε κἀγὼ ἀλυπότερος. Paul also reassures the Philippians of Epaphroditus' sympathy and affection in 2:26: ἐπειδὴ ἐπιποθῶν ἦν πάντας ὑμᾶς καὶ ἀδημονῶν, διότι ἠκούσατε ὅτι ἠσθένησεν.

[23] Kassel, *Untersuchungen*, 51, 98 n. 1; Scourfield, *Consoling Heliodorus*, 80–1, and chapter 3 above.

[24] Favez, "Le sentiment."

[25] Julian's ποθεινότατος recalls Paul's ἐπιπόθητοι at Phil. 4:1 (cf., 1:7: ἐπιποθῶ; and 2:26: ἐπιποθῶν). This example is admittedly late.

[26] *De nepote amisso* 1.

affection (σπλάγχνα) and camaraderie (συγκοινωνός) in 1:7–8 to supplement his consolation of the Philippians is confirmed later in Phil. 2:1 where both ideas (σπλάγχνα and κοινωνία) are explicitly linked with consolation.[27]

Intercessory prayer-report: the need for discernment (Phil. 1:9–11)

Paul returns to his prayer for the Philippians, mentioned in passing in verse 4, in verses 9–11. He reports the content of the prayer in 1:9: καὶ τοῦτο προσεύχομαι, ἵνα ἡ ἀγάπη ὑμῶν ἔτι μᾶλλον καὶ μᾶλλον περισσεύῃ ἐν ἐπιγνώσει καὶ πάσῃ αἰσθήσει. This is followed in 1:10–11 by two final clauses. The first of these is closely related to the prayer of 1:9, further specifying the "knowledge and perception" that Paul wishes the Philippians to acquire: εἰς τὸ δοκιμάζειν ὑμᾶς τὰ διαφέροντα (1:10a).[28] The second final clause is more remotely tied to Paul's prayer. It indicates the ultimate eschatological consequences he has in view: ἵνα ἦτε εἰλικρινεῖς καὶ ἀπρόσκοποι εἰς ἡμέραν Χριστοῦ κτλ. (1:10b–11).

Two problems of interpretation

The prayer-report of Phil. 1:9–11 has proven surprisingly difficult for interpreters. There are two problems: (1) how to understand the relationship of love and knowledge in 1:9: ἵνα ἡ ἀγάπη ὑμῶν ἔτι μᾶλλον καὶ μᾶλλον περισσεύῃ ἐν ἐπιγνώσει καὶ πάσῃ αἰσθήσει,

---

[27] εἴ τις παράκλησις . . . εἴ τι παραμύθιον . . . εἴ τις κοινωνία . . . εἴ τις σπλάγχνα.

[28] I translate 1:10a: "that you might be able to discern the things that matter." I defend my translation of τὰ διαφέροντα as "the things that matter" below. I have chosen to translate δοκιμάζειν "to discern" for the following reasons. δοκιμάζειν has two basic meanings: "to test" or "to examine," and by way of consequence, "to approve" or "to accept" as having been tested. Epictetus uses the term in the first sense at *Diss.* 1.20.7, 12 when he exhorts his students "to test impressions" (δοκιμάζειν τὰς φαντασίας) to see if they are what they appear to be, that is, to see if they are in fact things that matter (τὰγαθὰ καὶ καλά) or if they are simply things that appear to matter but in reality do not (τὰ ἀδιάφορα); see also: *Diss.* 2.5.1; 2.8.20; 2.18.24; esp. *Ench.* 1.3–5, where the failure to test impressions is said to be the cause of grief (πενθήσεις); cf. *Diss.* 2.13.2; 3.3.15; 4.7.40; Lohmeyer, *An die Philipper*, 32. This is obviously not the sense in which Paul uses the term in Phil. 1:10a, since one does not "test" the things that matter, but rather, having tested one's experiences in general, one "approves" those that matter while rejecting those that do not. I would express this notion of approval-on-the-basis-of-testing as "discernment," and so I translate δοκιμάζειν as "to discern." See further Adolf F. Bonhöffer, *Epictet und das Neue Testament* (RVV 10; Giessen; Töpelmann, 1911) 298–9.

and (2) how then to relate this understanding to the immediately following purpose clause in 1:10: εἰς τὸ δοκιμάζειν ὑμᾶς τὰ διαφέροντα. Barth puts his finger on the first problem when he writes, "Daß die Liebe zunehmen soll an Erkenntnis . . . scheint schwierig."[29] It is easy to think of Paul calling for knowledge to be tempered or otherwise informed by love (cf. 1 Cor. 8:1: ἡ γνῶσις φυσιοῖ, ἡ δὲ ἀγάπη οἰκοδομεῖ), but that love might somehow be deficient in knowledge sounds singularly un-Pauline.

Most commentators solve this problem by reversing Paul's meaning, interpreting Paul's prayer to be a call for "überfließende Liebe" that will eventually produce in the Philippians a type of spiritual discernment.[30] But this is an impossible interpretation. In the construction τινὰ περισσεύειν ἐν τινί, it is not the subject (τινά) that increases but the object of the preposition ἐν. So, for instance, when in Rom. 15:13 Paul writes εἰς τὸ περισσεύειν ὑμᾶς ἐν τῇ ἐλπίδι, he is not calling for the Romans themselves (ὑμᾶς) to increase – whatever this might mean – but for their hope (ἐν τῇ ἐλπίδι) to do so. Similarly, in 1 Cor. 15:58 the expression περισσεύοντες ἐν τῷ ἔργῳ τοῦ Κυρίου πάντοτε envisions an increase "in the work of the Lord."[31] If Paul's prayer in Phil. 1:9 had been

[29] *Erklärung des Philipperbriefes* (Munich: Kaiser, 1928) 13.

[30] Gnilka, *Philipperbrief*, 51: "Der erste Gebetwunsch für die Gemeinde ist überfließende Liebe"; cf. Spicq, *Agapè*, 2:238: "l'accroissement de la charité rend la connaissance . . . plus pénétrante et le sens moral plus délicat et plus aigu"; ibid., 234: "Ces trois versets [Phil. 1:9–11] sont les plus denses et les plus précis du Nouveau Testament sur l'influence de l'*agapè* au point de vue intellectuel et moral." O'Brien, *Philippians*, 77, is even more explicit: "Paul's prayer, then, was not that some fresh elements such as knowledge and insight might be introduced into their love . . . Rather, the content of the petition was that the love of God within the readers might increase beyond all measure." A number of commentators admit that the grammar calls for knowledge to be added to love but later define knowledge in terms of love: Beare, *Philippians*, 54; Collange, *Philippiens*, 49; cf. Gnilka, *Philipperbrief*, 52.

[31] Cf. 2 Cor. 8:7: ὥσπερ ἐν παντὶ περισσεύετε ἵνα καὶ ἐν ταύτῃ τῇ χάριτι περισσεύητε. Περισσεύω occurs twenty-four times in the recognized letters of Paul (Rom. 3:7; 5:15; 15:13; 1 Cor. 8:8; 14:12; 15:58; 2 Cor. 1:5 [twice]; 3:9; 4:15; 8:2, 7 [twice]; 9:8 [twice], 12; Phil. 1:9, 26; 4:12 [twice]; 18; 1 Thess. 3:12; 4:1, 10; cf. Eph. 1:8; Col. 2:7). Twice it is transitive (2 Cor. 9:8a; 1 Thess. 3:12); in its remaining twenty-two occurrences it is intransitive. Of these, it occurs seven times without further modification, twice it is modified by a noun in the dative, and thirteen times by a prepositional phrase: εἰς (six times), ἐν (six times), and πρός (once). Typically, when it is modified by εἰς or πρός the subject of the verb is the thing undergoing increase. Thus when in Rom. 5:15 Paul writes ἡ χάρις τοῦ θεοῦ . . . εἰς τοὺς πόλλους ἐπερίσσευσεν, it is ἡ χάρις τοῦ θεοῦ that undergoes increase. An exception to this is 2 Cor. 9:8 where εἰς is equivalent to ἐν (cf. 1 Cor. 15:58). On the other hand, when περισσεύω is modified by ἐν it is typically the object of the preposition that increases (cf. Rom. 15:13; 1 Cor. 15:58; 2 Cor. 3:9; 8:7 [twice]; Phil. 1:6). Phil. 1:26 is an exception to this. Here Paul's idiom ἐν Χριστῷ functions adverbially.

for the Philippians' love to increase and thus inform their knowledge, he would have written: ἵνα ἡ ἐπίγνωσις ὑμῶν . . . περισσεύῃ ἐν ἀγάπῃ. As it stands, however, his prayer acknowledges their love and calls for an increase in knowledge.[32]

This brings us to the second problem, namely, how to relate the prayer of 1:9 to the purpose clause of verse 10a: εἰς τὸ δοκιμάζειν ὑμᾶς τὰ διαφέροντα. This passage has been a challenge to interpreters who have sensed its importance for the letter, but, encumbered with the traditional reading of verse 9 as a prayer for the Philippians to increase in love, have had to explain how love will give the Philippians discernment. Two explanations have traditionally been offered depending on the meaning given to τὰ διαφέροντα. The first, traceable to John Chrysostom, takes τὰ διαφέροντα to mean "things differing" and understands Paul to be speaking of *a distinction in kind* between Christian truth and pagan error discernible on the basis of ἀγάπη.[33] The second, traceable to Chrysostom's schoolmate Theodore of Mopsuestia, translates "things excelling" and understands *a difference in degree* between things that are good and those that are better, again discernible on the basis of ἀγάπη.[34]

But there is a third option that immediately recommends itself once we have disentangled ourselves from the traditional interpretation of 1:9: namely, that Paul here invokes the familiar Stoic distinction between things that matter (τὰ διαφέροντα) and things

---

[32] Collange, *Philippiens*, 48: "reconnaissant les qualités d'affection de ses lecteurs (ἀγάπη), l'apôtre leur demande de gagner en intelligence et en discernement."

[33] *In Epist. ad Phil.*, hom. 2.1 (*PG* 62.191.2): δέος γὰρ μή τις παραφθαρῇ ὑπὸ τῆς τῶν αἱρετικῶν ἀγάπης; cf. Theophyl., *Expositio Epist. ad Phil.* (*PG* 1124.147A–1148B); W. A. van Hengel, *Commentarius Perpetuus in Epistolam Pauli ad Philippenses* (Amsterdam: Luchtmanns & Müller, 1838) 61: "discernere quae probanda et improbanda"; W. M. L. de Wette, *Kurze Erklärung der Briefe an die Kolosser, an Philemon, an die Epheser und Philipper* (2nd edn. Leipzig: Weidmann, 1847) 182: "um zu prüfen, was recht und unrecht ist"; Vincent, *Philippians*, 12–13: "to put to proof the things that differ"; Collange, *Philippiens*, 49: "Les Philippiens sont donc appelés à faire le tri dans ce que leur présentent les prédicateurs étrangers entre ce qui découle de l'Evangile, de l'*agapè* et ce qui n'est qu'accessoires vues humaines."

[34] *PG* 66.921C: δοκιμάζοντας τίνα τὰ κρείττονα (= Swete, 1:204); cf. Theodoret, *Interpr. Epist. ad Phil.* (*PG* 82.561C): ὥστε εἰδέναι τίνα μὲν καλά, τίνα δὲ κρείττονα; Bengel, *Gnomon*, 766: *non modo prae malis bona, sed in bonis optima*; Meyer, *An die Philipper*, 19: "um zu billigen das (sittlich) Vorzügliche"; Weiss, *Philipper-Brief*, 63: "nicht um den Unterschied von Böse und Gut, sondern unter den guten Dingen, *quae potiora sunt*"; and Lightfoot, *Philippians*, 86–7: "not 'things which are opposed,' as good and bad – for it requires no keen moral sense to discriminate between these – but 'things that transcend'"; Gnilka, *Philipperbrief*, 52.

that do not (τὰ ἀδιάφορα).³⁵ We have already discussed the significant role that this distinction played in ancient consolation.³⁶ If Philippians is consolatory, then for Paul to organize his consolation around the thesis that the Philippians have not clearly discerned the things that matter makes excellent sense. Furthermore, for him to advance this thesis in the introductory prayer-report of 1:9–11 is exactly what we should expect, given what we know about the epistolary function of these reports in Paul's letters.³⁷

Most modern commentators, following Lohmeyer, recognize that τὰ διαφέροντα "ist eindeutiger Ausdruck hellenistischer Moralphilosophie."³⁸ However, like Lohmeyer, they quickly lose sight of the philosophical connotations of this term when they go on to interpret the larger clause εἰς τὸ δοκιμάζειν ὑμᾶς τὰ διαφέροντα in light of two similar expressions in Romans. The first of these is Rom. 2:18, which offers an almost exact parallel: δοκιμάζεις τὰ διαφέροντα. The context is Paul's caricature of Jewish confidence in the Law, from which it has been inferred that τὰ διαφέροντα should be "understood against the religious background of Judaism."³⁹ Just as the Jew finds moral direction from the Law, so the Christian makes decisions on the basis of ἀγάπη.⁴⁰ But this

³⁵ Cf. Epict., *Diss.* 2.5.7: ἡ ὕλη οὐ διαφέρουσα; Stob., *Ecl.* 2.80.8–9 (in Arius Didymus' synopsis of stoic ethics); Marc. Aur., *Med.* 9.10, 27; 11.16. For the term's wider philosophical usage, cf. Ps.-Plato, *Eryx.* 394D5–6; Plut., *De rect. aud.* 12.43.E, who criticizes those who attend philosophical lectures for their entertainment value and not for personal benefit: they enjoy hearing others criticized, but when "a philosopher leaves others aside and speaks personally and directly to them reminding them of things that really matter (περὶ τῶν διαφερόντων)" they are put off. For the non-philosophical use of the term, cf. Plut., *Caes.* 65; Plut., *Quom. adul.* 73A; POxy. 9.1204 (299 CE): τὸ διαφέρον μέρος; H. W. Waddington, ed., *Inscriptions Grecques et Latines de Syrie* (Paris, F. Didot, 1870) 410.2.

³⁶ See chapter 3 above.

³⁷ Wiles, *Intercessory Prayers*, 229. We have already noted that, on this theory, Phil. 1:9–11 is analogous both in terms of its function and its content to *Ad Helv.* 4.1, where Seneca announces his thesis that his exile is a matter of indifference to him and should be such to others in a formal *propositio*: "that I have suffered nothing on account of which I myself can be called wretched, much less make those related to me wretched."

³⁸ Lohmeyer, *An die Philipper*, 32–3; cf. W. Michaelis, *Der Brief des Paulus an die Philipper* (THNT; Leipzig: Deichert, 1935) 16–17; Gnilka, *Philipperbrief*, 52; Collange, *Philippiens*, 49; Ralph Martin, *Philippians* (NCBC; London: Marshall, Morgan & Scott, 1976; Grand Rapids: Eerdmanns, 1980) 69; Schenk, *Die Philipperbriefe*, 112–13. Cf. Jaquette, *Discerning What Counts*; idem, "Indifference to Status"; Sampley, *Walking Between the Times*, 77–83.

³⁹ O'Brien, *Philippians*, 77–8; following Lohmeyer.

⁴⁰ By this account τὰ διαφέροντα does not announce Paul's argumentative strategy, but simply one point, albeit a central point, of his parenesis. In the end this differs little from the second traditional interpretation that sees in τὰ διαφέροντα a

raises at least two problems. For not only does it require that we interpret Paul's prayer in Phil. 1:9 as a call for love and not knowledge, it obscures the most natural reading of Rom. 2:18, which is that Judaism has here appropriated current philosophical terminology for apologetic purposes. The Jew, by means of the Law, is like the philosopher who knows the things that really matter (τὰ διαφέροντα), while the pagan, without the Law, is unable to make these distinctions.[41] Read this way, Rom. 2:18 supports our reading of Phil. 1:10a.

The second text appealed to by interpreters of Phil. 1:9–10a is Rom. 12:2. The term τὰ διαφέροντα does not occur here, but δοκιμάζειν does. Paul promises that those who have been transformed by the renewing of their minds will be able to discern (δοκιμάζειν) the will of God (τὸ θέλημα τοῦ θεοῦ), which he defines as "that which is good, well pleasing, and perfect" (τὸ ἀγαθὸν καὶ εὐάρεστον καὶ τέλειον). By a simple act of substitution the τὰ διαφέροντα of Phil. 1:10a becomes the τὰ διαφέροντα of Rom. 2:18 and then (because of the occurrence of δοκίμαζειν in both texts) the τὸ θέλημα τοῦ θεοῦ of Rom. 12:2, which is finally equated with τὸ ἀγαθὸν καὶ εὐάρεστον καὶ τέλειον.[42] Schenk writes: "θέλημα . . . ist synonym mit διαφέροντα . . . hier vertritt θέλημα das διαφέροντα."[43] Of course, the correct procedure is to interpret Phil. 1:10a in its own context before appealing to some verbal congruence (δοκιμάζειν) in Rom. 12.[44]

---

difference in degree (cf. Lightfoot's "keen moral sense" or Bengel's "in bonis optima").

[41] Hans Lietzmann, *An die Römer* (4th edn.; HNT 8; Tübingen: Mohr [Siebeck], 1933) 43, who sees the pagan philosophical connection. For the *topos* of indifferent things in Hellenistic Judaism see Philo, *Det.* 122; *Post.* 81; *Mos.* 2.40f.; *L. A.* 2.17; *Op.* 74; *Sac.* 99; *Fug.* 152; *Her.* 253; *Praem.* 70; *Spec.* 2.46; *Prob.* 61; 83 (collected by Betz, *Galatians*, 94 n. 351).

[42] This connection precedes Lohmeyer; cf. van Hengel, *Commentarius Perpetuus*, 61; C. Bruston, "De quelques passages obscurs de l'épître aux Philippiens," *RThPh* 42 (1909) 196–9.

[43] *Die Philipperbriefe*, 113.

[44] To his credit G. W. Peterman, *Paul's Gift from Philippi: Conventions of Gift-Exchange and Christian Giving* (SNTSMS 92; Cambridge: Cambridge University Press, 1997) 106–7, 113, resists interpreting Phil. 1:10 in light of Rom. 2:18 and 12:2. Instead he sees in τὰ διαφέροντα, which he correctly translates "things that really matter," a reference to ἐριθεία and κενοδοξία in 2:3, citing in support Dio, *Or.* 38.29: "we pity those who do not understand wherein false glory differs from true" (ἐλεοῦμεν τοὺς οὐκ ἐπισταμένους τινι διαφέρει δόξα ψευδὴς ἀληθοῦς). But this is not a relevant parallel since διαφέρει here means "it differs" not "it matters." Furthermore, for Paul ἐριθεία and κενοδοξία are *not* "things that do not really matter" but things that matter a great deal and are wrong!

τὰ διαφέροντα in context

It should at this point be clear that both the immediate epistolary context of 1:9–11 and Paul's larger rhetorical (i.e., consolatory) purposes support our view that τὰ διαφέροντα in Phil. 1:10a should be translated "the things that matter" and that the philosophical connotations of this expression should, as far as possible, be taken seriously.[45] It only remains to see whether our interpretation of τὰ διαφέροντα is borne out by the rest of the letter. Before proceeding with our exegesis of 1:12–2:30, however, it will be helpful to consider one further piece of evidence from ancient consolation which will allow us to bring into even sharper focus Paul's consolatory strategy as adumbrated in the prayer-report of 1:9–11. The text is Seneca, *Ep.* 107.1.[46]

The occasion for *Ep.* 107 may easily be reconstructed.[47] Seneca has received word from Lucilius that several of Lucilius' most trusted slaves have run away. Lucilius feels deeply betrayed by this, and Seneca writes to console him. Seneca takes the position that his friend has lost sight of the fact that things like this do not really matter.[48] He begins his letter abruptly with the following pointed questions:

> Where is that prudence of yours? Where is that skill in making the necessary distinctions? Where is that ability to rise above circumstance? Does a matter of such insignificance affect you so much? (*Ubi illa prudentia tua? Ubi in*

[45] Troels Engberg-Pedersen, "Stoicism in Philippians," in *idem*, ed., *Paul in His Hellenistic Context* (Minneapolis: Fortress, 1995) 262 n. 10, warns against those who under the rubric of *Popularphilosophie* "[do not take] Paul's use of various moral [= philosophical] terms seriously at all." He cites as an example Gnilka's treatment of διαφέροντα in Phil 1:10 (*Philipperbrief*, 51–2), as well as his interpretation of Phil. 4:11 (*Philipperbrief*, 174–6). See in general the discussion in J. N. Sevenster, *Paul and Seneca* (NovTSup 4; Leiden: Brill, 1961); Bonhöffer, *Epictet und das Neue Testament*; 98–179, 195–390; Lightfoot, *Philippians*, appendix 2: "St. Paul and Seneca," 270–333. On the older debate regarding Epictetus and Paul, see Bonhöffer, *Epictet und das Neue Testament*; 4–81.

[46] We have already made reference to Seneca, *Ep.* 107 in our discussion of Cyrenaic consolation theory, and we shall have occasion to return to it below in our exegesis of Phil. 1:27–30. Here we are interested in the opening lines of the letter (§1), and in the striking parallel it provides to Phil. 1:9–10a.

[47] Whether this occasion is real or a literary creation is irrelevant to our purposes here.

[48] Cf. *Ep.* 42.5 (*supervacua*) and the comments on this text by D. A. Russell, "Letters to Lucilius" in C. D. N. Costa, ed., *Seneca* (London: Routledge, 1974) 76–7.

dispiciendis rebus subtilitas? Ubi magnitudo? Tam pusilla te res tangit?)

The progression of thought is reminiscent of Cleanthes' theory of consolation: practical knowledge (*prudentia*), leading to a certain subtlety or discernment (*subtilitas*), the objective of which is to distinguish the things that matter and the things that do not matter (*in dispiciendis rebus . . . pusilla res*), so as not to be distressed by the latter (*Tam . . . te . . . tangit*). By reversing the order we can see how Seneca arrived at his diagnosis: Lucilius is distressed over what is in reality a matter of insignificance, which implies that he has failed to make this distinction in his current circumstances, which in turn implies that he has faltered in his practical knowledge.

Ep. 107.1 obviously contains a number striking parallels to both the language and thought of Phil. 1:9–10a: (1) Paul like Seneca begins with a kind of practical knowledge (ἐπίγνωσις καὶ αἴσθησις);[49] (2) he also like Seneca calls for discernment (εἰς τὸ δοκιμάζειν ὑμᾶς); (3) this discernment has as its object the distinction between what does and does not matter (τὰ διαφέροντα), with the goal (implied) that the Philippians not be distressed by the latter. However, there are at least two significant differences. First, Paul is not as abrupt as Seneca. Although his point is basically the same, he does not indict the Philippians with a series of rhetorical questions, but reports his prayers for them.[50] This gentleness will characterize the rest of letter.[51] Second, Paul's focus is decidedly more positive than Seneca's. He does not approach his consolation through things that do not matter (cf. Seneca's "*pusilla res*"), but through the things that do (τὰ διαφέροντα).

This second difference is particularly instructive for our understanding of Paul's overall consolatory strategy. By focusing on "the things that matter" Paul effectively anticipates his positive approach to consolation in the remainder of the letter, where he urges the Philippians not simply to put aside their grief but to rejoice, first in the "progress of the gospel" (1:12–18a) and the "salvation" of the

[49] Malunowiczówna, "Les éléments stoïciens," 36: "La manque de la vraie connaissance est la cause de notre tristesse"; cf. Chrys., *In Epist. ad Thess.*, hom. 7.1 (*PG* 62.435); *Ad Stag.* 1.2 (*PG* 47.427).

[50] For this basic difference between Christian and pagan consolation, which Paul here initiates, see Scourfield, *Consoling Heliodorus*, 80–1; cf. Favez, "Le sentiment"; *idem*, *La consolation*, 84–9; Manning, "Consolatory Tradition."

[51] Here see especially our exegesis of 1:22–6 below. Paul's ethos is not contradicted in Phil. 3:2–4:1 where he continues to deal affirmingly with the Philippians themselves.

gospel messenger (1:18b–21) and also, ultimately, "in the Lord" (3:1; cf. 4:4). Paul's argument, therefore, is not that only the things that do not matter have been negatively affected by his current misfortune (à la Cleanthes), but that the things that do matter have actually been aided. To put it another way, Paul's consolation of the Philippians does not aim at the absence of grief (Stoic ἀπάθεια), but at the presence of joy.[52] Chrysostom adopts a similar aim in *Ep. ad Olymp.* 10: "This is what we are seeking for you, not simply to rid you of our despondency, but to fill you with a great and lasting joy."[53]

These differences aside, Paul's diagnosis of the Philippians' distress parallels to a remarkable degree Seneca's diagnosis of Lucilius' similar struggles: the Philippians are distressed over what is in reality a matter of insignificance (Paul's imprisonment), which implies that they have failed to distinguish accurately between the things that matter and the things that do not, which in turn implies that they are not thinking clearly. Paul writes to correct this.[54]

Consolation and ethical conduct

Phil. 1:10b–11 also calls for brief comment. If we are correct in our interpretation of 1:9–10a, then Paul's immediate objective in writing the Philippians, reflected in the final clause of 1:10a, was to provide them with the "knowledge and perception" necessary to "discern the things that matter" in order that they might more accurately assess their current circumstances and be consoled. But as the second final clause of 1:10b–11 indicates, Paul also had a more remote ethical/eschatological goal in mind: ἵνα ἦτε εἰλικρινεῖς καὶ ἀπρόσκοποι εἰς ἡμέραν Χριστοῦ, πεπληρωμένοι καρπὸν δικαιοσύνης κτλ.

Here Paul explicitly ties the ethical conduct of the Philippians, together with the eschatological consequences of that conduct, to their consolation.[55] The distress that the Philippians were feeling in

[52] Stoic εὐπάθεια. In this Paul unknowingly anticipates and paves the way for the *topos* of the "martyr's joy" characteristic of later martyrdom theology; cf. Lohmeyer, *An die Philipper*, 49–50, 113–14, 123–4, 167–8 and *passim*.

[53] *Ep. ad Olymp.* 10.1.21–3 Malingrey: τοῦτο γὰρ ἡμῖν τὸ σπουδαζόμενον οὐκ ἀθυμίας σε ἀπαλλάξαι μόνον, ἀλλὰ καὶ εὐφροσύνης ἐμπλῆσαι πολλῆς καὶ διηνεκοῦς. Cf. J. N. D. Kelly, *Golden Mouth: The Story of John Chrysostom: Ascetic, Preacher, Bishop* (Ithaca, NY: Cornell, 1995) 267.

[54] Phil. 1:12: γινώσκειν δὲ ὑμᾶς βούλομαι, ἀδελφοί, ὅτι . . .

[55] We have already noted this connection between consolation and conduct in our discussion of the rhetorical situation of Philippians.

their current circumstances was affecting their practical conduct as Christians. Paul does not specify in 1:10b–11 what the practical problems at Philippi were, though he is clear that the consequences were far reaching. But as we learn from elsewhere in the letter, there were divisions in the church which Paul associates with a kind of moral breakdown: τὸ αὐτὸ φρονῆτε . . . μηδὲν κατ᾽ ἐριθείαν μηδὲ κατὰ κενοδοξίαν ἀλλὰ τῇ ταπεινοφροσύνῃ ἀλλήλους ἡγούμενοι ὑπερέχοντας ἑαυτῶν (2:2–3).[56] At 2:14 Paul also speaks of "grumbling and disputing" against God.

The connection between consolation and conduct is also reflected in the body of the letter in the progression from consolation in ch. 1 to exhortation in ch. 2, the latter of which builds on the former (cf. 2:1: οὖν).

---

[56] Paul uses the same language (τὸ αὐτὸ φρονεῖν) of the quarrel between Euodia and Syntyche in 4:2–3. On the relationship of 4:2–3 with 2:1–4, see Meeks, "Man from Heaven in Philippians," 334; Nils A. Dahl, "Euodia and Syntyche and Paul's Letter to the Philippians," in L. Michael White and O. Larry Yarbrough, eds., *The Social World of the First Christians: Essays in Honor of Wayne Meeks* (Minneapolis: Augsburg Fortress, 1995) 7, 15.

5

DISCERNING THE THINGS THAT MATTER IN THE GOSPEL MISSION (PHIL. 1:12–2:30)

> In the beginning of his letter Paul offers the Philippians much consolation regarding his imprisonment, showing not only that they should not be troubled, but that they should rejoice.
>
> John Chrysostom, *In Epist. ad Phil.*, praef. 1

We come now to the first heading of the letter (1:12–2:30),[1] which falls naturally into two parts: consolation (1:12–30)[2] and exhortation (2:1–30). We are concerned primarily with the first (consolatory) part, which may be further divided into four smaller sections: 1:12–18a; 1:18b–21; 1:22–6; and 1:27–30. Here Paul applies his thesis that the Philippians must learn to discern "the things that matter" (1:10a) to the problem of his imprisonment. He invites the Philippians, "who have heard that he is in prison and are distressed,"[3] to rejoice with him in the progress (προκοπή) of the gospel (1:12–18a) and his own anticipated salvation (σωτηρία; 1:18b–21). These are the things that matter, and they have been furthered by his imprisonment. Again, our exegesis of this material will be selective, focusing on the various consolatory aspects of Paul's argument.

---

[1] Watson, "Rhetorical Analysis" calls Phil. 1:12–26 an exordium and 1:27–30 the proposition of the letter. But this is to force a rhetorical disposition on the letter. It is better to see the "proposition" of the letter in the prayer-report of 1:9–11 (esp. 1:10a) with 1:12 beginning the first heading of the argument.

[2] Thus Chrys., *In Epist. ad Phil.*, hom. 3.3 (*PG* 62.201.36–7): ταῦτα δὴ πάντα πρὸς παραμυθίαν τῶν Φιλιππησίων λέγει.

[3] Chrys., *In Epist. ad Phil.*, hom. 2.2 (*PG* 62.191.47): ἀκούσαντας ὅτι δέδεται, ἀλγεῖν.

Consolation: rejoicing in the progress of the gospel (Phil. 1:12–30)

Paul introduces the consolation that begins in 1:12 with a common epistolary "disclosure formula": γινώσκειν δὲ ὑμᾶς βούλομαι.[4] Similar formulas occur elsewhere in Paul, but none with the infinitive γινώσκειν.[5] Paul's choice of γινώσκειν here recalls the ἐπίγνωσις of 1:9. The implication is that he will now impart the "knowledge and perception" that, on his view, the Philippians need in order to distinguish the things that matter from the things that do not.

The progress of the gospel message (Phil. 1:12–18a)

The first thing Paul wants the Philippians to understand is that his imprisonment has in fact aided the progress of the gospel (1:12–18a). He states his thesis in 1:12: τὰ κατ᾽ ἐμὲ μᾶλλον εἰς προκοπὴν τοῦ εὐαγγελίου ἐλήλυθεν.[6] He supports his thesis with three arguments in 1:13–17. First, imprisonment has enhanced his reputation as a servant of Christ: τοὺς δεσμούς μου φανεροὺς ἐν Χριστῷ γενέσθαι ἐν ὅλῳ τῷ πραιτωρίῳ καὶ τοῖς λοιποῖς πᾶσιν (13).[7] Second, it has made him an example to other believers who have become more bold in their own witness: καὶ τοὺς πλείονας τῶν ἀδελφῶν ἐν κυρίῳ πεποιθότας τοῖς δεσμοῖς μου περισσο-

---

[4] See further, Terence Y. Mullins, "Disclosure: A Literary Form in the New Testament," *NovT* 7 (1964) 44–50.

[5] Thus: θέλω δὲ ὑμᾶς εἰδέναι (1 Cor. 11:3; cf. Col. 2.1); οὐ θέλω (θέλομεν) ὑμᾶς ἀγνοεῖν (1 Cor. 10:1; 2 Cor. 1:8; Rom. 1:13; 1 Thess. 4.13); γνωρίζω (γνωρίζομεν) ὑμῖν (1 Cor. 15:1; 2 Cor. 8:1; Gal. 1:11).

[6] εἰς ... ἐλήλυθεν should be understood causally: "My imprisonment has resulted in (caused) the progress of the gospel." Cf. Wisd. 15:5: εἰς ὄρεξιν ἔρχεται ("arouses desire").

[7] φανεροὺς ἐν Χριστῷ γενέσθαι is awkward. I would supply an εἶναι after φανεροὺς: "so that my chains have been manifest [to be] in Christ." Chrysostom interprets ἐν Χριστῷ to mean διὰ Χριστόν (*In Epist. ad Phil.*, hom. 2.2 [*PG* 62.192.13]). The meaning of ἐν ὅλῳ τῷ πραιτωρίῳ is much debated and cannot be solved independently of the question of provenance. If we accept a Caesarean origin then "Herod's praetorium" (Acts 23:35) is in view. If we accept an Ephesian origin then the reference is to the residence of the proconsul of Asia. Lightfoot (*Philippians*, 99–104) has argued convincingly in my judgment that if we accept a Roman provenance for the letter, the reference must be to the praetorian guards. For our purposes it is not necessary to decide the matter. Regardless of how we understand πραιτώριον, Paul's point is that his reputation has been enhanced. I would translate καὶ τοῖς λοιποῖς πᾶσιν "and among all the rest," not "and in every other place" (cf. 4:22; οἱ ἐκ τῆς Καίσαρος οἰκίας).

τέρως τολμᾶν ἀφόβως τὸν λόγον λαλεῖν (14). And third, it has caused even certain of his rivals to step up their proclamation of Christ: τινὲς μὲν καὶ διὰ φθόνον καὶ ἔριν ... τὸν Χριστὸν κηρύσσουσιν ... οἰόμενοι θλῖψιν ἐγείρειν τοῖς δεσμοῖς μου (15–17).[8] He concludes in 1:18a that his imprisonment, far from being a source of discouragement, is an occasion for rejoicing: ἐν τούτῳ χαίρω.

At least five *topoi* from contemporary consolation may be identified in Phil. 1:12–18a. The first and most important of these is the distinction between the things that matter and the things that do not. Without this distinction Paul's positive evaluation of his imprisonment would have been impossible. Paul states the general terms of this distinction in 1:12. They are: his own "situation" (τὰ κατ' ἐμέ),[9] which does not matter,[10] and "the progress of the gospel" (προκοπὴν τοῦ εὐαγγελίου), which does.[11] He further specifies these terms in 1:13–17.[12] In 1:13 he contrasts his "chains" (δεσμοί) with his enhanced reputation as a servant of Christ ἐν

---

[8] The reference to rivals in 1:15–17 is particularly relevant in light of the rivalry at Philippi between Euodia and Syntyche (4:2–3). The language of 1:15–17 is picked up again in 2:1–4, which in turn anticipates 4:2–3. See Dahl, "Euodia and Syntyche," 7, 15. The sub-text of 1:15–17 is that personal rivalry is a matter of indifference as long as Christ is proclaimed. Cf. Chrys., *In Epist. ad Phil.*, hom. 2.2 (*PG* 62.191.47).

[9] τὰ κατ' ἐμέ, "my situation" or "my circumstances"; cf. τὰ περὶ ὑμῶν (1:27; 2:19); τὰ κατ' ἐμέ (Col. 4:7). Efforts to further specify τὰ κατ' ἐμέ have not been convincing; e.g., the suggestion by Collange (*Philippiens*, 52–3) that Paul is here referring to his recent appeal to Roman citizenship which has been opposed by some as cowardly. More reasonable is the proposal by Nigel Turner (*Grammar of New Testament Greek*, vol. III: *Syntax* [Edinburgh: T. & T. Clark, 1963] 15) that we translate "my lawsuit" on the basis of Acts 25:14 (τὰ κατὰ Παῦλον); cf. Acts 24:22 (τὰ κατ' ὑμᾶς); PEleph. 13.3 (τὰ κατὰ σέ).

[10] Paul's claim that imprisonment is a matter of indifference, while impressive, would not have sounded strange to his audience. Imprisonment – along with death, exile, and poverty – was one of the stock hardships (περιστάσεις) discounted as an ἀδιάφορον by philosophers. Cf. Epict., *Diss.* 1.30.2–3: "'What did you call exile and prison and chains and death and dishonor in your school?' 'I called them "matters of indifference" (ἀδιάφορα).'" Similarly, *Diss.* 1.29.5: "When the tyrant threatens and summons me, I say 'What is he threatening?' If he says, 'I will bind you with chains,' then I say, 'He is threatening my hands and my feet.' If he says, 'I will cut off your head,' then I say, 'He is threatening my neck.' If he says, 'I will throw you in prison,' then I say, 'He is threatening my paltry flesh,' and so on if he threatens me with exile, etc." See further, *Diss.* 1.1.22–4; 2.1.38; 2.6.5; Tert., *Ad Mart.* 2; Cyp., *Ep.* 33.2. Cf. Craig S. Wansink, *Chained in Christ: The Experience and Rhetoric of Paul's Imprisonments* (JSNTSup 130; Sheffield: Sheffield Academic Press, 1996) 74 n. 159.

[11] Cf. Acts 20:24.

[12] Three times in 1:13–17 Paul relativizes his "chains" (δεσμοί; 13, 14, 17) to various means by which the gospel is advanced.

ὅλῳ τῷ πραιτωρίῳ καὶ τοῖς λοιποῖς πᾶσιν. In 1:14 he contrasts his "chains" (δεσμοί) with his example to other believers, who now "speak the word" even more boldly than before. Finally, in 1:15–17 he contrasts the spitefulness of certain rivals who have sought to "add affliction to my chains" (θλῖψιν ἐγείρειν τοῖς δεσμοῖς μου) with their wrongly motivated but nonetheless increased proclamation of Christ. In 1:18a he philosophically concludes: τὶ γάρ; πλὴν ὅτι παντὶ τρόπῳ, εἴτε προφάσει εἴτε ἀληθείᾳ, Χριστὸς καταγγέλλεται, καὶ ἐν τούτῳ χαίρω.[13]

The construction εἴτε . . . εἴτε, which Paul uses in 1:18a to dismiss as unimportant the antipathy of his rivals, has parallels in contemporary Stoicism where it was sometimes used as an indication of things that do not matter. Musonius, frag. 38 Hense reads:[14]

> We ought to become like God and, dividing (διελόντας) matters in the same way that he does, lay hold of the things that are within our control (τὰ ἐφ' ἡμῖν) and relinquish to the cosmos the things not in our control (τὰ μὴ ἐφ' ἡμῖν), whether it asks for our children, or our homeland, or our body, or anything else (εἴτε τῶν παίδων εἴτε τῆς πατρίδος εἴτε τοῦ σώματος εἴτε ὁτουοῦν).

Epictetus uses the expression at *Diss.* 3.22.21:

> My paltry body is nothing to me (οὐδὲν πρὸς ἐμέ). Its parts are nothing to me (οὐδὲν πρὸς ἐμέ). Death? Let it come whenever it wishes, whether (εἴτε) it be the death of the whole or (εἴτε) of some part.

Seneca uses the Latin equivalent (*sive . . . sive*) in *Ep.* 74.26:

> Whether (*sive*) a long old age is given to the wise man, or (*sive*) his end comes before old age, the measure of the greatest good to which he has obtained remains the same, notwithstanding the difference in years.

He uses the construction again at *Ep.* 111.4, speaking of the sage's equanimity "whether (*sive*) the course of his life is smooth, or (*sive*) is disrupted by adversity and hardship."[15] Paul repeats this construction again in 1:20 to show his indifference to death (εἴτε διὰ

---

[13] Cf. Theophyl., *Expositio Epist. ad Phil.* ad loc. (*PG* 124.1152A): μόνον γὰρ φησὶ, τὸν Χριστὸν καταγγελλέτω τις, καὶ οὐδὲν διαφέρει.

[14] Stob., *Ecl.* 2.8.30 (= Epict., frag. 4 Schenkl).

[15] Cf. *Ep.* 36.6.

ζωῆς εἴτε διὰ θανάτου), and then again in 1:27, where he exhorts
the Philippians to be indifferent to his return (εἴτε ἐλθών . . . εἴτε
ἀπών . . .). Commenting on 1:18, Chrysostom writes:[16]

> Just look at the philosophy (τὸ φιλόσοφον) of this man!
> . . . What difference does it make to me (τί γὰρ ἐμοὶ
> διαφέρει), he says, whether it be done in this way or that
> way? Only that in every way whether in pretense or in truth
> Christ is proclaimed.

A second consolatory *topos* utilized in Phil. 1:12–18a is that
conventional misfortunes often actually advance the cause of things
that really matter. Paul takes this position in 1:12 when he claims
not only that his imprisonment has not hindered the gospel, but
that it has actually furthered the gospel's progress. We have already
seen this kind of argument in Musonius frag. 9 Hense (Ὅτι οὐ
κακὸν ἡ φυγή).[17] Musonius allows that exile may deprive us of
certain conventional goods, "things the masses consider to be
goods," but not of "things that are truly good." However, he adds
that exile can actually aid us in our pursuit of that which is truly
good "since it furnishes men leisure and a greater opportunity for
learning the good and practicing it than they formerly enjoyed."[18]
Similar arguments can be found in Seneca[19] and Plutarch.[20]
Consolers also argued that poverty, while depriving us of certain
extrinsic things, forces an austerity that is healthy both physically
and spiritually.[21]

A third *topos* from contemporary consolation lies in the observation that hardship enhances one's reputation. Paul employs this
topos in 1:13 when he reports that his reputation as a servant of
Christ had been disseminated ἐν ὅλῳ τῷ πραιτωρίῳ καὶ τοῖς
λοιποῖς πᾶσιν. One of the more celebrated benefits of exile was
an enhanced reputation. The most famous example of this was

---

[16] *In Epist. ad Phil.*, hom. 2.2 (*PG* 62.193.22–6). For the related expression τί γὰρ
cf. BDF §299.3; Gnilka, *Philipperbrief*, 63: "eine verbreitete Redefloskel, die auf die
Hauptsache hinlenkt," citing Rom. 3:3; LXX Job 16:3; 21:4; Xenoph., *Mem.* 2.6.2;
3.3.6 (after Lightfoot, *Philippians*, 90); cf. Epict., *Diss.* 1.12.18. The more common
expression in Paul is τί οὖν; (Rom. 3:9; 6:15; 1 Cor. 14:15, 26). Jerome translates:
Non mihi curae est (*In Epist. ad Phil.*, ad loc.; *PL* 30.843A).
[17] Muson., frag. 9.44.2–16 Hense.
[18] Muson., frag. 9.43.8–15 Hense.
[19] Sen., *De tran. an.* 9.3.
[20] Plut., *De ex.* 603E; 604B–D; *De cap. ex inimicis util.* 87A.
[21] Muson., frag. 9.43.14–15; Sen., *Ad Helv.* 10.3; 12.1–7; Chrys., *Ep. ad Olymp.*
1.1.12–18 Malingrey.

Diogenes of Sinope who, according to Musonius, "was transformed from an ordinary citizen to a philosopher during his exile" (ὃς ἐκ μὲν ἰδιώτου φιλόσοφος ἐγένετο φυγών).[22] Dio, in an effort to present himself as the new Diogenes, credits exile with his own reputation as a philosopher:[23]

> Gradually and with no planning or arrogance on my part, it happened that I acquired the name [of philosopher] . . . And perhaps it did turn out that I benefited from my reputation (ἀπολαῦσαι τῆς φήμης), for many began to approach me and ask what was my opinion on good and evil . . . Furthermore, they would invite me to stand before the public and speak.

Doxographic and consolatory tradition attributed similar beginnings to Zeno and Crates.[24]

Related to this is a fourth consolatory *topos*: that misfortune makes one an example to others.[25] Paul employs this *topos* in Phil. 1:14 when he reports that his imprisonment has made him an example to other believers: καὶ τοὺς πλείονας τῶν ἀδελφῶν ἐν κυρίῳ πεποιθότας τοῖς δεσμοῖς μου περισσοτέρως τολμᾶν ἀφόβως τὸν λόγον λαλεῖν. Prison, says Epictetus, is a place where Zeus "trains the philosopher and uses him as a witness to others" (γυμνάζων καὶ μάρτυρι πρὸς τοὺς ἄλλους χρώμενος).[26] Socrates was, of course, the classic example of this. Seneca reminds an anxious Lucilius of Socrates' example in *Ep.* 24.4:[27]

> In prison Socrates held philosophical discussions and was unwilling to leave when some offered him a way of escape.

---

[22] Frag. 9.43.16–7 Hense; cf. Diog. Laert. 6.49; Plut., *De tran. an.* 467C.

[23] *Or.* 13.10–13.

[24] For Zeno, see Plut., *De tran. an.* 467D and *Ad ux.* 603D; for Crates, see Diog. Laert. 6.85.

[25] Grollios, Τέχνη ἀλυπίας, 80–1, who cites: Sen., *Ad Poly.* 5.4–5; 6.1–5; *Ad Marc.* 4.4; *Ep.* 43.3ff.; Epict., *Diss.* 3.22.14; Ps.-Ovid, *Cons. ad Liv.* 343–56 cf. Cic., *Ad Brut.* 1.9.2; Jer., *Ep.* 60.14.5. See also Kurth, *Senecas Trostschrift*, 71–89; Esteve-Forriol, *Trauer- und Trostgedichte*, 153. Favorin., frag. 22.1.28–45 Barigazzi, after citing the examples of Diogenes, Crates, and Musonius, offers himself as an example: τῷ οἰκείῳ παραδείγνατι προτρέπων (43–4); personal experience was the basis of Musonius' instruction in frag. 9.50.4–5 Hense: οἷς δὲ λογισμοῖς χρῶμαι πρὸς ἐμαυτόν . . . τούτους καὶ πρὸς σὲ εἴποιμι ἄν.

[26] *Diss.* 3.24.113.

[27] Cf. Ps.-Soc., *Ep.* 14.5–6 (= Abraham J. Malherbe, *The Cynic Epistles: A Study Edition* [SBLSBS 12; Missoula, MT: Scholars Press, 1977] 256.8–15).

> Rather, he remained that he might [by his example] remove from men the two most grievous fears, prison and death.

At *Ep.* 70.9 he writes:[28]

> Socrates might have ended his life by fasting, he might have died by starvation rather than poison. However, he spent thirty days in prison expecting death . . . that he might show himself submissive to the laws and *that he might make his death a source of strength to his friends.*

Socrates was also remembered for writing paeans in prison: "we shall be followers of Socrates, when we are able to write paeans in prison."[29] Following Socrates' example, the appropriate response to prison was thus to rejoice: "it behooves you to go off to prison rejoicing" (εἰς φυλακήν σε δεῖ χαίροντα ἀπιέναι).[30]

This brings us to the fifth and final consolatory *topos* that Paul employs in 1:12–18a: the "joy" (χαρά, *gaudium*) that one who has been instructed in the things that do and do not matter is able to experience even in the midst of crisis. In 1:18a Paul writes: τί γάρ; πλὴν ὅτι παντὶ τρόπῳ, εἴτε προφάσει εἴτε ἀληθείᾳ, Χριστὸς καταγγέλλεται, καὶ ἐν τούτῳ χαίρω. Here Paul combines the two central themes of the letter, joy and educated indifference. Because he is indifferent to his circumstances Paul is able to rejoice in the progress of the gospel even though he himself is in prison. This, as we have already seen, is a significant philosophical claim.[31] We may recall Seneca's instruction of Lucilius:[32]

> Do you want to know the basis of a good mind? It is that you do not find joy in things that do not matter. Did I say basis? It is the pinnacle. He has reached the top who knows what is to be the object of his joy.

We may also recall again Chysostom's comments on Phil. 1:18:[33]

---

[28] Cf. Sen., *Ep.* 71.17; 104.28; Epict., *Diss.* 1.4.24; 29.16; 2.13.24; Plut., *De tr. an.* 466E (cf. *De ex.* 607F); Max. Tyr., *Or.* 34.9B Hobein. See further: Sen., *Ad Marc.* 10.6; *Ep.* 26.10; 65.24; 76.33; 85.26, 41; *De prov.* 5.3; Epict., *Diss.* 1.29.22–9; 2.6.24–6; 3.8.5; 24.105; 4.1.133; 4.34.

[29] Epict., *Diss.* 2.6.26; cf. *Diss.* 4.4.22; Pl., *Phr.* 60D; Diog. Laert. 2.42; cf. Acts 16:25!

[30] Epict., *Diss.* 3.24.77.

[31] See our discussion above in chapter 3.

[32] *Ep.* 23.1–2.

[33] *In Epist. ad Phil.*, hom. 3.1 (*PG* 62.197.37ff.).

The great and philosophic soul is vexed by none of the
grievous things in the present life: not enmities, not accusations, not slanders, not perils or plots . . . And such
was the soul of Paul; it had taken possession of a place
higher than any fortress, the seat of spiritual philosophy,
true philosophy . . . That blessed man had not only the
emperor waging war against him, but many others attempting to grieve him in many ways, even with bitter
slander. But what does he say? Not only "I am not hurt or
overcome by these things," but "I rejoice and I will
rejoice!"

The salvation of the gospel messenger (Phil. 1:18b–21)

With the change of tense in 1:18b (χαρήσομαι)[34] Paul introduces
the second major grounds for encouragement, his anticipated
"salvation" (σωτηρία).[35] Commentators have understood Paul's
use of σωτηρία here in a variety of ways. Some have understood
Paul to be speaking of his eventual release from prison.[36] Others
see a reference to Paul's "vindication" in court.[37] Others interpret
Paul to be speaking of his final salvation, "his vindication in the
heavenly court."[38] However, Paul himself spells out the content of
his expected σωτηρία in 1:20 when he goes on to speak of his eager
expectation (ἀποκαραδοκία) "that in nothing I shall act shamefully
(αἰσχυνθήσομαι)[39] but that with all boldness of speech (ἐν πάσῃ

[34] Setting aside the maxim of 1:21, the future tense characterizes this section
ἀποβήσεται . . . αἰσχυνθήσομαι . . . μεγαλυνθήσεται.

[35] ἀλλὰ καὶ χαρήσομαι οἶδα γὰρ ὅτι τοῦτό μοι ἀποβήσεται εἰς σωτηρίαν. The
antecedent of τοῦτο is τὰ κατ' ἐμέ (1:12). εἰς σωτηρίαν [ἐμοί] is parallel to εἰς
προκοπὴν τοῦ εὐαγγελίου, while ἀποβήσεται continues ἐλήλυθεν. The expression
τοῦτό μοι ἀποβήσεται εἰς σωτηρίαν reproduces exactly LXX Job 13:16. The verb
ἀποβαίνω occurs only here in Paul.

[36] Most recently, Gerald Hawthorne, *Philippians* (WBC 43; Waco, Texas: Word
Books, 1987) 40. Phil. 1:20b (εἴτε διὰ ζωῆς εἴτε διὰ θανάτου) is evidence that tells
against this interpretation.

[37] R. Martin, *Philippians*, 75: "the word ['salvation'] is equivalent to his vindication at court. He hopes that his trust in God will be honored and his witness to
divine faithfulness will be attested by the turn of events. But this is not the same as
the hope of release from prison since in the next verse he envisages the possibility of
death."

[38] This seems to be the majority view: Wiles, *Intercessory Prayers*, 279 (cited by
O'Brien, *Philippians*, 110 n. 17); Beare, *Philippians*, 62; Gnilka, *Philipperbrief*, 66;
Collange, *Philippiens*, 57; cf. Th. Mop., *In Epist. ad Phil.*, ad loc. (Swete, 1.209).

[39] There are two possible ways to understand αἰσχυνθήσομαι: either subjectively
as "I shall be ashamed," or objectively as "I shall be put to shame." Either way,

παρρησίᾳ), as always, so now also, Christ will be magnified in my body, whether by life or by death." The σωτηρία Paul expects, therefore, is his continued courageous witness for Christ, a witness that may now be borne out, because of his imprisonment, ἐν τῷ σώματί μου.[40]

Viewed negatively, σωτηρία here means deliverance, not from imprisonment and possible death, neither of which matter, but from cowardice and shame.[41] Epictetus writes in similar terms of Socrates' last days in prison:[42]

> Socrates, who did not vote when the Athenians demanded it of him, who despised the Tyrants, who said such things as he did about virtue and moral excellence, this Socrates does not save himself by some shameful act (αἰσχρῶς οὐ σῴζεται). Indeed, it is impossible to save this man shamefully (σῶσαι αἰσχρῶς). Rather, it is in dying that he is saved (ἀποθνῄσκων σῴζεται).

According to Epictetus, Socrates' principal concern was not to escape death but to avoid any kind of shameful behavior. Indeed, death without capitulation is viewed as a form of salvation. Paul gives five reasons why his salvation, thus conceived, will come to pass. They are: (1) the prayers of the Philippians;[43] (2) the enablement of Christ's spirit;[44] (3) Paul's own ardent desire (τὴν ἀποκαραδοκίαν καὶ ἐλπίδα μου) not to act shamefully; (4) his past record of bold confession (ὡς πάντοτε καὶ νῦν); and (5) his firm conviction that "to die is gain."

Three of the consolatory *topoi* introduced in 1:12–18a continue in 1:18b–21. The first of these, the *topos* of "joy," occurs immediately in 1:18b: ἀλλὰ καὶ χαρήσομαι. This is followed in 1:19 by the

however, the overall sense is clear, since the expression is meant to be the opposite of ἐν πάσῃ παρρησίᾳ: Paul does not want to lose his nerve, to fail to speak boldly. If we understand αἰσχυνθήσομαι subjectively in the sense of feeling shame, then Paul does not want to be ashamed of Christ. If, on the other hand, we understand αἰσχυνθήσομαι objectively in the sense of being put to shame, then Paul does not want to act in a way that shames him. I have taken shame objectively (cf. Phil. 3:19) and have therefore translated, "that in nothing I shall act shamefully."

[40] Paul of course believed that his present "salvation" would bring with it certain eschatological consequences. But that is not his emphasis here.

[41] Cf. 2 Tim. 4:18: ῥύσεταί με ὁ κύριος ἀπὸ παντὸς ἔργου πονηροῦ καὶ σώσει εἰς τὴν βασιλείαν αὐτοῦ, on which see especially Chrys., *In II Epist. ad Tim.*, hom. 10 (ad loc.): ἀπὸ παντὸς ἁμαρτήματος.

[42] *Diss.* 4.1.164–5.

[43] Cf. Eph. 6:18–20; Col. 4:3–4.

[44] Cf. Matt. 10:19–20; Lk. 12:11–12; Acts 4:8.

topos that conventional misfortune often works for real good, the good in this case being Paul's "salvation." Finally, the *topos* of things that do not matter is repeated in Paul's indifference to death in 1:20, where Paul again uses the expression εἴτε . . . εἴτε: εἴτε διὰ ζωῆς εἴτε διὰ θανάτου.[45] Commenting on Paul's discussion of life and death in Phil. 1:20–4, Chrysostom writes:[46]

> For again life falls into the class of middle things (τῶν μέσων), of things that do not matter (ἀδιαφόρων) . . . For even death falls into the category of things that do not matter (ἀδιαφόρων), since death itself is not an evil.

A fourth *topos*, "freedom of speech" or παρρησία, is newly introduced in 1:20.

Consolers of exiles had to contend with the fact that political oppression and disenfranchisement typically meant the loss of freedom of speech (παρρησία).[47] Euripides' *Phoenissae* 391–4 was often quoted in support of this idea.[48] Here Jocasta asks her son Polyneices what misfortunes an exile has to bear, to which he replies: "One that is the greatest of all: not to have freedom of speech" (ἕν μὲν μέγιστον· οὐκ ἔχει παρρησίαν). She is appalled: "You have described the part of a slave! – not to speak one's mind" (δούλου τόδ᾽ εἶπας, μὴ λέγειν ἅ τις φρονεῖ). Polyneices agrees: "One must endure the folly of the powerful." Consolers offered a twofold response to Euripides. First, they pointed out that, while it is indeed the lot of a slave not to speak his mind, a wise man will

---

[45] Paul treats his "salvation" against the backdrop of his possible execution. Just as the perverse motivations of his rivals have not obstructed the proclamation of Christ (εἴτε προφάσει εἴτε ἀληθείᾳ, Χριστὸς καταγγέλλεται), so also, whether he lives or dies will have no effect on his anticipated "salvation" (εἴτε διὰ ζωῆς εἴτε διὰ θανάτου). For death as a matter of indifference, cf. Diog. Laert. 7.105, 7.189; Epict., *Diss.* 2.1.17; 2.5.14; 2.6.8; 2.19.13; 3.22.33; 3.26.4; Adolf F. Bonhöffer, *Die Ethik des Stoikers Epictet* (Stuttgart: Enke, 1894) 29–39; Jaquette, *Discerning What Counts*, 109–36; *idem*, "Life and Death, *Adiaphora*, and Paul's Rhetorical Strategies," *NovT* 38 (1996) 33: "Neither life nor death can hinder Paul's ultimate goal: honoring Christ." Cf. 1 Thess. 5:10: εἴτε γρηγορῶμεν εἴτε καθεύδωμεν; Rom. 14:8: ἐάν τε γὰρ ζῶμεν, τῷ κυρίῳ ζῶμεν, ἐάν τε ἀποθνήσκωμεν, τῷ κυρίῳ ἀποθνήσκομεν.

[46] *In Epist. ad Phil.*, hom. 3.3 (*PG* 62.202.31–2, 56–7): τὸ γὰρ ζῆν πάλιν τῶν μέσων ἐστὶ καὶ ἀδιαφόρων . . . καὶ γὰρ ὁ θάνατος τῶν ἀδιαφόρων ἐστίν.

[47] See E. L. Grasmück, *Exilium: Untersuchungen zur Verbannung in der Antike* (Paderborn: Schöningh, 1978), index, s.v. παρρησία; B. Häsler, *Favorin über die Verbannung* (Bottrop i.W: Postberg, 1935) 28–36; Alfred Giesecke, *De sententiis*, 36–43.

[48] Muson., frag. 9.48.1ff. Hense; Plut., *De ex.* 605F: ἀλλ᾽ ἐπεὶ πολλοὺς τὰ τοῦ Εὐριπίδου κινεῖ, δυνατῶς τῆς φυγῆς κατηγορεῖν δοκοῦντος.

also show discretion.[49] But more importantly, they insisted that it is not "the folly of the powerful" that silences those oppressed, but the oppressed's own fear of punishment and death, and that this fear robs men of παρρησία both at home and abroad.[50] "Are you not aware that I am an exile?" Musonius asks. "Have I then been deprived of freedom of speech (παρρησία)?"[51] Paul's consolation in 1:18b–21 turns on his similar claim that imprisonment will not deprive him of his "boldness" (παρρησία).[52]

The rhetoric of 1:18b–21 is similar to the rhetoric of 1:12–18a in that Paul reports his thoughts and feelings that the Philippians might imitate them and thus be encouraged. There is one difference, however, and that is that in 1:18b–21 Paul not only instructs the Philippians but begins to correct them. Paul heads his list of reasons why his salvation is assured with the Philippians' prayers (διὰ τῆς ὑμῶν δεήσεως; 1:19). At first glance this is natural enough; the Philippians were no doubt praying for Paul's "salvation." However, as soon as it becomes evident that by "salvation" Paul means not his physical release from prison but his continued courage to magnify Christ "whether through life or through death," the inclusion of the Philippians' prayer becomes problematic, for the Philippians, as Paul well knew, were praying for his release and return to Philippi (cf. 1:25–6). Paul here subtly and gently indicates to his readers that their prayers for him, and with those prayers their whole evaluation of his situation, were not what they should be.[53]

---

[49] Plut., *De ex.* 606B.

[50] Muson., frag. 9.48.15–19 Hense: "For it is not exiles who fear to speak their mind, but those who are terrified lest pain or death or punishment or some other such consequence befall them for what they say. Fear produces this behavior, by God, and not exile." As always, precepts are followed by example: Diogenes when he was an exile in Athens or when he was captured by pirates and sold to Xeniades of Corinth or brought before Philip of Macedon (Muson., frag. 9.49.4–9 Hense; Plut., *De ex.* 606B–C), Theodorus the Cyrenaic before Lysimachus (Plut., *De ex.* 606B; cf. Diog. Laert., 2.102; Philo, *Prob.* 129; Philodem., Περὶ θανάτου col. 32.23ff.), Hannibal before Antiochus (Plut., *De ex.* 606C; cf. Cic., *De div.* 2.24.52; Val. Max., 2.7.6). At 9.49.10ff. Musonius offers himself as an example.

[51] Muson., frag. 9.49.10–11 Hense.

[52] Indeed, on our reading of Phil. 1:18b–21, Paul's anticipated "salvation" (v. 19) consists precisely in his παρρησία.

[53] If we view 1:18b–21 from the perspective of the Philippians as readers, this discrepancy will not have been immediately obvious (1:19), but as Paul makes clear what he means by "salvation" they will have understood that their prayers were not what they should be. The subtlety and gentleness of Paul's correction here accords with his overall positive strategy of consolation, which, as we have already noted,

Paul's promised release and the Philippians' lack of progress (Phil. 1:22–6)

Paul offers the Philippians a third consolation in 1:22–6 when he assures them of his release from prison and eventual return to Philippi. For Paul "to die is gain" (1:21); but he also knows that there is a certain benefit to his living on: εἰ δὲ τὸ ζῆν ἐν σαρκί, τοῦτό μοι καρπὸς ἔργου (1:22). More importantly, he is convinced that a return visit to Philippi is necessary for the Philippians' sakes: τὸ δὲ ἐπιμένειν ἐν τῇ σαρκὶ ἀναγκαιότερον δι' ὑμᾶς (1:24). He assures them, therefore, that they will see him again: καὶ τοῦτο πεποιθὼς οἶδα ὅτι μενῶ καὶ παραμενῶ πᾶσιν ὑμῖν εἰς τὴν ὑμῶν προκοπὴν καὶ χαρὰν τῆς πίστεως, ἵνα τὸ καύχημα ὑμῶν περισσεύῃ ἐν Χριστῷ Ἰησοῦ ἐν ἐμοὶ διὰ τῆς ἐμῆς παρουσίας πάλιν πρὸς ὑμᾶς (1:25–6).

However, Paul's primary purpose in Phil. 1:22–6 is not to offer the Philippians additional consolation, but to make them aware of the hardship that their grief is working on him and to impress upon them the general inappropriateness of that grief. Here Paul confronts what we have identified as the first of two "rhetorical problems" facing him in writing the Philippians: namely, how to rebuke them for their emotional frailty when what they expect from him is a letter thanking them for their support and, if possible, reassuring them of his welfare.[54] Paul's solution to this problem is ingenious: he gives the Philippians the reassurance that they expect and need, but he bases that reassurance on a clear recognition of their weakness. The result is that the Philippians can take consolation in the likelihood that they will see Paul again, but they may do so only by acknowledging their failure to have responded correctly to his imprisonment.[55]

Crucial to Paul's rhetoric of reassurance (and rebuke) in 1:22–6

---

invites the Philippians to rejoice in the things that matter (τὰ διαφέροντα; 1:10a) and not simply to be indifferent to the things that do not (cf. Stoic apathy).

[54] See our discussion of this in chapter 2 above. For a discussion of the various indirect ways that rebuke was given in antiquity, see Stowers, *Letter Writing*, 125–41.

[55] Chrysostom senses the rhetorical force of this: ἐνταῦθα αὐτοὺς καὶ διανίστησιν, ὥστε προσέχειν ἑαυτοῖς. εἰ γὰρ δι' ὑμᾶς, φησί, μενῶ, ὁρᾶτε μὴ καταισχύνητέ μου τὴν παραμονήν (*In Epist. ad Phil.*, hom 4.4 [*PG* 62.207.28–30]). Cf. Brian J. Capper, "Paul's Dispute with Philippi: Understanding Paul's Argument in Phil 1–2 from His Thanks in 4.10–20," *ThZ* 49 (1993) 210 n. 35: "Paul's extraordinary presumption to be able to choose his fate (1.22) perhaps arises specifically from his desire to shame the Philippians."

is his striking deliberation on life and death in 1:22–4. Let us leave aside for the moment the fact that Paul here contemplates "choosing" (αἱρήσομαι) his own death, and let us focus instead on Paul's presentation of his dilemma, which takes the form of a thinly veiled complaint. Paul represents himself as "torn between" (συνέχομαι) two options. His strong preference (ἐπιθυμία)[56] is to depart and be with Christ which is "much better by far" (πολλῷ μᾶλλον κρεῖσσον).[57] But he feels constrained to remain in the flesh because this is "more necessary for you" (ἀναγκαιότερον δι᾽ ὑμᾶς). At stake are the Philippians' "progress and joy in the faith" (προκοπὴν καὶ χαρὰν τῆς πίστεως), and only by Paul's presence again at Philippi (διὰ τῆς ἐμῆς παρουσίας πάλιν πρὸς ὑμᾶς) will these be restored. Here then is Paul's dilemma: he must choose between what he very much *wants* to do and what he feels he *must* do for the sake of the Philippians. Paul never directly blames the Philippians for placing him in this situation. But he also leaves little doubt that it is their current lack of "progress and joy" that is forcing him to choose against his will.

Paul's rhetoric reaches a high point in 1:25 where, having concluded that "to remain in the flesh is more necessary for you," he writes: "and being confident of this (τοῦτο πεποίθως), I know that I shall remain [in the flesh] and continue with you all for your progress and joy in the faith." Two expressions in this verse call for comment. The first is the confidence formula τοῦτο πεποίθως ("being confident of this"). Twice elsewhere in Philippians Paul uses this formula to preface his reassurance of the Philippians. In 1:6 he writes: "being confident of this very thing (πεποίθως αὐτὸ τοῦτο), that he who began a good work among you will complete it until the day of Jesus Christ." In 2:24: "And I am confident in the Lord (πέποιθα ἐν κυρίῳ) that I too shall come soon." In both of these instances God is the object of Paul's confidence. In 1:25, however, Paul's confidence is not in God but in the emotional frailty of the Philippians who are dependent upon his physical return for their progress and joy in the faith.[58] "I am confident that

[56] *Contra* Collange, *Philippiens*, 61–2, ἐπιθυμία here is not used in a negative sense; cf. 1 Thess. 2:17; Gnilka, *Philipperbrief*, 73.
[57] Paul's pleonastic use of the triple comparative is almost unprecedented; cf. BDF §246. Compare Socrates' similar sentiment at Xenoph., *Ap.* 33: ἐπεὶ γὰρ ἔγνω τοῦ ἔτι ζῆν τὸ τεθνάναι αὐτῷ κρεῖττον εἶναι.
[58] The antecedent of τοῦτο in verse 25 is verse 24: τὸ δὲ ἐπιμένειν ἐν τῇ σαρκὶ ἀναγκαιότερον δι᾽ ὑμᾶς.

you will not make progress without seeing me again," Paul says, "and therefore I am confident that I shall see you again."

The reference in 1:25 to the Philippians' current lack of "progress and joy in the faith" (προκοπὴν καὶ χαρὰν τῆς πίστεως) also calls for comment. In using these two terms to characterize the Philippians' response to his imprisonment Paul brings the Philippians into explicit verbal contrast with what he says earlier about the gospel and himself. In 1:12 he reports that the gospel was still making "progress" despite his imprisonment (προκοπὴν τοῦ εὐαγγελίου), and in 1:18 he confesses that his joy has remained unbroken throughout his ordeal (χαίρω ἀλλὰ καὶ χαρήσομαι). But with the Philippians things are different. Like the gospel they should be making progress, and like Paul they should be rejoicing, but they are doing neither, and, as things now stand, they will continue in this manner until they see Paul again (cf. 1:26). This is in a very real sense unworthy of the gospel (cf. μόνον ἀξίως τοῦ εὐαγγελίου; 1:27!), and it is precisely for this reason that Paul is not free to do as he wishes.[59] It is characteristic of Paul's overall rhetorical strategy and his positive approach to consolation that he here suggests this unflattering comparison and then leaves the Philippians to draw the conclusion for themselves.

Let us now return to the problem of Paul's claim in 1:22 that life and death are his to "choose" (αἱρήσομαι) and that he might in the near future choose the latter. Commentators have resisted strongly the idea that Paul is here actually deliberating life and death. Lohmeyer, for instance, restricts Paul's choice to a totally inward act.[60] Similarly, Gnilka interprets Paul's choice as an act taken before God alone.[61] Beare translates τί αἱρήσομαι "what I shall prefer" instead of "what I shall choose,"[62] an acceptable translation, were it not for the fact that Paul states his preference clearly in 1:23: τὴν ἐπιθυμίαν ἔχων εἰς τὸ ἀναλῦσαι καὶ σὺν Χριστῷ εἶναι, πολλῷ μᾶλλον κρεῖσσον. Recently, Arthur Droge has taken Paul's language in 1:22 at face value and has concluded that Paul was in fact contemplating suicide.[63] There is much to recommend Droge's

---

[59] A moment's reflection on 1:12–26 would have led the Philippians to see that while neither imprisonment, nor rivals, nor the possibility of death were hindering Paul, they themselves were.

[60] *An die Philipper*, 61.   [61] *Philipperbrief*, 72.

[62] *Philippians*, 63; cf. BAGD, s.v. αἱρέω.

[63] "*Mori Lucrum*: Paul and Ancient Theories of Suicide," *NovT* 33 (1988) 268–86; cf. James L. Jaquette, "A Not-So-Noble Death: Figured Speech, Friendship and Suicide in Philippians 1:21–26," *Neot* 28 (1994) 177–92.

interpretation which locates Paul's deliberations in the context of ancient discussions of suicide, especially when we allow, as Droge does, that the ancient notion of "suicide" included martyrdom.[64] The obvious analogy is Socrates who, when arraigned on capital charges, knowingly sealed his fate by the manner of defense he employed.[65] Jesus' trial before Pilate was portrayed in similar terms.[66] It is not possible to be certain, but our interpretation of 1:18b–21 makes it likely that Paul entertained some similar idea of forcing his own fate, perhaps by a courageous exhibition of παρρησία in court (cf. 1:20).[67]

Behaving in a manner worthy of the gospel (Phil. 1:27–30)

In 1:27 Paul turns from his own situation (τὰ κατ᾽ ἐμέ; 1:12) to that of the Philippians (τὰ περὶ ὑμῶν). He has conceded – largely for rhetorical reasons – that their full recovery of "progress and joy" must await his return (1:25–6). However, even now (μόνον)[68] they can relinquish their unreasonable demand to see him again (εἴτε ἐλθὼν . . . εἴτε ἀπὼν) and begin to behave "in a manner worthy of the gospel" (ἀξίως τοῦ εὐαγγελίου; 1:27a).[69] Specifically, Paul

[64] See here the larger study, Arthur J. Droge and James D. Tabor, *A Noble Death: Suicide and Martyrdom among Christians and Jews in Antiquity* (San Francisco: Harper, 1992).

[65] Xenophon explicitly states this at *Ap.* 32: Σωκράτης δὲ διὰ τὸ μεγαλύνειν ἑαυτὸν ἐν τῷ δικαστηρίῳ φθόνον ἐπαγόμενος μᾶλλον καταψηφίσασθαι ἑαυτοῦ ἐποίησε τοὺς δικαστάς. Cf. also *Ap.* 1; 9; Plato, *Ap.* 38E. Like Paul (cf. Phil. 1:20), Socrates is also concerned to avoid shameful (αἰσχρόν) behavior (cf. Plato, *Ap.* 35A; Epict., *Diss.* 4.1.164–5). See also Sen., *Ep.* 104.3–5 which speaks of lingering in life for the sake of his wife and friends.

[66] Mk. 15:2–5; Matt. 27:11–13; Lk. 23:1–4; also Jesus before Herod in Lk. 23:9. John 10:18: "No one takes [my life] from me, but I lay it down of my own accord." There is a good discussion of this in Wansink, *Chained in Christ*, 120–4, which I have for the most part followed.

[67] Collange, *Philippiens*, 26, 59, sees Paul deliberating about whether or not to appeal to his Roman citizenship. However, the emphasis on παρρησία in 1:18b–21 suggests that some sort of courtroom display was in view. According to Epictetus, *Diss.* 2.2.8–20 (cf. *Diss.* 1.9.22–24), Socrates intentionally provoked (προσερεθίζειν) his judges. For such bravado among early Christians, cf. Marc. Aur., *Med.* 11.3; Pliny, *Ep.* 10.96; *Martyr. Apoll.* 14–23; Wansink, *Chained in Christ*, 123; G. E. M. de Ste Croix and A. N. Sherwin-White, "Why Were the Early Christians Persecuted? – An Amendment," *Past and Present* 27 (1964) 23–33; Herbert Musurillo, ed., *The Acts of the Christian Martyrs* (Oxford: Clarendon, 1972) lviii–lxii; Droge and Tabor, *A Noble Death*, 132–5.

[68] H. A. Steen, "Les clichés épistolaires dans les lettres sur papyrus grècques," *C&M* I.153 (1938).

[69] The "gospel" has been a central theme in Phil. 1:12–26, and Paul's behavior has centered around its proclamation. If things are going well with the gospel, things

wishes to hear "that [the Philippians] are standing firm in one spirit, striving together with one mind for the faith of the gospel, and in no way frightened by [their] opponents" (1:27b–28a). He supports the last of these injunctions, that the Philippians not be frightened by their opponents, with three arguments: (1) that their equanimity in the face of opposition signals a victorious outcome to their current ordeal, that is, the destruction of their opponents and their own σωτηρία: ἥτις ἐστὶν αὐτοῖς ἔνδειξις ἀπωλείας, ὑμῶν δὲ σωτηρίας (1:28b);[70] (2) that their suffering has been ordained by God: ὑμῖν ἐχαρίσθη τὸ ὑπὲρ Χριστοῦ . . . πάσχειν (1:29); and (3) that he himself has suffered and continues to suffer similar opposition in his service to Christ: τὸν αὐτὸν ἀγῶνα ἔχοντες, οἷον εἴδετε ἐν ἐμοὶ καὶ νῦν ἀκούετε ἐν ἐμοί (1:30).[71]

At least five *topoi* from ancient consolation are discernible in 1:27–30. We have already noted the *topos* of indifferent things present in the expression εἴτε ἐλθὼν . . . εἴτε ἀπὼν in 1:27.[72] A second *topos* may be identified in Paul's charge that the Philippians

are going well with Paul (1:12–18a); if Paul can but live out his commitment to proclaim the gospel boldly, then, whether or not this means his death, he has lived well (1:18b–21). The gospel is to assume a similar centrality in the life of the Philippians.

[70] Paul uses σωτηρία here in the same sense as 1:19, that is, not to act shamefully in the face of external threats, but to continue to boldly magnify Christ. Obviously, to meet initial threats with calm resolve signals such an outcome.

[71] Most commentators take 1:27–30 with the exhortation of 2:1–18, and indeed Paul's general charge in 1:27 to strive together with one mind (μιᾷ ψυχῇ) anticipates his exhortation to unity in 2:1–4 (cf. σύμψυχοι 2:2). But there is also much to link the material in 1:27–30 to the consolation of 1:12–6. To begin with, the οὖν *paraeneticum* of 2:1 marks a major break and indicates that a significant shift in thought occurs at 2:1. By comparison, the weaker μόνον in 1:27 suggests a continuation of thought between 1:25–6 and 1:27–30. Moreover, the reference to Paul's present circumstances in 1:30 (τὸν αὐτὸν ἀγῶνα ἔχοντες, οἷον . . . νῦν ἀκούετε ἐν ἐμοί) forms a natural inclusion with 1:12 (τὰ κατ᾽ ἐμέ), linking 1:27–30 with what precedes. In addition, the theme of indifference so prominent in 1:12–26 (εἴτε προφάσει εἴτε ἀληθείᾳ, 1:18; εἴτε διὰ ζωῆς εἴτε διὰ θανάτου, 1:20) is continued in the same terms in 1:27 (εἴτε ἐλθὼν . . . εἴτε ἀπών), as is the theme of "gospel" (1:12; 27 [twice]). However, the most significant feature of 1:27–30 tying it to the consolation of 1:12–26 is the remarkable concentration of consolatory *topoi* in these four verses. Chrysostom, who is attuned to the consolatory nature of 1:12–30, treats all of 1:27–30 with 1:12–26 (*In Epist. ad Phil.* 4.3 [*PG* 62.208.3ff.]); cf. Walter, "Die Philipper und das Leiden," 421, 432.

[72] With the possible exception of 3:1, Paul's charge in 1:27 to behave in a manner worthy of the gospel independent of his return is the most basic exhortation of the letter. Just as Paul is indifferent to the antipathy of his rivals (εἴτε προφάσει εἴτε ἀληθείᾳ; 1:18a) and to the ultimate outcome of his trial (εἴτε διὰ ζωῆς εἴτε διὰ θανάτου; 1:20), so the Philippians must accept as a matter of indifference his presence or absence (εἴτε ἐλθὼν . . . εἴτε ἀπών . . .). To continue their inordinate dependence on him is not to live "in a manner worthy of the gospel."

behave "in a manner worthy" (ἀξίως) of the gospel.[73] Consolers regularly challenged those distressed by misfortune to act in a manner "worthy" (*dignus*) of their status or office. At *Ad Brut.* 1.9.2 Cicero reminds Brutus of his *officia* as a military and political leader. Similarly, Seneca charges Claudius' secretary *a libellis* Polybius "to do nothing unworthy of his claim to be a sage and a scholar" (*nihil . . . indignum facere perfecti et eruditi viri professione*),[74] and cites as "worthy of a great man" (*dignam magno viro*) the words of Telamon at the death of Ajax: "I knew when I fathered him that he would die."[75] Philiscus rebukes the exiled Cicero that he is behaving in an unworthy manner:[76]

> Are you not ashamed, Cicero, to be weeping and behaving like a woman?[77] Really, I should never have expected that you, who have enjoyed such an excellent and varied education, and who have acted as advocate to many, would grow so faint-hearted.

The argument that grief is unworthy of us as rational beings is scattered throughout the tradition, often in the form of short asides that one should bear misfortune with manly courage and patience (*patientia*).[78]

A third consolatory *topos* appears in 1:28 where Paul exhorts the Philippians not to be "frightened" (μὴ πτυρόμενοι) by their opponents. The term Paul chooses, πτύρομαι, is a NT hapax that denotes an element of surprise as well as fear. LSJ suggests "start at" and "be alarmed at" as possible translations. The imagery is that of an animal frightened by a loud noise,[79] and in particular of

---

[73] ἀξίως . . . πολιτεύεσθε in 1:27 may be helpfully compared with the expression γενναίως φέρε found in several papyrus letters of consolation (SB 14.11646.9–10 [= P.Yale inv. 663; Chapa letter 1], BGU 3.801 [= P.Berol. inv. 8636; Chapa letter 3]; PSI 1248.11 [= Chapa letter 6]); Chapa, *Letters of Condolence*, 38–43.

[74] *Ad Poly.* 6.3; Cic., *Tusc.* 3.27.65–66: *Ergo in potestate est adiicere dolorem, cum velis, tempori servientem.* Cf. Sen., *Ad Poly.* 6.1; Pind., *Pyth.* 1.86–8; Jer., *Ep.* 60.14.5; cf. Ennius frag. 158 Vahlen = frag. 215 Jocelyn); Cic., *Ad Att.* 12.10; 12.11.

[75] *Ad Poly.* 11.2: *Ego cum genui, tum moriturum scivi* (from the lost tragedy of Ennius); cf. *Ep.* 107.7: *viro bono dignum.*

[76] Cass. Dio 38.18.1.

[77] A favorite comparison: Sen., *Ad Marc.* 1.1; 7.3; *Ad Poly.* 6.2, Cic., *Ad Brut.* 1.9.1 (*ferre . . . quam deceret virum*).

[78] Horace, *Carm.* 1.24.19–20; Ov., *Met.* 8.633; Sen., *Ad Marc.* 13; Fern, *The Latin Consolatio Mortis,* index, s.v. *patientia* and *patientia et constantia*; cf. Tolman, *Sepulchral Inscriptions,* 76.

[79] Philo Bybl. *apud* Euseb., *Praep. Ev.* 1.10.4 (= Jacoby, *FGrHist* 790 frag. 2, p. 807.5): πρὸς τὸν ἦχον (= τὸν πάταγον τῶν βροντῶν) ἐπτύρη; Plut., *Praec. ger.*

a horse startled by the first clash of battle.[80] But the term also occurs in consolatory contexts where it describes the element of surprise that comes about with unexpected misfortune. At Ps.-Plato, *Ax.* 370A Axiochus is presented to Socrates as one panicked by the sudden onset of a terminal illness: οὐκ ἄν ποτε πτυρείης τὸν θάνατον.[81] Similarly, Marcus Aurelius wants a soul not panicked by adversity: ἡ ψυχή . . . πτυρομένη.[82] At *Ep.* 107.4 Seneca speaks of a person unprepared for adversity who is "thrown into a panic" by even the slightest misfortune: *inparatus etiam levissima expavit.* Underlying this language is the Cyrenaic theory of consolation which, as we have already seen, traced distress (*aegritudo*) not to misfortune as such but to "misfortune that is unforeseen and takes one by surprise" (*insperatum et necopinatum malum*).[83] Paul's charge that the Philippians not be surprised by their opponents expresses this *topos.*[84]

Paul supports his exhortation that the Philippians not be taken off guard by their opponents in 1:28 with two further consolatory *topoi* in 1:29–30: (1) that suffering has been ordained by God (ὑμῖν ἐχαρίσθη . . . πάσχειν; v. 29),[85] and (2) that others (here Paul) have suffered similar things beforehand (τὸν αὐτὸν ἀγῶνα ἔχοντες, οἷον εἴδετε ἐν ἐμοί; v. 30).[86] Both of these *topoi* were used in

reip. 800C: μήτε ὄψει μήτε φωνῇ πτυρόμενος ὥσπερ θηρίον ὕποπτον. Cf. *Hom. Clem.* 2.39: πτύραντες ἀμαθεῖς ἄχλους (*PG* 2.104B); *PNess* 1.778 (vi A.D.) where it glosses *terreo* (cf. Vulg. of Phil. 1:28).

[80] Diod. Sic. 2.19; Plut., *Fab.* 3; *Marc.* 6; *Phil.* 12. At Hip., *Mul.* 1.25 it is a severe form of fright that may induce a miscarriage. The term was popular with Epiphanius (see *PGL* s.v. πτύρω); cf. *Acta Pauli*: Παῦλος οὐκ ἐπτύρη; Euseb., *Hist. Ev.* 5.24: οὐ πτύρομαι ἐπὶ τοῖς καταπληθσσομένοις. Apart from the fact that the term will have evoked such a vivid picture, commentators offer little explanation why Paul chooses this rare word: cf. Bonnard, *Philippiens*, 35; Beare, *Philippians*, 67; Gnilka, *Philipperbrief*, 99.

[81] Cf. *Ax.* 364B.

[82] *Med.* 8.45.

[83] Cic., *Tusc.* 3.14.29; cf. 3.31.76; Grollios, *Ad Marciam*, 44–51. Grief is the fruit of unrealistic expectation: Sen., *Ad Poly.* 10.5 (*spes avida*); *Ep.* 99.3–5; *Ad Marc.* 12.1–2; Lucr. 3.931–67. Cf. Johann, *Trauer und Trost*, 85–92.

[84] This *topos* figures prominently in the consolation of 1 Peter; cf. 1 Pet. 4:12: μὴ ξενίζεσθε . . . ὡς ξένου ὑμῖν συμβαίνοντος; cf. John 16:1, 33. For the *praemeditatio futuri mali* in Paul, see Abraham Malherbe, "Exhortation in I Thessalonians," *NovT* 25 (1983) 254–6 (reprinted in *idem, Paul and the Popular Philosophers* [Minneapolis: Fortress, 1989] 49–66) who adduces 1 Thess. 3:3–4; but see the criticism by Chapa, "Consolatory Patterns?," 220–228.

[85] ἐχαρίσθη constitutes a divine passive. For suffering as a "gift" (ἐχαρίσθη), see also Phil. 1:7 (χάρις); cf. 2:17–18; 3:10.

[86] For the observation that others have suffered before, see esp. Sen., *Ad Marc.* 2.1–5.6; *Ad Poly.* 14.1–17.6, cf. Grollios, Τέχνη ἀλυπίας, 67–71; Kurth, *Senecas*

support of the Cyrenaic thesis that misfortune should not be unexpected. Seneca uses them in this manner in *Ep.* 107.2–9, which offers a striking parallel to Phil. 1:28–30.[87] He first reminds Lucilius that the misfortune that has befallen him is not unusual (*nihil horum insolitum; nihil inexpectatum est*) and that he is distressed, not because his slaves have fled, but because he had not prepared for it: *inparatus etiam levissima expavit.*[88] He then cites in support of this the example of others who have suffered similar if not worse things:[89]

> "My slaves have run away!" you cry. Well, others have been robbed; others have been blackmailed, others have been slain, others have been betrayed, others have been stamped underfoot, others have been attacked by poison, by slander. Whatever misfortune you name, it has happened to many.

Finally, he cites a divine law (*lex*)[90] that all are subject to suffering, concluding with his well-known translation of Cleanthes' famous *Hymn to Zeus*:

> *Duc, o parens celsique dominator poli,*
> *Quocumque placuit; nulla parendi mora est.*
> *Adsum inpiger. Fac nolle, comitabor gemens*
> *Malusque patiar, facere quod licuit bono.*
> *Ducunt volentem fata, nolentem trahunt.*

Paul follows the same procedure in Phil. 1:28–30, with the exception that he reverses the order of the last two supporting *topoi*, citing first the divine law of suffering for all (believers) in 1:29, and then his own example in 1:30.

Trostschrift, 26–34; 167–216; Abel, *Bauformen*, 88–91; Johann, *Trauer und Trost*, index, s.v. *exemplum.*

[87] We have already looked at Sen., *Ep.* 107.1 in our exegesis of Phil. 1:9–10a above. We are here concerned with Seneca's argumentation from §§2–12.

[88] *Ep.* 107.4.

[89] *Ep.* 107.5.

[90] *Ep.* 107.9: *Ad hanc legem animus noster aptandus est.* All are subject to this law. Significantly, this subjection was to manifest itself "without murmuring" (*sine murmuratione*) and "grumbling" (*gemens*). We discuss this *topos* below in our exegesis of Phil. 2:14: Πάντα ποιεῖτε χωρὶς γογγυσμῶν καὶ διαλογισμῶν.

Exhortation: combating the fruits of discouragement (Phil. 2:1–30)

Exhortation to rational and responsible behavior in the face of emotional distress was, as we have already noted, an important part of ancient consolation, and in Phil. 2:1–30 Paul follows the consolatory arguments of 1:12–30 with a number of explicit hortatory injunctions and *exempla*.[91] He discerns two problems: (1) disunity in the church and (2) grumbling against God. In answer to the first of these, he urges a self-sacrificing humility (2:1–4). In answer to the second, he encourages a spirit of uncomplaining obedience (2:12–18). He adduces Christ as an example for both of these qualities (2:5–11). Timothy (2:19–24) and Epaphroditus (2:25–30) are also exemplary, though to a lesser degree.[92] Our comments on 2:1–30 will be selective. We are primarily interested in the ways Paul continues his efforts at consolation.

Discharging one's duties to other believers (Phil. 2:1–4)

Paul begins the exhortation of 2:1–4 with an explicit reference to the consolation of the Philippians: Εἴ τις οὖν παράκλησις ἐν Χριστῷ, εἴ τι παραμύθιον ἀγάπης, εἴ τις κοινωνία πνεύματος, εἴ τις σπλάγχνα καὶ οἰκτιρμοί . . . (2:1).[93] It is tempting to read this

[91] The move from consolatory argument to exhortation has already occurred in 1:27. However, the exhortation of 1:27–30 is very closely tied to the arguments of 1:12–26 as the continuation of so many consolatory *topoi*, especially the *topos* of indifference (εἴτε . . . εἴτε, 1:27; cf. 1:18, 20), in 1:27–30 makes plain. Nevertheless, the exhortation of 2:1–18 develops directly out of 1:27–30, especially the charge of 1:27: ὅτι στήκετε ἐν ἑνὶ πνεύματι, μιᾷ ψυχῇ συναθλοῦντες τῇ πίστει τοῦ εὐαγγελίου (cf. 2:2). Perhaps the best way to explain this is to see the focus of the exhortation shifting in 2:1. If 1:27 urges the Philippians to be indifferent to all but the progress of the gospel and so to remain focused as a group (μιᾷ ψυχῇ συναθλοῦντες τῇ πίστει τοῦ εὐαγγελίου), 2:1–4 explores attitudes and behaviors that are disrupting that group effort (μηδὲν κατ᾿ ἐριθείαν μηδὲ κατὰ κενοδοξίαν . . .).

[92] The sending of Timothy and Epaphroditus also serves a consolatory function; cf. 2:28: σπουδαιοτέρως οὖν ἔπεμψα αὐτόν, ἵνα ἰδόντες αὐτὸν πάλιν χαρῆτε. Timothy is a surrogate for Paul (cf. 2:23–4). For a similar use of surrogates in consolation, see Sen., *Ad Helv.* 18–19.

[93] There is disagreement among commentators on how to translate παράκλησις. Most (e.g., Lightfoot, Vincent, Beare, Gnilka, Schenk) render "exhortation" because of the obvious hortatory context of 2:1–4. But this confuses the basis of Paul's exhortation (i.e., consolation) with the exhortation itself. Furthermore, we have shown that the preceding context (1:12–30) is consolatory. It is better to translate "consolation" (with Lohmeyer, *An die Philipper*, 82; Bonnard, *Philippiens*, 38; Collange, *Philippiens*, 72); cf. 2 Cor. 1:3–7. Cf. C. J. Bjerkelund, *Parakalô: Form,*

as a general reference to the consolation he has just offered in 1:12–30, and this makes good sense of the expressions παράκλησις ἐν Χριστῷ and κοινωνία πνεύματος, both of which may be related back to themes in 1:12–30.[94] However, this does not explain παραμύθιον ἀγάπης, which looks ahead to 2:2 (τὴν αὐτὴν ἀγάπην ἔχοντες), nor does it account for the reference to σπλάγχνα καὶ οἰκτιρμοί which seem to anticipate the fruits of restored unity in the Philippian community.[95] In at least some sense, therefore, the consolation described in Phil. 2:1 is proleptic, that is, to come about when the Philippians follow the advice Paul is about to offer. The exhortation of 2:1–30 thus continues in a very practical way the consolation of 1:12–30.

Paul also continues the *topos* of joy in 2:1–4. However, this time he does not hold up his joy as exemplary but alludes to its deficiency. Paul's joy is not yet full (πληρώσατε), because of the disunity that exists among the Philippians (2:2). Rather than working together with unity of purpose (τὸ ἓν φρονοῦντες) in the cause of the gospel, there is personal rivalry (ἐριθεία; 2:3) among Paul's supporters at Philippi that reminds him of the rivalry (ἐριθεία; 1:17) he is currently experiencing in the place of his imprisonment. He has tried to restore their confidence in his mission (1:12–30). He now exhorts them to recultivate their former spirit of cooperation in the cause of Christ: τῇ ταπεινοφροσύνῃ . . . μὴ τὰ ἑαυτῶν ἕκαστος σκοποῦντες ἀλλὰ καὶ τὰ ἑτέρων ἕκαστοι (2:3–4).[96]

The example of Christ (Phil. 2:5–11)

Paul adduces in support of his exhortation in 2:1–4 the example of Christ: τοῦτο φρονεῖτε ἐν ὑμῖν, ὃ καὶ ἐν Χριστῷ Ἰησοῦ, "Have this attitude among yourselves, which was also in Christ Jesus"

Funktion und Sinn der Parakalô-Satze in den paulinischen Briefe (Bibliotheca Theologica Norvegica 1; Oslo: Universitetsforlaget, 1967) 175.

[94] For παράκλησις ἐν Χριστῷ, cf. 1:13, 23, 29; for κοινωνία πνεύματος, cf. 1:19, 27.

[95] οἰκτιρμοί are associated with consolation in 2 Cor. 1:3: ὁ πατὴρ τῶν οἰκτιρμῶν καὶ θεὸς πάσης παρακλήσεως. For consolation from love, cf. Col. 2:2: ἵνα παρακληθῶσιν αἱ καρδίαι αὐτῶν συμβιβασθέντες ἐν ἀγάπῃ.

[96] It has often been noted that Paul's more general instructions in 2:1–4 prepare for his specific admonition of Euodia and Syntyche in 4:2–3 (e.g., ἵνα τὸ αὐτὸ φρονῆτε, 2:2; τὸ αὐτὸ φρονεῖν, 4:2). See most recently, Dahl, "Euodia and Syntyche."

(2:5).[97] He cites as evidence of Christ's example an early hymn
(2:6–11), the original form and meaning of which are much
debated.[98] For our purposes, however, it is sufficient that we
understand the meaning of the hymn in its present context in
Philippians, which is that Christ in his incarnation and death
exemplifies the qualities that Paul wishes to see in the Philippians.[99]
The hymn of 2:6–11 thus looks back to the exhortation to humility
in 2:1–4 (cf. 2:8a: ἐταπείνωσεν ἑαυτόν)[100] and forward to the
exhortation to obedience in 2:12–18 (cf. 2:8b: γενόμενος ὑπήκοος
μέχρι θανάτου). Terms from the hymn are also echoed in the
descriptions of Timothy and Epaphroditus in 2:19–30, whose
examples further substantiate Paul's exhortation in 2:1–4 and
2:12–18.[101] There is little in the hymn that might function by way

[97] I supply an ἦν after ὅ: ὃ ἦν καὶ ἐν Χριστῷ Ἰησοῦ. Against this it is argued that
some form of φρονεῖν is more naturally supplied since it produces a neat parallelism
with the first part of the sentence (τοῦτο φρονεῖτε ἐν ὑμῖν). The problem with this
view is that elsewhere when Paul wants to produce such a parallelism he usually does
so explicitly. Cf. Rom. 6:3: ὅσοι ἐβαπτίσθημεν εἰς Χριστὸν Ἰησοῦν εἰς τὸν θάνατον
αὐτοῦ ἐβαπτίσθημεν; 1 Cor. 3:17: εἴ τις τὸν ναὸν τοῦ θεοῦ φθείρει, φθερεῖ τοῦτον ὁ
θεός; Gal. 6:8: ὁ σπείρων εἰς τὴν σάρκα ἑαυτοῦ ἐκ τῆς σαρκὸς θερίσει φθοράν, ὁ
δὲ σπείρων εἰς τὸ πνεῦμα ἐκ τοῦ πνεύματος θερίσει ζωὴν αἰώνιον; but especially,
Rom. 12:3: μὴ ὑπερφρονεῖν παρ᾽ ὃ δεῖ φρονεῖν ἀλλὰ φρονεῖν εἰς τὸ σωφρονεῖν. It
is more natural, I think, to see some form of εἶναι implied.
[98] See here especially the landmark studies of Ernst Lohmeyer, *Kyrios Jesus: Eine
Untersuchung zu Phil. 2,5–11* (Heidelberg: Carl Winter, 1928; 2nd edn., 1961) and
Ernst Käsemann, "Kritische Analyse." There are various surveys of scholarship on
Phil. 2:5–11. See in particular, Ralph Martin, *Carmen Christi*, 24–41; cf. Morna
Hooker, "Philippians 2,6–11," 151–64, whose skepticism is by no means unjustified.
[99] Cf. 2 Cor. 8:9. R. Martin (*Carmen Christi*, 68–74, 84–8) denies that the hymn
of 2:6–11 is exemplary even in its current setting in Philippians. But he can do this
only by ignoring the larger context. Granted that the translation of 2:5 is difficult,
there is no doubt, however, that the hymn describes in Christ the very "attitude" (cf.
ἡγήσατο; 2:6) that Paul's wishes to see in the Philippians in 2:1–4. Furthermore, it is
clear that the exhortation of 2:12–16 (which begins Ὥστε, ἀγαπητοί μου, καθὼς
πάντοτε ὑπηκούσατε . . .) derives from the example of Christ in 2:6–11 (cf. 2:8:
γενόμενος ὑπήκοος). Käsemann, who insists that the hymn is not an *exemplum*,
resorts to a play on words (as noted by Martin himself: *Carmen Christi*, 86) in
accounting for the obvious relationship between the hymn of 2:5–11 and the
exhortation of 2:12–16: "Gehorsam werden wir jedoch nicht durch ein Vorbild,
sondern durch das Wort, das uns als ihm gehörig bezeugt" ("Kritische Analyse,"
95).
[100] The ἑαυτόν in 2:7 and again in 2:8 also pick up the ἑαυτῶν in 2:3 and 2:4. We
may also see in 2:3–4 (ἀλλήλους ἡγούμενοι ὑπερέχοντας ἑαυτῶν, μὴ τὰ ἑαυτῶν
ἕκαστος σκοποῦντες ἀλλὰ καὶ τὰ ἑτέρων ἕκαστοι) the mindset of a δοῦλος (2:7).
[101] Like Christ, Timothy is a servant (ὡς πατρὶ τέκνον σὺν ἐμοὶ ἐδούλευσεν εἰς
τὸ εὐαγγέλιον) who is genuinely concerned for the interests of others (ὅστις γνησίως
τὰ περὶ ὑμῶν μεριμνήσει). Epaphroditus, in his efforts to deliver the Philippians'
gift to Paul, put his life at risk, "even to the point of death" (μέχρι θανάτου). See my
discussion of these texts below. Timothy seems to exemplify best the exhortation to

of consolation, except for the implicit promise in 2:9–11 that those
who follow Christ's example will be rewarded.[102]

Discharging one's duties to God (Phil. 2:12–18)

Paul returns to explicit exhortation in 2:12–18. Whereas the
exhortation of 2:1–4 concerned the Philippians' relationships with
one another, the exhortation of 2:12–18 concerns the Philippians'
relationship with God.[103] It falls into three parts (2:12–13, 14–16,
17–18), the first two of which may be further divided into an
imperatival clause (vv. 12 and 14) followed by a supporting reason
(vv. 13 and 15–16). In the first part (2:12–13) Paul characterizes the
Philippians' relationship with God in general terms as obedience
μετὰ φόβου καὶ τρόμου. In the second part (2:14–16) he focuses
more specifically on the problem at hand: πάντα ποιεῖτε χωρὶς
γογγυσμῶν καὶ διαλογισμῶν. Paul concludes in 2:17–18 with an
explicit charge (already implicit in 1:18) that the Philippians join
him in rejoicing over his present circumstances and their possible
outcome, whatever that may be.[104]

In 2:12–13 Paul exhorts the Philippians to continue in their
obedience to God.[105] In their current circumstances this means,

self-negation in 2:1–4, and Epaphroditus the exhortation to extreme obedience in
2:12–18.

[102] I see no problem with extending the so-called ethical interpretation of 2:5–11
to include the exaltation of Christ in verses 9–11. The Philippians can expect
analogous reward when they follow Christ's example and are found εἰλικρινεῖς καὶ
ἀπρόσκοποι εἰς ἡμέραν Χριστοῦ, πεπληρωμένοι καρπὸν δικαιοσύνης τὸν διὰ
Ἰησοῦ Χριστοῦ εἰς δόξαν καὶ ἔπαινον θεοῦ (1:10b–11). Indeed, their support of
Paul has already caused fruit to abound in their account: τὸν καρπὸν τὸν
πλεονάζοντα εἰς λόγον ὑμῶν (4:17). For the idea of reward with Christ, cf. Rom.
8:17: εἴπερ συμπάσχομεν ἵνα καὶ συνδοξασθῶμεν. It might also be argued that
Christ's example is consolatory in so far as it supplements Paul's example in 1:30
which is clearly consolatory. But it does not seem to me that Paul is using the
example of Christ in this way; that is, Christ is not here adduced as an example of
others who have suffered similar hardship, but as a moral example to be followed.

[103] Paul is apparently concerned that his forced separation from the Philippians
has not only disrupted their cooperative efforts as a church (2:1–4), but that it has
intruded upon their relationship with God (2:12–16): καθὼς πάντοτε ὑπηκούσατε,
μὴ ὡς ἐν τῇ παρουσίᾳ μου μόνον ἀλλὰ νῦν πολλῷ μᾶλλον ἐν τῇ ἀπουσίᾳ μου . . .

[104] In the context, rejoicing with Paul should be understood as precluding the
"grumbling and disputing" of 2:14.

[105] The one to whom the Philippians are to render their obedience is not explicitly
stated in 2:12a. Gnilka, *Philipperbrief*, 148, suggests that Paul has obedience to
himself in mind. Bonnard, *Philippiens*, 48, understands him to mean obedience to
the leaders in the church mentioned in 1:1. Collange, *Philippiens*, 98, understands
obedience "de la foi contrète." But if ὑπηκούσατε in verse 12 picks up the ὑπήκοος

among other things, seeking their own "salvation" with fear and trembling: καθὼς πάντοτε ὑπηκούσατε . . . μετὰ φόβου καὶ τρόμου τὴν ἑαυτῶν σωτηρίαν κατεργάζεσθε. The key term here is "salvation" (σωτηρία). The Philippians no doubt conceived their salvation, as they did Paul's,[106] in quite literal terms: the cessation of their difficulties, including the physical return of Paul.[107] But Paul has already defined this important term in his earlier discussion of his own suffering in 1:19–20, where he equates it not with physical deliverance but with moral victory in the face of threatening circumstances.[108] The Philippians are to seek a similar "salvation" in their current hardship,[109] which by definition must be pursued with a proper reverence toward God (μετὰ φόβου καὶ τρόμου). They will be helped in this pursuit by seeing in their present circumstances the hand of God, who is producing in the Philippian community both the desiring and the doing of his will: θεὸς γὰρ ἐστιν ὁ ἐνεργῶν ἐν ὑμῖν καὶ τὸ θέλειν καὶ τὸ ἐνεργεῖν ὑπὲρ τῆς εὐδοκίας (v. 13).[110]

In 2:14–16 Paul focuses more specifically on the problem of the Philippians' impiety. In particular, he does not want the Philippians (1) to complain against God: πάντα ποιεῖτε χωρὶς γογγυσμῶν καὶ διαλογισμῶν, and thus (2) mar their reputation: ἵνα γένησθε ἄμεμπτοι καὶ ἀκέραιοι, τέκνα θεοῦ ἄμωμα μέσον γενεᾶς σκολιᾶς καὶ διεστραμμένης, ἐν οἷς φαίνεσθε ὡς φωστῆρες ἐν κόσμῳ.[111] Both of these motifs, complaining against God and coping with hardship in an exemplary fashion, are consolatory *topoi*. We have

of the hymn in 2:8, as almost all interpreters agree that it does, then the implied recipient of the Philippians' obedience is God. God then also becomes the natural object of the φόβος καὶ τρόμος in verse 12b, as well as γογγυσμοὶ καὶ διαλογισμοί in 4:14.

[106] See my discussion of 1:18b–21 above in chapter 5.

[107] Cf. 2:12: ὡς ἐν τῇ παρουσίᾳ μου μόνον ἀλλὰ νῦν πολλῷ μᾶλλον ἐν τῇ ἀπουσίᾳ μου; also 1:27.

[108] Paul invites comparison with this earlier discussion of his salvation when in 2:12 he refers to "your own salvation" (τὴν ἑαυτῶν σωτηρίαν).

[109] The Philippians' circumstances are, of course, not as severe as Paul's but it is still appropriate to speak of their "salvation" in moral terms.

[110] As in Phil. 1:6, I render ἐν ὑμῖν "among you." Cf. Gnilka, *Philipperbrief*, 150.

[111] Paul does not directly cite the OT in Philippians. Here, however, his language reflects the LXX. For γογγυσμός, see Exod. 16:7–12; Num. 17:5; cf. 1 Cor. 10:10 (μηδὲ γογγύζετε καθάπερ τινὲς αὐτῶν ἐγόγγυσαν . . .). Compare Phil. 2:15 (τέκνα θεοῦ ἄμωμα μέσον γενεᾶς σκολιᾶς καὶ διεστραμμένης) with Deut. 32:5 (τέκνα μώμητα γενεὰ σκολιὰ καὶ διεστραμμένη). Bonnard, *Philippiens*, 51, suggests that the grumbling here took the form of "insubordination ou de mécontentement." This would apparently bring into play the ἐπίσκοποι καὶ διάκονοι mentioned in Phil. 1:1. This is a speculative but attractive suggestion; but see Collange, *Philippiens*, 98.

already discussed the *topos* of being an example to others in connection with Phil. 1:13.[112] Let us, therefore, briefly consider the *topos* of complaining against God.

Ancient consolers regularly pointed out that unmitigated grief brought with it various character flaws, not the least of which was ingratitude.[113] Thus Seneca to Marullus: "Grief like yours has this among other evils: it is not only useless (*supervacuus*), but thankless (*ingratus*)."[114] Such ingratitude most often manifests itself in complaining:[115]

> If you confess that you have experienced great pleasures from him, then it is your duty not to complain (*queri*), but to give thanks (*gratias agere*) for what you have had.

The injunction not to complain against God (or fate) was therefore quite common. Marcia is to endure the death of her son "without complaint" (*sine querella*).[116] Similarly, Lucilius is to accept suffering "without murmuring" (*sine murmuratione*) and "grumbling" (*gemens*).[117] *Ad Poly.* 2–3 is an extended mock indictment (*litem*) of fate, in which Seneca brings forward a list of complaints (*querellae*) in accusation (*accusare*) for the death of Polybius' brother. At *Ad ux.* 610E–611B Plutarch urges his wife not "to complain and be disconsolate" (ἐγκαλεῖν καὶ δυσφορεῖν) over the death of their young daughter, but to maintain "a reverent language toward God" (ἡ περὶ τὸ θεῖον εὐφημία) and "a serene and uncomplaining attitude toward fate" (τὸ πρὸς τὴν τύχην ἵλεων καὶ ἀμεμφές). She is to avoid those who are "always complaining" (πάντα καὶ πάντως μεμφομένοις). Marcus Aurelius' injunction to himself at *Med.* 2.3 recalls Paul's language in Phil. 2:14: "you should not face death grumbling (μὴ γογγύζων) but graciously, with integrity, and from a heart thankful to the gods."[118]

At the end of 2:16 Paul voices his concern that he will not have "run in vain or labored in vain" at Philippi. This will happen if the

---

[112] See chapter 5 above.

[113] Cf. *Ad Poly.* 10.2, where in addition to ingratitude Seneca mentions injustice, greed, and stupidity; cf. *Ep.* 99:6.

[114] *Ep.* 99.4; cf. *De benef.* 3.4.1; Cic., *De fin.* 1.57, 62; Lucr. 3.931–67, esp. 957ff.; Plut., *Ad ux.* 610E–611D; Johann, *Trauer und Trost*, 85–92.

[115] Sen., *Ad Marc.* 12.1.

[116] *Ad. Marc.* 10.2.

[117] *Ep.* 107.9.

[118] Cf. Chrys., *In Epist. ad Phil.*, hom. 8.4 (*PG* 63.246.10–13): πάντοθεν οὖν ἡμῖν ὁ κοπετὸς ἐκκεκόφθω, πάντοθεν ὁ θρῆνος λυέσθω· ἐπὶ πᾶσιν εὐχαριστῶμεν τῷ θεῷ, χωρὶς γογγυσμῶν πάντα πράττωμεν.

Philippians ruin their reputation through complaining. However, should the Philippians follow Paul's advice and "do all things without grumblings and disputes," Paul will have his "boast" in the "day of Christ." In verses 17–18 he presses this one step further. Not only will Paul exult in the Philippians in the day of Christ, he even now in the face of death will find joy in their faith: ἀλλὰ εἰ καὶ σπένδομαι ἐπὶ τῇ θυσίᾳ καὶ λειτουργίᾳ τῆς πίστεως ὑμῶν,[119] χαίρω καὶ συγχαίρω πᾶσιν ὑμῖν.[120] He explicitly urges the Philippians to join him in this: τὸ δὲ αὐτὸ καὶ ὑμεῖς χαίρετε καὶ συγχαίρετέ μοι. This marks a turning point in the rhetoric of the letter, for from this point Paul will be explicit in urging the Philippians to rejoice (2:28–9; 3:1; 4:4; but see 4:10), whereas this has earlier only been implied (cf. 1:5; 18, 25). At the same time, by reintroducing the *topos* of joy here Paul further ties the exhortation of 2:1–30 with the consolation of 1:12–30.[121]

Timothy to come soon (Phil. 2:19–24)

Paul returns to the topic of his release and eventual return to Philippi in 2:19–24. Having already assured the Philippians that he will see them again (1:25–6), he now addresses the question of when that will be. His immediate plan is to send Timothy as soon as he knows something more definitive about his case (2:23). Timothy will then bring news of the Philippians back to Paul (2:19). Before long Paul hopes that he himself will be able to come (2:14).

In addition to conveying news of Paul's and Timothy's travel plans, 2:19–24 serves both a consolatory and hortatory function. Timothy will bring more up-to-date news about Paul. But more importantly, Timothy is Paul's surrogate: ὡς πατρὶ τέκνον.[122] His presence itself will be consolation to the Philippians. Paul will therefore send him "quickly" (ταχέως), "at once" (ἐξαυτῆς), as soon as he has more definitive news about his own circumstances. We find a similar use of surrogates by Seneca at *Ad Helv.* 18–19 where he advises his mother to find comfort in his brothers. They

---

[119] For faithful death as sacrifice, cf. Wisd. 3:6: ὡς ὁλοκάρπωμα θυσίας προσεδέξατο αὐτούς; 2 Macc. 7:38; 4 Macc. 17:22; *T. Benj.* 3:8; 1QS 5.6; 8.3–4; Randall Otto, "'If Possible I May Attain the Resurrection from the Dead' (Philippians 3:11)," *CBQ* 57 (1995) 335.

[120] Recalling 2:2: πληρώσατέ μου τὴν χαράν.

[121] Cf. Walter, "Die Philipper und das Leiden," 432.

[122] Cf. Lohmeyer, *An die Philipper*, 111–22.

remain with her and will compensate the loss she is suffering because of his exile: *nihil tibi deerit praeter numerum*.[123] In Phil. 2:19a Paul further consoles the Philippians by sharing in their anxiety: ἵνα κἀγὼ εὐψυχῶ γνοὺς τὰ περὶ ὑμῶν.[124] He has told them of his circumstances (τὰ κατ᾽ ἐμέ) in order to console them (1:12–21); he now wants to hear more of their circumstances (τὰ περὶ ὑμῶν) in order that he too might be comforted (ἵνα κἀγὼ εὐψυχῶ).[125] Of course, Paul's promise that he too will come "quickly" (ταχέως) will also have consoled the Philippians.

The hortatory function of 2:19–24 has not always been adequately emphasized by commentators who have tended to read it as "eine Art Empfehlungsbrief für Timotheus."[126] Without denying that 2:19–24 does indeed recommend Timothy, it is worth noting the precise terms that Paul's recommendation takes. We have already seen that, like Christ in 2:7 (μορφὴν δούλου λαβών), Timothy is an example of a servant: ὡς πατρὶ τέκνον σὺν ἐμοὶ ἐδούλευσεν εἰς τὸ εὐαγγέλιον. He also illustrates Paul's injunction in 2:4: μὴ τὰ ἑαυτῶν ἕκαστος σκοποῦντες ἀλλὰ καὶ τὰ ἑτέρων ἕκαστοι. For he is exemplary in his concern for others: οὐδένα γὰρ ἔχω ἰσόψυχον, ὅστις γνησίως τὰ περὶ ὑμῶν μεριμνήσει· οἱ πάντες γὰρ τὰ ἑαυτῶν ζητοῦσιν, οὐ τὰ Ἰησοῦ Χριστοῦ (2:20–1).

The return of Epaphroditus (Phil. 2:25–30)

Paul hopes to come to Philippi soon, and he plans to send Timothy even sooner; but for now he is sending Epaphroditus, the Philip-

---

[123] Seneca also reminds Helvia of her grandchildren, great-grandchildren, sister and the memory of her father. Like Timothy, Helvia's sister cares genuinely for her grief (19.1–2) and provides a moral example for her to follow (19.4–7).

[124] For εὐψυχω; in consolation, cf. BGU 4.1097.15: ἐγὼ γὰρ οὐχ ὀλιγωρῶ, ἀλλὰ εὐψυχοῦσα πα[ρα]μένω; POxy 1.115, a letter of consolation from the second century CE, begins: Εἰρήη Ταοννώφρει καὶ Φίλωνι εὐψυχεῖν; cf. Herm., *Vis.* 1.3.2: εὐψύχει καὶ ἰσχυροποίει σου τὸν οἶκον; Dibelius, *An die Philipper*, 65; Lohmeyer, *An die Philipper*, 115 n. 1; Gnilka, *Philipperbrief*, 158 n. 7. MM, s.v. εὐψυχῶ, report that εὐψυχῶ is a common term in funerary inscriptions, citing by way of example F. Preisigke, *Sammelbuch Griechischer Urkunden aus Ägypten I, II, III* (Strassburg and Berlin: Trübner, 1915–27) no. 46: Νίγερ μαχαιροφόρος, εὐψύχι, (ἐτῶν) ξ.

[125] This, of course, confirms our reading of 1:12–21 as consolatory. Cf. Chrys., *In Epist. ad Phil.*, hom. 9.1 (*PG* 62.245.46–51): ὥσπερ ὑμᾶς, φησίν, ἀνεκτησάμην ταῦτα ἀκούσαντας, ἅπερ ηὔχεσθε περὶ ἐμοῦ, ὅτι τὸ Εὐαγγέλιον ἐπέδωκεν, ὅτι κατησχύνθησαν ἐκεῖνοι, ὅτι δι᾽ ὧν ἐνόμιζον βλάπτειν, διὰ τούτων εὔφραναν· οὕτω βούλομαι καὶ τὰ καθ᾽ ὑμᾶς μαθεῖν, ἵνα κἀγὼ εὐψυχῶ, γνοὺς τὰ περὶ ὑμῶν.

[126] Dibelius, *An die Philipper*, 65; cf. Gnilka, *Philipperbrief*, 157; Collange, *Philippiens*, 103.

pians' own representative, back to them. In 2:25–30 he explains
why. As in 1:22–6, it appears that the Philippians' emotional state
has forced (ἀναγκαῖον) Paul's hand.[127]

Epaphroditus has faithfully, indeed heroically (παραβολευσάμενος τῇ ψυχῇ), carried out his service to Paul, and Paul commends
him as τὸν ἀδελφὸν καὶ συνεργὸν καὶ συστρατιώτην μου, ὑμῶν δὲ
ἀπόστολον καὶ λειτουργὸν τῆς χρείας μου. Nevertheless, Paul has
felt constrained to send him back to Philippi: ἀναγκαῖον δὲ
ἡγησάμην Ἐπαφρόδιτον . . . πέμψαι πρὸς ὑμᾶς.[128] The reason is
that Epaphroditus has become worried about the Philippians who
have received word that he has fallen ill: ἐπειδὴ ἐπιποθῶν ἦν
πάντας ὑμᾶς καὶ ἀδημονῶν, διότι ἠκούσατε ὅτι ἠσθένησεν. Paul
confirms this report: Epaphroditus had indeed fallen ill (καὶ γὰρ
ἠσθένησεν), and in fact he was worse than the Philippians had
heard: παραπλήσιον θανάτῳ. But he has since recovered: ἀλλὰ ὁ
θεὸς ἠλέησεν αὐτόν. Even so Paul has been diligent to return
Epaphroditus to the Philippians "in order that seeing him again
you might rejoice and I might be less burdened with grief" (ἵνα
ἰδόντες αὐτὸν πάλιν χαρῆτε κἀγὼ ἀλυπότερος ὦ).

It is clear from this last line – ἵνα ἰδόντες αὐτὸν πάλιν χαρῆτε
κἀγὼ ἀλυπότερος ὦ – that Paul believes that news of Epaphroditus'
illness will have further quashed the Philippians' joy, and that this
is what motivated his prompt return of Epaphroditus. Furthermore, it is clear that this response on the part of the Philippians is a
source of grief to Paul. Paul's purpose in returning Epaphroditus is
therefore explicitly consolatory: first, to console the Philippians
who, already distressed over Paul's imprisonment, are now further
distressed by word of Epaphroditus' illness, and second, to console
Paul himself who, like Epaphroditus, is concerned about the
Philippians.[129]

[127] The first word in 2:25–30 is ἀναγκαῖον: ἀναγκαῖον δὲ ἡγησάμην Ἐπαφρόδιτον . . . πέμψαι πρὸς ὑμᾶς. Recall Paul's use and our discussion of ἀναγκαιότερον
in 1:24.
[128] It might be objected that returning Epaphroditus at this point was simply in
keeping with the fact that he has fulfilled his commission, i.e., he has delivered the
gift. But the fact that Paul insists that Epaphroditus has indeed fulfilled his mission
suggests that the Philippians had intended him to stay on and help Paul for a while.
But whatever the case, Paul explains why he is sending Epaphroditus back and uses
this as an opportunity once more to point up the inconvenience of the Philippians'
emotional state.
[129] The expression ἵνα μὴ λύπην ἐπὶ λύπην σχῶ at the end of 2:27 calls for
comment. It is somewhat odd to hear Paul speak here of grief, since he earlier
presents himself as indifferent to the things that normally cause grief, including

As in the case of Timothy's commendation in 1:19–24, Paul's commendation of Epaphroditus also serves a hortatory function.[130] The Philippians are to welcome Epaphroditus back with joy: προσδέχεσθε οὖν αὐτὸν ἐν κυρίῳ μετὰ πάσης χαρᾶς. However, they are also to reflect upon his example: καὶ τοὺς τοιούτους ἐντίμους ἔχετε. Like Christ, who was "obedient to the point of death" (ὑπήκοος μέχρι θανάτου), Epaphroditus also in discharging his duty "to the point of death drew near" (μέχρι θανάτου ἤγγισεν).[131]

death. It may be that we should not read too much into his words here. On the other hand, Paul does allow in 2:2 that he lacks joy (and thus presumably experiences grief) over the Philippians' response to his imprisonment. And in 2:28 he explicitly states that the Philippians' distress over Epaphroditus' illness grieves him. It may be, therefore, that in 2:27 Paul's possible λύπη ἐπὶ λύπην is the grief he is already experiencing over the Philippians' distress about his imprisonment supplemented by the grief that he would feel over their distress if Epaphroditus were to die. This would explain the comparative ἀλυπότερος in 2:28. The Philippians' joy at the return of Epaphroditus will remove the second source of Paul's grief (the Philippians' distress over Epaphroditus) but not the first source of grief (the Philippians' distress over Paul's imprisonment). It is striking that the Philippians, who will rejoice only when Paul is present with them again (cf. 1:26; διὰ τῆς ἐμῆς παρουσίας πάλιν πρὸς ὑμᾶς), will rejoice only when they have seen Epaphroditus again (ἵνα ἰδόντες αὐτὸν πάλιν χαρῆτε).

[130] That the paragraphs about Timothy and Epaphroditus serve both a consolatory and a hortatory function further ties the exhortation of 2:1–18 to the consolation of 1:12–30.

[131] Whereas Timothy's example appears to substantiate the exhortation to care for others in 2:1–4, Epaphroditus' example substantiates the exhortation to uncomplaining obedience in 2:12–18.

6

DISCERNING THE ONE THING THAT MATTERS IN THE CHRISTIAN LIFE (PHIL. 3:1–4:1)

Believe me, real joy is a matter of the utmost importance.

Seneca, *Ep.* 23.4

With the command to "rejoice in the Lord" in Phil. 3:1a, Paul returns to the theme of "the things that matter," things that may legitimately be made the object of one's joy, and introduces the second heading of his letter (3:1–4:1). He has so far instructed the Philippians in the things that matter relative to the gospel mission, namely, the "progress" (προκοπή) of the gospel message and the "boldness" (παρρησία) of the gospel messenger (1:12–2:30). But he has more to say on this topic, and in 3:1–4:1 he takes up the question of what matters relative to one's Christian existence as such. Here the proper object of joy is not the proclamation of Christ (cf. 1:18b: Χριστὸς καταγγέλλεται, καὶ ἐν τούτῳ χαίρω), but Christ himself (cf. 3:1a: χαίρετε ἐν κυρίῳ). Paul thus moves in the second part of his letter from penultimate to ultimate concerns, or, to continue with the theme announced in 1:10a, from the things (plural) that matter to the "one thing" (ἕν)[1] that matters most: "the surpassing greatness of the knowledge of Christ" in comparison to which all else is "refuse."[2] In Christ, Paul offers the Philippians a

---

[1] Phil. 3:13.

[2] Phil. 3:8: ἡγοῦμαι πάντα ζημίαν εἶναι διὰ τὸ ὑπερέχον τῆς γνώσεως Χριστοῦ Ἰησοῦ τοῦ κυρίου μου, δι' ὃν τὰ πάντα ἐζημιώθην, καὶ ἡγοῦμαι σκύβαλα. It should be noted that Stoics also spoke of things mattering in both a penultimate and an ultimate sense. Ultimately, that is, relative to one's moral choice, they distinguished between virtue and vice on the one hand, and everything else, including conventional goods and evils, on the other. Penultimately, that is, relative to life "according to nature" (κατὰ φύσιν), they further distinguished between conventional goods and evils and matters of absolute indifference. By thus allowing for the relative value of conventional goods, goods "according to nature," the Stoics distinguished themselves from the Cynics for whom all things outside of virtue and vice were equally indifferent.

source of joy that is altogether independent of the measurable
successes of the gospel mission.

We will divide 3:1–4:1 into five parts: (1) an introductory
exhortation to "rejoice in the Lord" (3:1); (2) a warning against
those who do not "boast in Christ" but "have confidence in the
flesh" (3:2–3); (3) Paul's testimony relativizing both his past status
in Judaism and his present achievements as a Christian apostle to
the knowledge of Christ (3:4–16); (4) an exhortation to adopt as a
public ideal Paul's goal of knowing Christ (3:17–21); and (5) a
concluding exhortation to "stand thus in the Lord" (4:1). Our
exegesis will again be selective, our primary interest being in how
3:1–4:1 develops the thesis of 1:10a that the Philippians must learn
to identify the things that truly matter.

Introductory exhortation: "rejoice in the Lord" (Phil. 3:1)

Phil. 3:1 is transitional and serves to introduce the material that
follows in 3:2–4:1.[3] It falls into two parts. In the first part (3:1a),
Paul summarizes his hortatory concerns[4] in an exhortation to
"rejoice in the Lord" (χαίρετε ἐν κυρίῳ). This exhortation carries
forward the theme of joy (χαρά) prominent in chs. 1–2 and forms
an *inclusio* with the similar exhortation to "stand thus in the Lord"
(οὕτως στήκετε ἐν κυρίῳ) in 4:1.[5] In the second part (3:1b), Paul
assures the Philippians that the exhortation which follows does not
imply any ignorance on their part, since they have already heard
what he is about to say (τὰ αὐτὰ γράφειν).[6] Rather, he offers his

---

[3] Weiss, *Philipper-Brief*, 214.

[4] Thus Meeks, "The Man from Heaven in Philippians," 332: "the section as a
whole [= chapter 3] is not polemical but hortatory"; cf. Weiss, *Philipper-Brief*,
214–15; *pace* Helmut Koester, "The Purpose of the Polemic of a Pauline Fragment
(Philippians III)," *NTS* 8 (1961–62) 317–32.

[5] Schenk, *Die Philipperbriefe*, 274, sees an "Imperativ-Rahmen" in 3:2 and 4:1. Of
course, χαίρετε in 3:1 is also an imperative.

[6] This is a common hortatory idiom, and Paul employs it elsewhere in Rom.
15:14–15; 1 Thess. 4:9; 5:1, 2 Cor. 9:1. Cf. Stowers, "Friends and Enemies," 116–17,
and Abraham J. Malherbe, *Paul and the Thessalonians* (Philadelphia: Fortress,
1987), 70–2, who cite Isocr., *Nic.* 40; *Phil.* 105; Cic., *Ad fam.* 1.4.3; 2.4.2; Sen., *Ep.*
94.26; Dio Chrys., *Or.* 17.1–2. Because he misinterprets the hortatory idiom of Phil.
3:1b, Goodspeed is able to underestimate the force of 3:1a: "In 3:1 all is serene; they
must not mind Paul repeating himself, for it is for their good" (*Introduction*, 90–1).
However, the idiom of Phil. 3:1b no more trivializes the command of 3:1a, than the
same idiom in Rom. 15:14–15 (τολμηρότερον δὲ ἔγραψα ὑμῖν ἀπὸ μέρους ὡς
ἐπαναμιμνῄσκων) trivializes the letter to the Romans, to which it refers.

instruction by way of a reminder,[7] as a matter of precaution (ἀσφαλές).[8]

The seriousness of Paul's command to rejoice in the Lord in Phil. 3:1a has often been underestimated.[9] However, as we have already seen, ancient consolers viewed "joy" (*gaudium*) as "a matter of the utmost importance" (*res severa*).[10] Furthermore, Paul has employed the term with a similar philosophical seriousness in Phil. 1–2.[11] It is only natural that he should continue to use the term in this sense in 3:1a.[12] Particularly relevant to Paul's use of joy in Phil. 3:1a is Seneca's charge to Lucilius at *Ep.* 23.3 that before all else he must learn how to rejoice: *Hoc ante omnia fac, mi Lucili: disce gaudere.* Seneca here summarizes his entire philosophical program in a simple imperative: "Learn how to rejoice." Paul's command to rejoice in the Lord in Phil. 3:1a is an analogous summary of Christian existence. For Paul, of course, the proper object of joy is not Stoic virtue but Christ.[13] Nevertheless, for both Paul and Seneca "joy" is an indication of one's real values and thus of one's spiritual or philosophical progress: *tantum tibi ex sapientia, quantum ex gaudio deesse.*[14] Lucilius will learn how to rejoice only when he has learned not to overestimate the value of things that do not really matter: *ne gaudeas vanis.*[15] Paul's command to rejoice in the Lord in 3:1a calls for a similar "revaluation of values."[16]

---

[7] Cf. Phil. 3:18: οὒς πολλάκις ἔλεγον ὑμῖν.

[8] The warning of 3:2 should be interpreted as precautionary. The opponents here are not a live threat at Philippi. Rather, Paul sees in the Philippians certain tendencies that remind him of these opponents, whom both he and the Philippians repudiate. Paul adduces them in order to drive the Philippians away from their error.

[9] See our discussion of this problem above in chapter 1.

[10] *Ep.* 23.4: *Mihi crede, verum gaudium res severa est.* Joy is for Seneca the very basis (*fundamentum*) of happiness (*Ep.* 23.1–2). To find joy in things that do not matter is to place one's happiness at the whim of circumstances. However, to rejoice only in the things that truly matter, lifts one above the everyday give and take of chance and secures a more stable happiness.

[11] See our discussion of Phil. 1:18 above in chapter 5, and in particular Chrys., *In Epist. ad Phil.*, hom. 3.1 (*PG* 62.197.37ff.).

[12] τὸ λοιπόν in 3:1 ties the exhortation to rejoice in the Lord in 3:1a to Paul's earlier implicit and explicit exhortations to rejoice (1:18a and b; 2:17–18, and 28–9) as the last, and in this case most important term in a series.

[13] Cf. Sen. *Ep.* 23.6: *ad verum bonum specta et de duo gaude.*

[14] Sen., *Ep.* 59.14; cf. Phil. 1:12–26, especially 25, where Paul joins the concepts of "joy" (χαρά) and "progress" (προκοπή).

[15] *Ep.* 23.1.

[16] Gnilka, *Philipperbrief*, 191: "Umwertung der Werte." See our discussion of Phil. 3:4–16 below.

Warning against those who do not "boast in Christ" (Phil. 3:2–3)

Paul follows the exhortation to "rejoice in the Lord" in 3:1 with a stern warning against those who would teach otherwise. The warning proper comes in 3:2 and is actually a series of three warnings repeated for effect: βλέπετε τοὺς κύνας; βλέπετε τοὺς κακοὺς ἐργάτας; βλέπετε τὴν κατατομήν. It is followed in 3:3 with a supporting reason, the elements of which take up in reverse order the warnings of 3:2: ἡμεῖς γὰρ ἐσμεν ἡ περιτομή, οἱ πνεύματι θεοῦ λατρεύοντες καὶ καυχώμενοι ἐν Χριστῷ Ἰησοῦ καὶ οὐκ ἐν σαρκὶ πεποιθότες.

The sternness of Paul's warning in Phil. 3:2 cannot be denied. The threefold βλέπετε almost certainly means "beware of" or "watch out for" and not merely "consider,"[17] and Paul's opponents are unequivocally denigrated as "dogs . . . evil workers . . . the mutilation." However, it is possible to overstate Paul's pathos. His warning does not convey "an intensity unsurpassed even in Galatians,"[18] where both the readers and the opponents are chastised, nor does he lash out against his opponents in "violent hysteria."[19] To be sure, Paul's invective is biting – what else can invective be? – but he is by no means out of control, as the effective use of anaphora (βλέπετε . . . βλέπετε . . . βλέπετε . . .), assonance (κύνας . . . κακοὺς ἐργάτας . . . κατατομήν), and paronomasia (κατατομή/περιτομή), as well as parsicolon and chiasmus,[20] make plain. Paul's tone in 3:2 is best described as impassioned but measured, reflecting the seriousness of his exhortation in 3:1.

Because Paul engages in invective in 3:2 and again in 3:18–19, it is difficult to be specific about his opponents.[21] Indeed, Paul casts

[17] *Contra* Kirkpatrick, "ΒΛΕΠΕΤΕ," 146–8.

[18] Goodspeed, *Introduction*, 91. Koester, "Purpose of the Polemic," 319, likewise overstates the case when he speaks of the "unrelenting harshness" with which Paul attacks his opponents; Paul's "harshness" ends as quickly as it begins in 3:2 and does not resurface until 3:19; E. P. Sanders, "Paul on the Law, His Opponents, and the Jewish People" in Peter Richardson and David Granskou, eds., *Anti-Judaism in Early Christianity*, vol. I: *Paul and the Gospels* (Studies in Judaism and Christianity 2; Waterloo, Ontario: Wilfrid Laurier University, 1986) 81, similarly posits "a sustained polemic."

[19] J. L. Houlden, *Paul's Letters from Prison: Philippians, Colossians, Philemon, and Ephesians* (WPC; Philadelphia: Westminster, 1977) 41, who nonetheless holds to integrity on grounds that Philippians is an "informal letter, in which the writer . . . allows his thought to hop and drift easily" (95).

[20] Parsicolon in 3:2; chiastic parallelism between 3:2 and 3:3.

[21] I assume Paul has the same opponents – however amorphous a group they

his own net rather widely in 3:18, speaking of "many (πολλοί) . . . who are enemies of the cross of Christ." We have already seen that the opponents of ch. 3 cannot be the political ἀντικείμενοι of 1:28–30, nor the rivals of 1:15–17, whose formulation of the gospel cannot have differed significantly from Paul's. That they practiced circumcision (cf. κατατομή) is clear, and that they engaged in some sort of mission (cf. κακοὶ ἐργάται) is likely.[22] The reference to "enemies of the cross of Christ" in 3:18 may also suggest that Paul's opponents repudiated his claim that suffering leads to knowing Christ (cf. 3:10) and thus embraced a so-called triumphalist Christology.[23] But beyond this Paul's description is vague.[24]

Furthermore, it is not clear whether the opponents of Phil. 3 were an active threat to the Christian community at Philippi, or whether they were simply adduced as foils to Paul's own position.[25] The former view cannot be excluded as a possibility; however, the latter has much to commend it, including the fact that Paul explicitly characterizes the exhortation/warning of ch. 3 as precautionary (ἀσφαλές). Watson has also pointed out that Paul relies almost exclusively in ch. 3 on the force of his own example,[26] which he presumably would not have done if he were concerned that his position had been undermined in the community. This requires, at the very least, that the Philippians have remained loyal to Paul and that, if the opponents are threatening at all, they do so at a distance, the situation at Philippi being nowhere nearly as acute as in Galatia, where Paul's competitors had established a presence in the community. Finally, it should be noted that the high emotion

---

might have been – in view throughout chapter 3. This is the view of Schmithals, Koester, Gnilka, Collange. Against this view, see Robert Jewett, "Conflicting Movements in the Early Church as Reflected in Philippians," *NovT* 12 (1970) 362–90.

[22] The comparison has often been made between κακοὶ ἐργάται here in Phil. 3:2 and ἐργάται δόλιοι (= ψευδαπόστολοι) in 2 Cor. 11:13; cf. further: ὁ μὲν θερισμὸς πολὺς οἱ δὲ ἐργάται ὀλιγοί (Matt. 9:37–8; Lk. 10:2); ἄξιος γὰρ ὁ ἐργάτης τῆς τροφῆς/τοῦ μισθοῦ αὐτοῦ (Matt. 10:10; Lk. 10:7; 1 Tim. 5:18); Lk. 13:27 (ἐργάται ἀδικίας); 2 Tim. 2:15 (ἐργάτης ἀνεπαίσχυντος).

[23] J. Gnilka, "Die antipaulinische Mission in Philippi," *BZ* (1965) 258–76; Collange, *Philippiens*, 110, 120–1.

[24] Thus 3:2: κύνας; 3:19: ὧν τὸ τέλος ἀπώλεια, ὧν . . . ἡ δόξα ἐν τῇ αἰσχύνῃ αὐτῶν, οἱ τὰ ἐπίγεια φρονοῦντες. The reference to the "perfect" in 3:12–16 pertains to a tendency in certain of the Philippians and not in the opponents. In context, the indictment ὧν ὁ θεὸς ἡ κοιλία may well refer to Jewish dietary laws.

[25] D. Garland, "Composition and Unity," 166; G. B. Caird, *Paul's Letters from Prison* (Oxford: Oxford University Press, 1976) 131, and more recently, Stowers, "Friends and Enemies," 116.

[26] "Rhetorical Analysis," 75.

with which Paul writes, and which has led so many interpreters to
assume that he is in the midst of a heated polemic, derives in part at
least from his new topic, "the surpassing greatness of the knowledge of Christ," about which he felt very strongly.[27] Indeed, the
most sustained display of pathos in ch. 3 comes not in Paul's
description of his opponents in 3:2 and 18, but in 3:7–11 where
Paul recounts his desire to gain Christ.[28]

But even if we cannot identify Paul's opponents with any
precision, their function in the larger argument of the chapter is
clear enough. Koester has shown that Paul's description of his
opponents in 3:2 stands in point-for-point contrast to his own
position articulated in 3:3, with "circumcision" (περιτομή) being
the opposite of "mutilation" (κατατομή), "those ministering by the
Spirit of God" (οἱ πνεύματι θεοῦ λατρεύοντες) the opposite of
"evil workers" (κακοὶ ἐργάται), and "those boasting in Christ
Jesus and not taking confidence in the flesh" (καυχώμενοι ἐν
Χριστῷ Ἰησοῦ καὶ οὐκ ἐν σαρκὶ πεποιθότες) the opposite of
"dogs" (κύνες).[29] Koester uses this observation to establish a kind
of external control for interpreting Paul's invective. But the antithetical relationship between verses 2 and 3 that Koester describes
also allows us to locate the opponents of 3:2 in the larger argument
of ch. 3, since the last contrast made in verse 3 is picked up
immediately in verse 4, where it becomes the rubric for the
catalogue of verses 5–6: καίπερ ἐγὼ ἔχων πεποίθησιν καὶ ἐν
σαρκί. εἴ τις δοκεῖ ἄλλος πεποιθέναι καὶ ἐν σαρκί, ἐγὼ μᾶλλον. In
terms of the larger argument, therefore, Paul's opponents in 3:2
represent those who place confidence in the flesh and who therefore
do not boast in Christ Jesus. They constitute an extreme violation
of the exhortation of 3:1a to "rejoice in the Lord."[30]

---

[27] On this point, compare the emotion of 3:2 with that of 3:7–11.

[28] Also, as we shall argue below, the thrust of Paul's argument comes in 3:12–16,
which is not offered in response to the opponents of 3:2, but in response to the
Philippians themselves.

[29] "Purpose of the Polemic," 319–21. Koester uses this as an external control to
interpret Paul's invective. For λατρεύειν in a missionizing sense, cf. Rom. 1:9: ὁ
θεὸς ᾧ λατρεύω ἐν τῷ πνεύματί μου ἐν τῷ εὐαγγελίῳ.

[30] Paul connects "boasting" and "rejoicing" in 1:25–6: καὶ τοῦτο πεποιθὼς οἶδα
ὅτι μενῶ καὶ παραμενῶ πᾶσιν ὑμῖν εἰς τὴν ὑμῶν προκοπὴν καὶ χαρὰν τῆς πίστεως,
ἵνα τὸ καύχημα ὑμῶν περισσεύῃ ἐν Χριστῷ Ἰησοῦ. Schoon-Janßen, *Umstrittene
"Apologien,"* 132; cf. Weiss, *Philipper-Brief,* 226.

Paul's counter-example: "the surpassing greatness of the knowledge of Christ" (Phil. 3:4–16)

As a counter-example to those warned against in 3:2–3, that is, as a positive example of one who has come to "rejoice in the Lord," Paul cites his own testimony in 3:4–16. The testimony falls into two parts. In the first part (3:4–11), Paul reports the change in values he experienced in his conversion from Pharisaic Judaism to Christ.[31] In the second (3:12–16), he reports how this shift in values has continued to inform his life as an apostle. He urges those among the Philippians who consider themselves to be "mature" to adopt a similar set of values.

Paul's testimony relativizing his accomplishments in Judaism to the knowledge of Christ (Phil. 3:4–11)

Paul's conversion to Christ brought with it a radical change in values, and in the first part of his testimony in Phil. 3:4–11 he uses this change to underscore the difference between "boasting in Christ Jesus" (καυχώμενοι ἐν Χριστῷ Ἰησοῦ) and "having confidence in the flesh" (ἐν σαρκὶ πεποιθότες).[32] He treats the notion of "having confidence in the flesh" in 3:4–6, where he lists seven things that made up his former confidence in Judaism. The first four items listed describe his inherited standing: περιτομῇ ὀκταήμερος, ἐκ γένους Ἰσραήλ, φυλῆς βενιαμίν, Ἑβραῖος ἐξ Ἑβραίων (3:5a). The last three mark his personal achievements as a Pharisee: κατὰ νόμον Φαρισαῖος, κατὰ ζῆλος διώκων τὴν ἐκκλησίαν, κατὰ δικαιοσύνην τὴν ἐν νόμῳ γενόμενος ἄμεμπτος (3:5b–6). "Having confidence in the flesh" may thus be defined as placing a high value on one's privileges (e.g., ethnicity and birth) and accomplishments in a particular religion, in this case, Judaism.[33]

---

[31] On the change of values that typically accompanied conversion, especially philosophical conversion, in the ancient world, see Abraham J. Malherbe, "Conversion to Paul's Gospel," in *idem*, Frederick W. Norris and James W. Thompson, eds., *The Early Church in Its Context: Essays in Honor of Everett Ferguson* (NovTSup 90; Leiden: Brill, 1998) 233, who cites: Lucian, *Nigr.* 3–5; *Bis acc.* 17; Hor., *Sat.* 2.3.253–7; Epict., *Diss.* 3.1.14; Diog. Laert., 4.16.

[32] Robert C. Tannehill, *Dying and Rising with Christ: A Study in Pauline Theology* (BZNW 32; Berlin: Töpelmann, 1967) 115; Peter Siber, *Mit Christus leben: Eine Studie zur paulinischen Auferstehungshoffnung* (ATANT 61; Zurich: Theologischer Verlag, 1971) 110.

[33] It has been plausibly suggested that the opponents cautioned against in 3:2 made similar status claims. The parallel to 2 Cor. 11:22–3 is striking: Ἑβραῖοί εἰσιν;

Paul develops the notion of "boasting in Christ Jesus" in 3:7–11.[34] He approaches the topic negatively in verses 7–8 where he describes how boasting in Christ caused him to reject his former values. He traces his "revaluation of values" in three stages. In verse 7 he reports how at his conversion[35] he rejected his earlier confidence as a Pharisee: ἀλλὰ ἅτινα ἦν μοι κέρδη, ταῦτα ἥγημαι διὰ τὸν Χριστὸν ζημίαν.[36] In verse 8a he extends this critique to include all non-Christological bases for confidence: ἀλλὰ μενοῦνγε καὶ ἡγοῦμαι πάντα ζημίαν εἶναι διὰ τὸ ὑπερέχον τῆς γνώσεως Χριστοῦ Ἰησοῦ τοῦ κυρίου μου. Finally, in verse 8b he declares that he has actually lost all things for the sake of Christ and that he has only increased in his contempt for them: δι᾽ ὃν τὰ πάντα ἐζημιώθην, καὶ ἡγοῦμαι σκύβαλα, ἵνα Χριστὸν κερδήσω. At each stage in this progression the values Paul rejects are contrasted with the ideal of knowing Christ[37] or, as he puts it in the final clause of verse 8, of "gaining" Christ. This has become for him the *summum*

κἀγώ. Ἰσραηλῖταί εἰσιν; κἀγώ. σπέρμα Ἀβραάμ εἰσιν; κἀγώ. διάκονοι Χριστοῦ εἰσιν; . . . ὑπὲρ ἐγώ. However, this should not lead us to assume that the claims of Paul's opponents are necessarily mirrored in Paul's list. 2 Cor. 11:22–3 is obviously offered in response to competing claims: Ἑβραῖοί εἰσιν; . . . Ἰσραηλῖταί εἰσιν; . . . σπέρμα Ἀβραάμ εἰσιν; whereas Phil. 3:4 is more general: εἴ τις δοκεῖ ἄλλος πεποιθέναι καὶ ἐν σαρκι, ἐγὼ μᾶλλον.

[34] As the antithesis of "having confidence in the flesh," the expression "boasting in Christ Jesus" must mean at the very least taking pride in the privileges and accomplishments of Christ. Paul goes on to define the expression in terms of knowing Christ. We have seen this expression earlier in Phil. 1:26: ἵνα τὸ καύχημα ὑμῶν περισσεύῃ ἐν Χριστῷ Ἰησοῦ ἐν ἐμοὶ διὰ τῆς ἐμῆς παρουσίας πάλιν πρὸς ὑμᾶς. Here we learn that the Philippians' boasting in Christ is mediated by Paul (ἐν ἐμοί), and in particular by his return to them (διὰ τῆς ἐμῆς παρουσίας πάλιν πρὸς ὑμᾶς). The Philippians do not yet share Paul's radical valuing of Christ, and it is this error that he ultimately attempts to correct in 3:1–4:1.

[35] The use of the perfect ἥγημαι brings the consequences of Paul's change of mind into the present in a way that the aorist ἡγησάμην would not have done; even so Paul's past experience of conversion is in view; cf. Gnilka, *Philipperbrief*, 191.

[36] What Paul means by the phrase διὰ τὸν Χριστόν is not immediately clear. At the very least he is saying that his present experience of Christ has led him to devalue radically his former attainments (cf. 3:8: σκύβαλα). However, the language of "asset" and "liability" suggests something more, namely, that Paul now sees his success in Judaism as having somehow kept him from Christ, either because he felt satisfied in his life as a Pharisee, or because such confidence in the flesh by definition precluded "confidence" in Christ. The fact that Paul here treats the notions of "confidence in the flesh" and "boasting in Christ Jesus" as radically antithetical, even mutually exclusive, suggests the latter view. Cf. Phil. 3:9; Rom. 9:30–2. Against this view, see E. P. Sanders, "Paul on the Law," 78–80.

[37] διὰ τὸν Χριστόν . . . διὰ τὸ ὑπερέχον τῆς γνώσεως Χριστοῦ Ἰησοῦ . . . δι᾽ ὅν . . .

bonum (τὸ ὑπερέχον) in comparison to which all else pales in importance (σκύβαλα!).

Paul treats the positive side of "boasting in Christ" in 3:9–11.[38] He envisions a twofold process. The first part of this process is justification (v. 9): καὶ εὑρεθῶ ἐν αὐτῷ, μὴ ἔχων ἐμὴν δικαιοσύνην τὴν ἐκ νόμου ἀλλὰ τὴν διὰ πίστεως Χριστοῦ, τὴν ἐκ θεοῦ δικαιοσύνην ἐπὶ τῇ πίστει.[39] The second part is a set of experiences of which the ultimate aim is "to know [Christ]" (vv. 10–11):[40]

> τοῦ γνῶναι αὐτὸν καὶ τὴν δύναμιν τῆς ἀναστάσεως αὐτοῦ καὶ [τὴν] κοινωνίαν τῶν παθημάτων αὐτοῦ, συμμορφιζό-μενος τῷ θανάτῳ αὐτοῦ, εἴ πως καταντήσω εἰς τὴν ἐξανάστασιν τὴν ἐκ νεκρῶν.

Here Paul's testimony reaches a climax and recalls the ideal of verse 8a: τὸ ὑπερέχον τῆς γνώσεως Χριστοῦ Ἰησοῦ τοῦ κυρίου μου.

Paul's striking reflections on knowing Christ in 3:10–11 call for comment. Two problems in particular deserve special attention: (1) the unusual arrangement of Paul's ideas, and (2) the tentativeness with which Paul expresses his hope of resurrection in verse 11.[41] The arrangement of verses 10–11 has never been adequately explained, commentators noting the problem, but struggling to offer a definitive solution. Recently, Schenk has proposed that verses 10–11 follow a chiastic arrangement:[42]

(A)   resurrection (τὴν δύναμιν τῆς ἀναστάσεως αὐτοῦ)
(B)   suffering ([τὴν] κοινωνίαν τῶν παθημάτων αὐτοῦ)

[38] Whereas the intensity of the invective in 3:2 subsides immediately in 3:3ff., the intensity reached at the end of 3:8 (cf. σκύβαλα!) is sustained throughout 3:9–11. This is the real source of emotion in 3:1–4:1, not the alleged threat of the "dogs" of 3:2. Indeed, the passion Paul expresses in 3:2 and again in 3:18 is a function of his desire to know Christ described in almost wistful terms in 3:9–11. To put the matter another way, the shift in tone in 3:2ff. (which actually begins in 3:1) derives not from the fact that the epistolary situation has changed, but from the fact that Paul has changed his subject, that he has taken up a topic about which he could not have felt more strongly!

[39] Bonnard, *Philippiens*, 65: "être en Christ n'est pas autre chose que d'avoir (ἔχων) la justice qui vient de Dieu." In keeping with the larger argument Paul here conceives of justification in relational terms ("and might be found in him").

[40] Most commentators agree that the first καί after τοῦ γνῶναι αὐτόν is epexegetical, so that everything from τὴν δύναμιν κτλ., with the possible exception of the last clause (εἴ πως καταντήσω εἰς τὴν ἐξανάστασιν τὴν ἐκ νεκρῶν), explicates the notion of knowing Christ.

[41] Most recently, Otto, "'If Possible I May Attain.'"

[42] *Die Philipperbriefe*, 251, 320. In this he follows Siber, *Mit Christus leben*, cf. Lightfoot, *Philippians*, 150–1; Houlden, *Paul's Letters from Prison*, 107.

(B′)   death (συμμορφιζόμενος τῷ θανάτῳ αὐτοῦ)
(A′)   resurrection (τὴν ἐξανάστασιν τὴν ἐκ νεκρῶν)

The clarity of Schenk's proposal is welcome. But there are difficulties.

Schenk's proposal requires that in the first expression (τὴν δύναμιν
τῆς ἀναστάσεως αὐτοῦ) we emphasize the genitive ἀναστάσεως
and not the accusative δύναμιν. We are no doubt justified in doing
this in the second expression ([τὴν] κοινωνίαν τῶν παθημάτων
αὐτοῦ) where κοινωνίαν by its very meaning looks forward to
παθημάτων. But the semantics of τὴν δύναμιν τῆς ἀναστάσεως
αὐτοῦ are different. Here the emphasis would seem to be upon
δύναμιν, Paul's aim being to know the *power* of Christ's resurrection. A further difficulty lies in the fact that Schenk must equate the
sufferings of Christ (B) and the death of Christ (B′), which Paul
elsewhere does not do.[43] These are not insuperable difficulties, but
perhaps a more natural reading is to see a progression of ideas:
from power (δύναμις), to suffering (παθήματα), to death (θάνατος),
and then finally to resurrection (ἐξανάστασις),[44] each element
marking a more intimate knowledge of Christ through a kind of
shared experience.[45] Paul employs this same progression (from
power, to suffering, to death, to resurrection) in 2 Cor. 4:7–11.[46]

The parallel passage in 2 Cor. 4:7–11 may also help to explain
the tentativeness (εἴ πως) with which Paul expresses his hope of
resurrection in Phil. 3:11. Without exception commentators have
interpreted Phil. 3:11 eschatologically, as a reference to the future
resurrection of the dead. Thus the problem: Paul was not tentative
in his hope of resurrection. However, if we interpret the progression
of terms in Phil. 3:10–11 in light of 2 Cor. 4:7–11, the reference to
resurrection in 3:11 is not to be taken literally and eschatologically,
but metaphorically as the experience of those missionaries of the

[43] O'Brien, *Philippians*, 405–7; cf. Michaelis, πάθημα, *TDNT* V.932 (1967), who
nonetheless forces the chiasm. These terms, suffering and death, should retain their
natural sequential relationship.
[44] On this reading the "power" (δύναμις) of Phil. 3:10 pertains to the power of the
resurrection that enables the believer "to walk in newness of life" (Rom. 6:4).
[45] Note that Paul emphasizes "*his* resurrection . . . *his* sufferings . . . *his* death"
(ἀναστάσεως αὐτοῦ . . . παθημάτων αὐτοῦ . . . θανάτῳ αὐτοῦ).
[46] ἔχομεν δὲ τὸν θησαυρὸν τοῦτον ἐν ὀστρακίνοις σκεύεσιν, ἵνα ἡ ὑπερβολὴ
τῆς **δυνάμεως** ᾖ τοῦ θεοῦ καὶ μὴ ἐξ ἡμῶν· ἐν παντὶ **θλιβόμενοι** ἀλλ' οὐ στενοχωρού-
μενοι . . . πάντοτε τὴν **νέκρωσιν** τοῦ Ἰησοῦ ἐν τῷ σώματι περιφέροντες, ἵνα καὶ ἡ
ζωὴ τοῦ Ἰησοῦ ἐν τῷ σώματι ἡμῶν φανερωθῇ.

gospel who find new life in the midst of extreme conditions. This is the sense of 2 Cor. 4:10–11:

> πάντοτε τὴν νέκρωσιν τοῦ Ἰησοῦ ἐν τῷ σώματι περιφέ-
> ροντες, ἵνα καὶ ἡ ζωὴ τοῦ Ἰησοῦ ἐν τῷ σώματι ἡμῶν
> φανερωθῇ. ἀεὶ γὰρ ἡμεῖς οἱ ζῶντες εἰς θάνατον παραδιδό-
> μεθα διὰ Ἰησοῦν, ἵνα καὶ ἡ ζωὴ τοῦ Ἰησοῦ φανερωθῇ ἐν
> τῇ θνητῇ σαρκὶ ἡμῶν.

In 2 Corinthians this experience is adduced to explain the paradox-ical nature of apostolic existence[47] and is therefore treated as a fact: ὁ ἔξω ἡμῶν ἄνθρωπος διαφθείρεται, ἀλλ᾽ ὁ ἔσω ἡμῶν ἀνακαι-νοῦται ἡμέρᾳ καὶ ἡμέρᾳ (4:16). In Philippians, on the other hand, it is held out as the ultimate experience of those seeking to know Christ. Here it is treated as a goal that is never fully attainable (εἴ πως καταντήσω . . .), a kind of "impossible possibility," to take a phrase from Niebuhr,[48] since it is only those who have actually "departed" who can truly "be with Christ" (so Phil. 1:23).

Paul's testimony relativizing his accomplishments as an apostle to the knowledge of Christ (Phil. 3:12–16)

In the second part of his testimony in Phil. 3:12–16, Paul describes how the change of values that took place at his conversion has continued to inform his life as a Christian apostle. Verses 12–14 are an extended *correctio* (οὐχ ὅτι . . . δέ)[49] developed in two anti-theses, the first of which (v. 12):

---

[47] Erhardt Güttgemanns, *Der leidende Apostel und sein Herr: Studien zur pauli-nischen Christologie* (Göttingen: Vandenhoeck & Ruprecht, 1996) 121–3. However, it is not simply that the life of Jesus is manifest in Paul's suffering, but that Paul himself participates in, is sustained by, that life (ὁ ἔσω ἡμῶν ἀνακαινοῦται ἡμέρᾳ καὶ ἡμέρᾳ).

[48] Reinhold Niebuhr, *An Interpretation of Christian Ethics* (San Francisco: Harper & Row, 1963) 71–83.

[49] *Correctio* (ἐπιδιόρθωσις, ἐπανόρθωσις) took a number of forms and had various uses; cf. H. Lausberg, *Handbuch der literarischen Rhetorik*, 2 vols. (2nd edn.; Munich: Hueber, 1967) §§784–6. Though frequently used, little survives of the ancient discussion of this figure (cf. *Rhet ad Her.* 4.26.36). Quintilian does not discuss the figure, but at *Inst.* 9.3.89 he mentions those who have: Caecilius, Dionysius, Rutilius, Cornificius, Visellius, as well as others who are his contempor-aries. For instances of *correctio* in Paul, see BDF §495.2–3. Paul's concern here is to correct a disposition expressing itself in certain Philippians who are looking to their past achievements in the Pauline mission (see our discussion of the rhetorical situation of the letter in chapter 2 above) and not their ongoing and developing relationship with Christ as their source of satisfaction.

οὐχ ὅτι ἤδη ἔλαβον ἢ ἤδη τετελείωμαι, διώκω δὲ εἰ καὶ καταλάβω, ἐφ᾿ ᾧ καὶ κατελήμφθην ὑπὸ Χριστοῦ Ἰησοῦ,

is significantly amplified in the second (vv. 13–14):

ἀδελφοί, ἐγὼ ἐμαυτὸν οὐ λογίζομαι κατειληφέναι· ἓν δέ, τὰ μὲν ὀπίσω ἐπιλανθανόμενος τοῖς δὲ ἔμπροσθεν ἐπεκτεινόμενος, κατὰ σκοπὸν διώκω εἰς τὸ βραβεῖον τῆς ἄνω κλήσεως τοῦ θεοῦ ἐν Χριστῷ Ἰησοῦ.

Verses 15–16 are a concluding exhortation: ὅσοι οὖν τέλειοι, τοῦτο φρονῶμεν.

Paul identifies himself in verse 12 (the first antithesis) as one who has not yet obtained his goal of fully knowing Christ but who continues to pursue it.[50] The imagery is athletic, in particular that of the race track.[51] He reiterates his lack of attainment in verses 13–14 (the second antithesis), but adds what seems to be his main point. While he has indeed not yet grasped the prize, there is "one

[50] It is often noted that τετελείωμαι is a Pauline hapax, from which it is concluded that the term derives from Paul's opponents, the "dogs" of 3:2, or from a new group appearing (without explanation) in 3:12–16. It is just as likely that the term derives from the Philippians themselves, if in fact it is not Paul's word. The exhortation of 3:15, where the same root appears (τέλειοι), is clearly not directed to the opponents in 3:2, but to certain of the Philippians, most likely, Euodia and Syntyche and others who shared their sense of accomplishment in the Pauline mission. Many ideologies used this terminology in the ancient world, including Stoicism. Stoics like Epictetus and Seneca readily and repeatedly denied that they had attained the perfection of the sage (Sen., *Ad Helv.* 5.2; *Ep.* 83.17 [*perfectus sapiens*]; 109.15 [*perfectus vir*]; 120.12 [*perfectus vir*]; 124.50; cf. *Ep.* 66.45; 76.30; Epict., *Diss.* 2.8.25; 24.9; 3.7.17; cf. 2.23.40; 3.1.25; *Ench.* 51.1–2; cf. Plut., *De Stoic. repugn.* 27.1046E [= SVF 3.299]. On the sage as perfect see Stob., *Ecl.* 2.65.7 [= SVF 1.556]; *Diog. Laert.*, 7.128 [= SVF 1.569]; Philo, *L. A.* 1.93 [= SVF 3.519]). What is perhaps most revealing is that the introduction of perfectionism serves to advance Paul's argument from his devaluing of accomplishments in Judaism to accomplishments in Christianity. Paul's reference to perfectionism has all appearances of being a foil to this argument.

[51] The precise imagery is not clear in verse 12, but it quickly becomes so in verses 13–14. Cf. 1 Cor. 9:24: οὐκ οἴδατε ὅτι οἱ ἐν σταδίῳ τρέχοντες πάντες μὲν τρέχουσιν, εἷς δὲ λαμβάνει τὸ βραβεῖον; οὕτως τρέχετε ἵνα καταλάβητε. Victor C. Pfitzner, *Paul and the Agon Motif. Traditional Athletic Imagery in the Pauline Letters* (NovTSup 16; Leiden: Brill, 1967) 139–53. The traditional interpretation of 3:12–14 understands the race imagery to convey the idea that Paul is not yet finished (perfected) and thus as an argument against a kind of perfectionism. But this misses the point. Paul's concern is with those whose focus has drifted away from Christ, those who do not share his single-minded race toward the goal, those who have not forgotten the things that lie behind, but instead derive their sense of self precisely from these earlier accomplishments and who are now discouraged because these accomplishments have been called into question.

thing" that he has firmly in hand,[52] namely, the single-minded pursuit of his objective: ἐν δέ, τὰ μὲν ὀπίσω ἐπιλανθανόμενος τοῖς δὲ ἔμπροσθεν ἐπεκτεινόμενος. This is the point that Paul has been driving at since 3:4. Others will derive some sense of accomplishment from their past achievements. But Paul purposefully forgets these things – and here his accomplishments as an apostle are in view! – and presses undistractedly ahead.[53] As in 3:9–11, his goal remains to "gain" Christ: κατὰ σκοπὸν διώκω εἰς τὸ βραβεῖον τῆς ἄνω κλήσεως τοῦ θεοῦ ἐν Χριστῷ Ἰησοῦ.

Paul concludes his testimony in 3:15–16 with an exhortation to the "mature" (τέλειοι) among the Philippians – a group in which Paul is willing to include himself (cf. φρονῶμεν) – to follow him in his single-minded pursuit of Christ. Paul obviously has in view those who, like himself, have made significant contributions to the gospel mission and who are thus in a position to derive a sense of accomplishment from their past efforts. Instead of looking to the past, however, they must forget their previous achievements and focus exclusively on what lies ahead.[54] To Paul's mind this was the most fundamental problem at Philippi: a backward-looking emphasis on the mission and not a present and forward-looking emphasis on Christ. Even so, his tone in addressing the Philippians continues to be non-confrontational: καὶ εἴ τι ἑτέρως φρονεῖτε, καὶ τοῦτο ὁ θεὸς ὑμῖν ἀποκαλύψει.[55] Furthermore, he does not lose sight of the very practical problem of disunity: πλὴν εἰς ὃ ἐφθάσαμεν, τῷ αὐτῷ στοιχεῖν.[56]

Exhortation to adopt Paul's Christological values (Phil. 3:17–21)

In Phil. 3:17–21 Paul urges the community as a whole to take his example to heart and offers reasons. In particular, he wishes them

[52] I would supply a κατείληφα after the ἐν δέ. Other suggestions are ποιῶ or διώκω.

[53] The two participles in verse 13, τὰ μὲν ὀπίσω ἐπιλανθανόμενος τοῖς δὲ ἔμπροσθεν ἐπεκτεινόμενος, define κατὰ σκοπόν in verse 14.

[54] That is, "to know" Christ for the time being in suffering, and then finally in the future "to be with Christ" in death (cf. 1:23).

[55] But note the shift from first person (φρονῶμεν) to second person (φρονεῖτε . . . ὑμῖν). Contrast this with Paul's tone toward his opponents in 3:2 and 19.

[56] The reference to unity here is not as tangential as it initially may seem. The rivalry that had come to characterize certain relationships at Philippi derived from an inordinate emphasis on personal accomplishment in the mission, which emphasis Paul is here seeking to correct. Cf. Phil. 4:4–5 where Paul links rejoicing in the Lord with "forbearance" (τὸ ἐπιεικές).

to adopt as a kind of publicly agreed-upon value his ideal of
knowing Christ and to elevate only those who exemplify his model:
συμμιμηταί μου γίνεσθε, ἀδελφοί, καὶ σκοπεῖτε τοὺς οὕτω περιπατοῦντας καθὼς ἔχετε τύπον ἡμᾶς (3:17).⁵⁷ Paul supports his
exhortation with two reasons: (1) the presence of many bad
examples who as "enemies of the cross of Christ" reject the
humiliation and suffering entailed in knowing Christ (3:18–19),
and (2) the Philippians' own heavenly "citizenship" and allegiance
to Christ: ἡμῶν γὰρ τὸ πολίτευμα ἐν οὐρανοῖς ὑπάρξει, ἐξ οὗ καὶ
σωτῆρα ἀπεκδεχόμεθα κύριον Ἰησοῦν Χριστόν (3:20–1).⁵⁸

Paul's exhortation in 3:17 recapitulates his initial charge in 3:1 to
"rejoice in the Lord." It calls upon the Philippians to join Paul in
his single-minded pursuit of Christ and to put into perspective any
measurable contributions that they may have made to the gospel
mission. We have already noted the obvious consolatory value of
this, namely, that it would have afforded the Philippians a source
of joy independent of their successes in the gospel mission. But
since Paul requires the Philippians not only to adopt his ideal for
themselves but to use it as a criterion in evaluating others (cf. καὶ
σκοπεῖτε τοὺς οὕτω περιπατοῦντας καθὼς ἔχετε τύπον ἡμᾶς), the
exhortation of verse 17 would also have challenged the hegemony
of any whose undue emphasis on accomplishment and status in the
mission was causing them to fall short of Paul's standard, which
included among other things the ability to overlook personal
rivalry (1:15–17).⁵⁹ One thinks here of Euodia and Syntyche, whose
quarrel must in some sense have been reducible to personal rivalry,
since they are both commended by Paul for their devotion to his
mission (4:3).⁶⁰

⁵⁷ συμμιμηταί here conveys the sense of becoming "imitators together" and
indicates that Paul wants the Philippians to adopt his single-minded pursuit of Christ
as a community ideal. In the larger context, this implies the replacement of the old
ideal which overvalued one's accomplishments in the gospel ministry with the new
ideal of knowing Christ. The effect of this will be twofold. Most obviously, it will
insulate the community from the "dogs" of 3:2. But it will also challenge the
hegemony of people like Euodia and Syntyche whose undue emphasis on accomplishment and status in the mission and its resulting competitiveness was causing
them to fall short of Paul's standard, which included the ability to overlook personal
rivalry (1:15–17).
⁵⁸ Both πολίτευμα and σωτήρ are political terms. Indeed, Caesar, to whom the
Roman colonists at Philippi owed complete allegiance, was commonly designated
σωτήρ.
⁵⁹ We have already noted the importance of Paul's example in 1:15–17 with
regard to the exhortation of 2:1–4, especially verse 3: μηδὲν κατ' ἐριθείαν.
⁶⁰ Here Paul's twofold objective in writing to the Philippians is again in view. He

It remains to say something about the "enemies of the cross of Christ" in 3:18. This expression may be approached in two ways. One way is to examine Paul's description of these enemies in the next verse: ὧν τὸ τέλος ἀπώλεια, ὧν ὁ θεὸς ἡ κοιλία καὶ ἡ δόξα ἐν τῇ αἰσχύνῃ αὐτῶν, οἱ τὰ ἐπίγεια φρονοῦντες (v. 19). But we learn very little from this contrived list of paradoxes except that Paul wants the Philippians to reject the position of these "enemies" as self-frustrating and absurd.[61] The second and more fruitful approach is to begin with Paul's testimony in 3:4–16, understanding the enemies of the cross in 3:18 to represent those who contradict Paul's Christological ideal. The point of contact with Paul's testimony is thus 3:10 where suffering and even death are embraced as means of knowing Christ.[62] On these grounds one becomes an "enemy of the cross" when one rejects the proposition that those who seek to know Christ must suffer as he did and that this "cross" is to be enthusiastically embraced as leading to the *summum bonum* of knowing Christ. It is possible to imagine various ways in which this false ideology might have manifested itself, but the view that these "enemies of the cross," however amorphous a group they might have been, have significant elements in common with the false apostles of 2 Cor. 10–13,[63] especially a triumphalist Christology, has much to commend it.

Concluding exhortation: "stand thus in the Lord" (Phil. 4:1)

In Phil. 4:1 Paul concludes the second heading of his letter with the exhortation to "stand thus in the Lord" (οὕτως στήκετε ἐν κυρίῳ). We have already noted that this exhortation forms an *inclusio* with 3:1a: χαίρετε ἐν κυρίῳ. It also reiterates the basic point of 3:1a,

---

wanted to console them, but also to exhort them to unity. The exhortation of 3:17 provides an additional basis for consolation while challenging the hegemony of those who were disrupting the community.

[61] The paradoxes of 3:19 reflect Paul's new perspective, his "revaluation of values," as articulated in 3:7–11. Following Paul's conversion the position of his opponents seems absurd. The unconventional values of the Stoics produced analogous paradoxes. Read in light of the reference to circumcision in 3:2 (κατατομή), the indictment ὧν ὁ θεὸς ἡ κοιλία may, however, refer to Jewish dietary laws.

[62] On the basis of 1:29–30 we may surmise that the Philippians had difficulty in accounting for suffering in the gospel mission. In this regard the suffering of Christ in 2:8 and of their representative Epaphroditus in 2:30 takes on special significance.

[63] The κακοὶ ἐργάται of Phil. 3:2 are often compared with the ἐργάται δόλοι of 2 Cor. 11:13. See the discussion of 3:2 above in this chapter.

though without reference to the motif of joy.[64] To rejoice in the Lord is to stand in the Lord in the manner (οὕτως) just described in 3:2–21. The affection that Paul continues to display toward the Philippians reflects his continued awareness of their need for consolation: ἀδελφοί μου ἀγαπητοὶ καὶ ἐπιπόθητοι, χαρὰ καὶ στέφανός μου.

---

[64] But see Paul's description of the Philippians in 4:1a: χαρὰ καὶ στέφανός μου.

7

CONCLUDING PARENESIS, CONSOLATION, AND THANK-YOU NOTE (PHIL. 4:2–23)

Pray to God and do not grieve.   Aesop, *Fab*. 288 Hausrath

Let us not overlook whatever is pleasant and attractive in our present circumstances.   Plutarch, *De tranq. an*. 469A

We come now to the conclusion of Paul's letter to the Philippians (4:2–23). The material may be divided into three parts: (1) concluding parenesis and consolation (4:2–9); (2) a postscripted "thank-you note" (4:10–20); and (3) final greetings (4:21–23). As usual, our exegesis will be selective. In particular, we are interested in (1) how Paul modifies the general parenesis of 4:2–9 to fit his immediate purpose of consolation, and (2) how in 4:10–20 he formally expresses his appreciation for the Philippians' most recent gift while not compromising his stand that he is – and they should be! – independent of such non-essentials.[1]

Concluding parenesis and consolation (Phil. 4:2–9)

Paul frequently concludes his letters with a few words of general exhortation.[2] He follows the same procedure in his letter to the Philippians, but with the exception that in Philippians his exhortations are more obviously linked to the specific circumstances of the letter.[3] He first addresses a dispute between two prominent women in the church, Euodia and Syntyche (4:2–3), after which he offers several consolatory precepts (4:4–9).

[1] In chapter 2 above we identified this as one of two "rhetorical problems" facing Paul in writing to the Philippians, the other being how to rebuke the Philippians for their emotional frailty when what they expect from him are words of encouragement (for which see my comments on Phil. 1:18b–26 and 2:25–30 in chapter 5 above).

[2] E.g. Gal. 5:25–6:10; 1 Thess. 5:14–22.

[3] I do not mean to imply by this any judgment on the specific applicability of Paul's parenesis elsewhere.

In Phil. 4:2–3 Paul identifies Euodia and Syntyche by name and urges them to be reconciled to one another: Εὐοδίαν παρακαλῶ καὶ Συντύχην παρακαλῶ τὸ αὐτὸ φρονεῖν ἐν κυρίῳ. He enlists the aid of a "true yoke-fellow" (γνήσιε σύζυγε), emphasizing Euodia's and Syntyche's previous service in the gospel mission: αἵτινες ἐν τῷ εὐαγγελίῳ συνήθλησάν μοι μετὰ καὶ Κλήμεντος καὶ τῶν λοιπῶν συνεργῶν μου.[4] The precise nature of the dispute between Euodia and Syntyche is not indicated. However, as Nils Dahl has correctly pointed out, Paul's admonition "to mind the same thing in the Lord" (τὸ αὐτὸ φρονεῖν ἐν κυρίῳ) in 4:2 and his reminder that both women had "struggled along with me in the gospel" (ἐν τῷ εὐαγγελίῳ συνήθλησάν μοι) in 4:3, recall his earlier charges to unity in 1:27 (στήκετε ἐν ἑνὶ πνεύματι, μιᾷ ψυχῇ συναθλοῦντες τῇ πίστει τοῦ εὐαγγελίου) and 2:2 (ἵνα τὸ αὐτὸ φρονῆτε, τὴν αὐτὴν ἀγάπην ἔχοντες, σύμψυχοι, τὸ ἓν φρονοῦντες).[5] The rivalry between Euodia and Syntyche also makes particularly relevant Paul's report of personal rivalry in the gospel mission in 1:15–17.[6] It is not surprising that the two people singled out as most disruptive in the church were also two of the most prominent supporters of Paul's mission. As long-term partners with Paul they would have been most negatively affected by his imprisonment.[7]

In 4:4–9 Paul turns to the Philippians as a group, skillfully mixing general parenesis with consolation.[8] He organizes his parenesis around three separate consolatory precepts. They are: (1) to

[4] In 4:2–3 three prominent members of Paul's mission are mentioned by name (Euodia, Syntyche, Clement), while a fourth is referred to as a "true yoke-fellow" (γνήσιε σύζυγε). Unfortunately, none of these can be identified with any certainty. See further the discussion in Pilhofer, *Philippi*, 234–45.

[5] "Euodia and Syntyche," 3–15. Other συν-compounds in 4:3 (σύζυγε . . . συλλαμβάνου . . . συνεργῶν) echo σύμψυχοι in 2:2, as well as Paul's positive description of Epaphroditus in 2:25 (συνεργὸν καὶ συστρατιώτην μου) and Timothy at 2:22 (σὺν ἐμοὶ ἐδούλευσεν).

[6] The reference to rivalry in 1:15–17 (ἐξ ἐρεθείας; 1:17) is also linked to the exhortation to unity in 2:1–4 (κατ᾽ ἐριθείαν; 2:3).

[7] This, as we have already noted (see chapter 2 above), supports our thesis that discouragement over Paul's imprisonment and other apparent setbacks to the mission underlay the fractiousness at Philippi.

[8] In 4:4–9 Paul adroitly weaves together practical counsel with consolation. For example, in 4:5 we find τὸ ἐπιεικὲς ὑμῶν γνωσθήτω πᾶσιν ἀνθρώποις (exhortation) followed by ὁ κύριος ἐγγύς (consolation). Similarly, 4:6: μηδὲν μεριμνᾶτε (exhortation), ἀλλ᾽ ἐν παντὶ τῇ προσευχῇ καὶ τῇ δεήσει μετὰ εὐχαριστίας τὰ αἰτήματα ὑμῶν γνωριζέσθω πρὸς τὸν θεόν (consolation). At other times he formulates specific *solacia* as principles of universal relevance, as in 4:4 where the addition of πάντοτε turns the consolation of 3:1 (χαίρετε ἐν κυρίῳ) into a maxim: χαίρετε ἐν κυρίῳ πάντοτε.

rejoice in the Lord and anticipate his return (4:4–5);[9] (2) to pray with thanksgiving (4:6–7); and (3) to identify what is good in one's circumstances and to "think on these things" (4:8–9).

In 4:4 Paul twice repeats the charge of 3:1 to "rejoice in the Lord": χαίρετε ἐν κυρίῳ πάντοτε· πάλιν ἐρῶ, χαίρετε. He has already interpreted this charge in 3:2–4:1, so he does not explain it here.[10] The addition of πάντοτε turns the earlier charge into a universal maxim, a procedure that Paul uses elsewhere.[11] In 4:5 Paul exhorts the Philippians to apply this Christological perspective to their relations with others: τὸ ἐπιεικὲς ὑμῶν γνωσθήτω πᾶσιν ἀνθρώποις. As in 3:20–1, he adds an eschatological motivation: ὁ κύριος ἐγγύς.

In 4:6–7 Paul offers a second consolatory precept: namely, prayer with thanksgiving. Paul's imprisonment on potentially capital charges, together with their own political persecution, had left the Philippians "anxious" (cf. μηδὲν μεριμνᾶτε).[12] Paul offers them "the peace of God which surpasses all understanding," but only if they will pray: τὰ αἰτήματα ὑμῶν γνωριζέσθω πρὸς τὸν θεόν. Aesop had offered similar advice: εὔχου τῷ θεῷ καὶ μὴ θρήνει.[13] In particular, Paul recommends prayer "with thanksgiving" (μετὰ εὐχαριστίας). Chrysostom comments: "Here is another consolation

---

[9] Note the connection between rejoicing in the Lord and the return of the Lord in 4:4–5. This connection is made earlier in 3:1–21 which begins with the former theme in verses 1ff. and concludes with the latter in verses 20–1.

[10] To rejoice in the Lord means to value the knowledge of Christ (ἡ γνῶσις Χριστοῦ) above all else as the *summum bonum* of Christian existence. This has the effect of radically devaluing all other concerns and is thus consolatory along Stoic lines, as we have already explained.

[11] Paul makes similar additions elsewhere in the final parenetic sections of his letters, most notably in 1 Thess. 5:16–22: **πάντοτε** χαίρετε, **ἀδιαλείπτως** προσεύχεσθε, **ἐν παντὶ** εὐχαριστεῖτε ... **πάντα** δὲ δοκιμάζετε ... **ἀπὸ παντὸς εἴδους** πονηροῦ ἀπέχεσθε. Cf. Phil. 4:6: ἐν παντὶ τῇ προσευχῇ καὶ τῇ δεήσει Col. 4:6: ὁ λόγος ὑμῶν πάντοτε ἐν χάριτι. For the moral maxim (γνώμη, *sentantia*) as a universal sentiment, see Arist., *Ars rhet.* 2.21; *Rhet. ad Alex.* 11.1430b.1; *Rhet. ad Her.* 4.17.24–25; Quint., *Inst.* 8.5.3–8; cf. Ps.-Demetr., *Eloc.* 9; Hermog., *Prog.* 4.24–27; Aphth., *Prog.* 4.67–72; Prisc., *Praeex. rhet.* 3.11–14.

[12] "Anxiety" is a common synonym for "grief" (λύπη, *aegritudo, maeror, tristitia*) in the consolatory literature; but Paul's use of μεριμνάω is somewhat anomalous. The term of choice is φροντίζω, φροντίς; e.g., Ps.-Plut., *Ad Apoll.* 109E (πάσης ἀπαλλαγὴ λύπης καὶ φροντίδος); Cass. Dio 38.20.1. However, μέριμνα does occur; cf. Plut., *De tran. an.* 477E: ἐν ὀδυρμοῖς ... καὶ βαρυθυμίαις καὶ μερίμναις ἐπιπόνοις. For *sollicitudo*, cf. Sen., *Ad Helv.* 17.5; 18.5, 9; *Ad Marc.* 24.4 (with *maeror*); *De. tran. an.* 7.3 (with *tristitia*); 16.1; Cypr., *De mort.* 2.33 (CCSL 3A; with *anxietas*).

[13] *Fab.* 288 Hausrath. Cf. Plut., *Cor.*, 35.2 (230E): ὃ δ' ἔστι ἄλλοις ἀτυχίας πάσης καὶ κακοπραγίας παραμύθιον, εὔχεσθαι θεοῖς.

(παραμυθία), a medicine that heals grief and hardship and all that is painful. And what is it? To pray, to offer thanks in all things."[14] Bultmann is more theoretical: "der Beter in eine eigentümliche Distanz zu seinen Wünschen tritt, wenn er sie μετὰ εὐχαριστίας vor Gott kundtut und sich damit von der Sorge befreit."[15]

To remain thankful (*gratias agere*) in the midst of hardship was a prominent theme in ancient consolation.[16] Cicero speaks of the wise man who "remembers the past with gratitude" and thus endures all suffering with equanimity.[17] Lucretius criticizes those who always crave what is absent and do not appreciate the things at hand.[18] Seneca urges Marcia not to complain about what she has lost, but to "give thanks" (*gratias agere*) for what she has had.[19] He offers similar advice to Polybius: "He is an ungrateful man (*ingratus*) who calls the end of what is pleasant an injustice."[20] He chides Marullus: "Your grief has this among other evils: it is not only useless, but thankless (*ingratus*)."[21] Plutarch reminds his wife, who is mourning with him the death of their young daughter, not to be "ungrateful for what God had given them" (περὶ τοῦ δοθέντος ἀχαριστεῖν).[22] Ingratitude was often construed as grumbling against fate or God, as when Marcus Aurelius exhorts himself to meet death "without grumbling" (μὴ γογγύζων), but "from a heart grateful to the gods" (ἀπὸ καρδίας εὐχάριστος τοῖς θεοῖς).[23] We have, of course, met this theme already in Phil 2:14: πάντα ποιεῖτε χωρὶς γογγυσμῶν.

Paul gives his third and final consolatory precept in 4:8–9 when he advises the Philippians to identify what is good in their present circumstances and to focus their attention on these things (4:8–9a):

---

[14] *In Epist. ad Phil.*, hom. 14.1 (*PG* 62.283.51–4). Chrysostom offers similar advice at *Ep. ad Olymp.* 7.3.4–5 Malingrey: μὴ τοίνυν θορυβοῦ, μηδὲ ταράττου, ἀλλὰ μένε διηνεκῶς ὑπὲρ πάντων αὐτῷ εὐχαριστοῦσα.

[15] *TWNT* 4.595, s.v. ἀμέριμνος.

[16] Johann, *Trauer und Trost*, 85–92.

[17] *De fin.* 1.62; cf. 1.57: *sapientes bona praeterita grata recordatione renovata delectant.* Cf. Epicur., *Sent. Vat.* 55: θεραπευτέον τὰς συμφορὰς τῇ τῶν ἀπολλυμένων χάριτι καὶ τῷ γινώσκειν, ὅτι οὐκ ἔστιν ἄπρακτον ποιῆσαι τὸ γεγονός.

[18] *De rer. nat.* 3.957: *semper aves quod abest, praesentia temnis.* Cf. Cyril Bailey, *Titi Lucreti Cari De rerum natura libri sex. Prolegomena, Critical Apparatus, Translation, and Commentary.* 3 vols. (Oxford: Clarendon, 1947) II:1154, who cites: Epicur., *Sent. Vat.* 14; frag. 490 Usener; Democr., frag. B 202 (Diels and Kranz); Lucr., 3.1082–3.

[19] *Ad Marc.* 12.1–2.   [20] *Ad Poly.* 10.2.

[21] *Ep.* 99.4.   [22] *Ad ux.* 610E.

[23] *Med.* 2.2–3; cf. 2.16; Sen., *Ad Marc.* 10.2; *Ad Poly.* 3.1; Plut., *Ad ux.* 610E–611B; Fronto, *De nepote amisso* 2.2.

150   *Consolation in Philippians*

τὸ λοιπόν,[24] ἀδελφοί, ὅσα ἐστὶν ἀληθῆ, ὅσα σεμνά, ὅσα δίκαια, ὅσα ἁγνά, ὅσα προσφιλῆ, ὅσα εὔφημα, εἴ τις ἀρετὴ καὶ εἴ τις ἔπαινος, ταῦτα λογίζεσθε,[25] ἃ καὶ ἐμάθετε καὶ παρελάβετε καὶ ἠκούσατε καὶ εἴδετε ἐν ἐμοί, ταῦτα πράσσετε.

He again promises peace from God: καὶ ὁ θεὸς τῆς εἰρήνης ἔσται μεθ' ὑμῶν (4:9b).[26] This technique (purposefully focusing on what is good in a difficult situation) is best understood as an instance of the Epicurean method of *avocatio-revocatio*, consolation by turning one's mind away from (*avocatio*) what is painful and to (*revocatio*) what is pleasant.[27] We have already briefly discussed this method above in chapter 3. Let us now consider it in more detail.[28]

Cicero examines Epicurean and Cyrenaic consolation theory together in *Tusc.* 3.13.28–22.52. Unlike the Cyrenaics who understood grief to be the result of unexpected misfortune (*insperatum et necopinatum malum*) and who thus made a practice of anticipating hardship (*praemeditatio futurorum malorum*),[29] Epicurus held that grief is the natural response to misfortune of any kind, unexpected

[24] τὸ λοιπόν marks the third and final consolatory precept (4:8–9).

[25] λογίζομαι typically has the sense of "calculate" or "reckon," but by our period it can also mean simply "think"; cf. MM. BAGD suggests "think about, consider, ponder, let one's mind dwell on." Chrysostom glosses: ἐν τούτοις εἶναι, ταῦτα μεριμνᾶν, ταῦτα ἐννοεῖν (*PG* 62.286.25–6). Chrysostom uses the term in connection with the technique of *avocatio* at *Ep. ad Olymp.* 1.1.9–11 Malingrey: ταῦτ' οὖν καὶ αὐτὴ λογιζομένη, δέσποινά μου θεοφιλεστάτη, ὑψηλοτέρα γίνου τῶν θορύβων τούτων καὶ τῶν κλυδώνων; and again at 7.5.39–41: καὶ καλὴν ἀσχολουμένη ἀσχολίαν (= λογίσασθαι μετὰ τῶν λυπηρῶν τὰ χρηστὰ [from lines 33–4]) οὕτως ἀπαγαγεῖν σαυτὴν τῆς ἀθυμίας· πολλὴν γὰρ καὶ ἐντεῦθεν δέξῃ τὴν παράκλησιν. In the latter instance it seems to retain its sense of "reckon" or "take into account." Seneca uses *computare* to similar effect at *Ep.* 99.4: *Sed plerique non computant, quanta perceperint, quantum gavisi sint*. We will discuss the second part of Paul's admonition – ἃ καὶ ἐμάθετε καὶ παρελάβετε καὶ ἠκούσατε καὶ εἴδετε ἐν ἐμοί, ταῦτα πράσσετε – below.

[26] Cf. 4:7. It might be objected that 4:9b is Paul's concluding "peace wish" (cf. Rom. 15:33; 16:20a; 2 Cor. 13:11; Gal. 6:16; 1 Thess. 5:23; cf. Eph. 6:23; 2 Thess. 3:16) and is thus not consolatory. But these are not mutually exclusive propositions, especially when we observe that the so-called "wish" of 4:9b is actually a "promise" (note the future tense: ἔσται) like 4:7 (φρουρήσει; cf. 2 Cor. 13:11).

[27] In addition to my description of this technique below, see Kassel, *Untersuchungen*, 31–2; Grollios, *Ad Marciam*, 26–7, 66, 86–8, 91; Johann, *Trauer und Trost*, index, s.v. *avocatio-revocatio*.

[28] The following largely reproduces my earlier study, "*Bona Cogitare*."

[29] *Tusc.* 3.13.28–14.29. See our discussion of the Cyrenaic theory of consolation above in chapters 3 and 5 (regarding Phil. 1:28–30). For the *praemeditatio* in Paul, see Malherbe, *Paul and the Thessalonians*, 57–8, who cites 1 Thess. 3:3–4 (cf. Phil. 1:28–30).

or otherwise, and that to anticipate hardship, far from preparing us for its arrival, only adds to our current sorrows (*Tusc.* 3.15.32). According to Epicurus the only way to avoid grief is to distract the mind from hardship by the contemplation of pleasure: *avocatione a cogitanda molestia et revocatione ad contemplandas voluptates.*[30]

Cicero raises a number of objections to Epicurus' method.[31] First, he says, it is unrealistic: "under the sting of circumstances which we regard as evil – circumstances that tear us, vex us, goad us, burn us, leave us unable to breathe – concealment or forgetfulness is not within our control."[32] Second, it is philosophically irresponsible: "Do you urge me to forget? This is contrary to nature!" Primarily, though, it is morally bankrupt:[33]

> You bid me to reflect on good things (*bona cogitare*) and to forget evil things. There would be something in what you say and something worthy of a great philosopher, were you sensible that those things are good which are most worthy of a human being (*ea bona esse, quae essent homine dignissima*) . . . But you are turning my thoughts towards pleasures (*ad voluptates*).

Cicero rejects Epicurus' method as it stands. But he does not reject the principle *bona cogitare* as such, provided that the goods in question are not the false goods of pleasure but the real goods of virtue. The result is a modified (Academic) form of the *avocatio-revocatio*: "But if, Epicurus, you call me back (*revocas*) to these goods (sc. courage, self-control, justice, prudence), I obey, I follow, I make you my leader, I shall even forget evil, as you urge".[34]

[30] *Tusc.* 3.15.33 (= 444 Usener); cf. 3.31.76: *Sunt qui abducant a malis ad bona, ut Epicurus*; 5.26.73–4: *se dicit [Epicurus] recordatione acquiescere praeteritarum voluptatum*; *De fin.* 1.57 (Torquatus speaking): *Est autem situm in nobis ut et adversa quasi perpetua oblivione abruamus et secunda iucunde ac suaviter meminerimus.* See chapter 3 above.

[31] *Tusc.* 3.16.34–21.51; cf. *De fin.* 2.30.96–8.

[32] Written within a year of Tullia's death, Cicero's words here obviously recall his unbearable loss. In his truly elegant letter of consolation to Cicero (*Ad fam.* 4.5) Servius Sulpicius Rufus had urged: *Etiam tu ab hisce rebus animum ac cogitationem tuam avoca, atque ea potius reminiscere, quae digna tua persona sunt*, but to no avail. See Cicero's pathetic reply at *Ad fam.* 4.6.2–3.

[33] *Tusc.* 3.16.35–3.17.37.

[34] *Tusc.* 3.17.37. Cicero's willingness to "forget evil" here seems to contradict his earlier criticism that to forget is contrary to nature. This may indeed be the case, done for rhetorical effect. However, under his modified version of the *avocatio* the evils "forgotten" need not be real evils any longer, but matters of indifference relative to the true goods (= the virtues) being contemplated.

Epicurus' method was popular with consolers, who were always
eclectic in their counsel.³⁵ Seneca, for instance, employs it in each
of his formal consolations. In the *Ad Polybium* he twice develops
the technique at length (chaps. 5–8 and 12–13),³⁶ urging Polybius
to direct his thoughts away from his brother's death to family
duties (5.4–5), public office (6.1–5), service to Caesar (7.1–4 and
12.3–13.4), literary pursuits (8.1–4 and 11.5–6), pleasant memories
of his brother (10.6), and, finally, his surviving brothers, wife, and
son (12.1–2). Similarly, in the *Ad Helviam matrem* he directs his
mother's attention away from his exile to her other sons who
remain with her (18.1–3), her grandchildren (18.4–6), especially
Novatilla who will soon bear her great-grandchildren (18.7–8), the
memory of her father (18.9), and her sister (19.1–7). In the *Ad
Marciam*, he criticizes Octavia who, after the death of Marcellus,
did not permit herself to be distracted (*avocari*) from her grief
(2.3–4) and recalls the philosopher Areus' counsel to Livia on the
death of Drusus that she remember the good times and occupy
herself with her children and grandchildren (4.3–5.6). He returns to
the theme in 24.1–4.³⁷ Twice, however, Seneca follows Cicero's
counsel and recommends the contemplation of virtue. Thus at *Ad
Poly.* 18.7 he writes: "Think about his modesty, think about his
ingenuity . . . his industry . . . his steadfastness."³⁸ And at *Ad
Marc.* 24.3–4: "Start thinking of him not in terms of his years, but
in terms of his virtues . . . and by the contemplation of these hold
your son as it were in your breast."³⁹

³⁵ *Tusc.* 3.31.76: *ut fere nos in Consolatione omnia in consolationem unam
coniecimus*; of *Ad Att.* 12.14.3.
³⁶ Johann, *Trauer und Trost*, 150–5. Seneca criticizes the method in its grosser
forms at *Ad. Helv.* 17.2. At *Ad Marc.* 1.5, 8 he refers to it as the "soft" (*molliter*)
approach to consolation. In open defiance of Epicurus he begins both *Ad Helv.*
(2.4–4.1) and *Ad Marc.* (1.2–5) by evoking past pain (!) in an effort "to conquer
grief not cheat it" (*vincere dolorem . . . non circumscribere*; *Ad Helv.* 4.1). Chrysostom
makes a similar beginning in *Ep. ad Olymp.* 7.1 Malingrey.
³⁷ The method may also be in view in 12.1–2; thus Grollios, *Ad Marciam*, 52–4;
cf. Abel, *Bauformen*, 26: "Die verschiedenen Erscheinungsformen des avocatio-
revocatio-Motivs bilden eine Kette, die sich über den ganzen Hauptteil (c. 2–25)
spannt." But see Johann, *Trauer und Trost*, 92. Elsewhere in Seneca: *Ep.* 63.4
(Attalus); 99.3–5; cf. *De ira*, 3.39.4; *De brev. vit.* 10.2ff.; *De vit. beat.* 6.1–2; *De benef.*
3.4.1.
³⁸ *Cogita modestiam eius, cogita . . . sollertiam . . . industriam . . . constantiam.*
³⁹ *Incipe virtutibus illum non annis aestimare . . . Harum contemplatione virtutum
filium gere quasi sinu!* Cf. Cic., *Ad fam.* 4.13: *Reliquum est, ut consoler et afferam
rationes, quibus te a molestiis coner abducere . . . quid sit forti et sapienti homine
dignum, quid gravitas, quid altitudo animi, quid acta tua vita, quid studia, quid artes . . .*;
Jer., *Ep.* 60.7.3: *ita in parvo isto volumine cernas adumbrata, non expressa, signa*

Plutarch also makes repeated use of Epicurus' method. He devotes a lengthy paragraph to the subject at *De tran. an.* 468F–469D, where in language reminiscent of Phil. 4:8 he urges Paccius "not to overlook whatever is pleasant and attractive in our current circumstances" (τὸ μὴ παρορᾶν ὅσα προσφιλῆ καὶ ἀστεῖα πάρεστιν ἡμῖν) and thus always to mix the good with the bad. Similarly at *De ex.* 600D he writes:

> Those of us who possess understanding make life more pleasant and potable by pouring good things into the bad, whereas with most, like filters, the worst things remain and stick to them while the best things flow away.

Again at *Ad ux.* 610E:[40]

> The person who in cases like this tries his best to remember his blessings, turning his mind way from (μεταστρέφων) dark and disturbing things and diverting it to (μεταφέρων) the bright and shining things of life, either extinguishes grief altogether or, by mixing it with these things, makes it small and dim by comparison.

Elsewhere the technique of *avocatio-revocatio* occurs in pseudo-Ovid, pseudo-Plutarch, Pliny, and Julian,[41] and in early Christian literature, in Ambrose, Jerome, Basil, and Paulinus of Nola.[42] Let us return to Phil. 4:8–9. We are now in a position not only to identify the consolation of 4:8–9 but also to describe its relationship to 4:6–7, to which it is linked by its almost identical promise of divine peace. In 4:6–7 Paul promises the Philippians peace if they will tell their worries to God, while at the same time not forgetting to thank him for his blessings.[43] But there is something else that

---

virtutum; Ps.-Phalaris, *Ep.* 103.1–2: Τοῦ πένθους τίνα ἄν τις ἄλλην ἱκανωτέραν ὑμῖν παράκλησιν εἰσενέγκοιτο, ὦ παῖδες, ἢ τὴν ἀρετὴν τοῦ γονέως, ἐφ᾽ ᾧ γε τὸ πένθος φέρεσθε; οὐ γὰρ δακρύεσθαι τὰ Στησιχόρου πρέπον, ἀλλ᾽ ὑμνεῖσθαι . . . φρονεῖτε μὲν ἄξια τοῦ τεκνώσαντος.

[40] Cf. 608A–B.

[41] Ps.-Ov., *Cons. ad Liv.* 377–400 and 411–16; cf. Schoonhoven, *AD LIVIAM*, 178–82; Ps.-Plut., *Ad Apoll.* 116A–B; Pliny, *Ep.* 8.5.2; Jul., *Or.* 8.246C–E.

[42] Ambr., *Exc. Sat.* 1.3; Jer., *Ep.* 60.7.3; 108.1.2; 118.4.2; Bas., *Ep.* 5.2; 269.2; Paul. Nol., *Ep.* 13.6; cited in Scourfield, *Consoling Heliodorus*, 133–4.

[43] To remain thankful (*gratias agere*) in the midst of hardship is not only a prominent theme in ancient consolation in general but in the *avocatio-revocatio* in particular: Cic., *De fin.* 1.57, 62; Lucr. 3.931–67, esp. 957ff.; Sen., *Ep.* 99.3–5; *Ad Marc.* 12.1–2; *Ad Poly.* 10.2; Plut., *Ad ux.* 610E–611D; cf. Johann, *Trauer und Trost*, 85–92.

they can do to fight anxiety. Having thanked God for what is good in their current circumstances, they can let their minds dwell upon these things: ὅσα ἐστὶν ἀληθῆ, ὅσα σεμνά, ὅσα δίκαια, ὅσα ἁγνά, ὅσα προσφιλῆ, ὅσα εὔφημα, εἴ τις ἀρετὴ καὶ εἴ τις ἔπαινος, ταῦτα λογίζεσθε (4:8). Here Paul employs Epicurus' *bona cogitare* (ταῦτα λογίζεσθε), but in its Academic (Ciceronean) version: namely, that we turn our minds not to the false goods of pleasure but to the real goods of virtue.[44] We have already noted the striking similarity between Paul's language in 4:8 and Plutarch's articulation of the *avocatio-revocatio* at *De tranquillitate animi* 469A: τὸ μὴ παρορᾶν ὅσα προσφιλῆ καὶ ἀστεῖα πάρεστιν ἡμῖν.[45] But even more importantly, Paul models this technique himself in Phil. 1:12–21 when he refuses to dwell on the (conventional) evils of his imprisonment but focuses instead on the (real) good of the gospel's continued progress. Following his own advice to contemplate the good, he develops a list of positive things that have resulted from his imprisonment and "rejoices"[46] in them: his enhanced reputation as a servant of Christ (1:13), the increased courage of other Christians (1:14), the unhindered proclamation of Christ, even by those whose motives are less than noble (1:15–18a), as well as the unique opportunity prison has given him to magnify Christ ἐν τῷ σώματι (1:18b–20).[47] The consolatory precept of Phil. 4:8 thus recalls the consolatory arguments of 1:12–20.[48]

This leaves us to account for the correlative exhortation of 4:9a – ἃ καὶ ἐμάθετε καὶ παρελάβετε καὶ ἠκούσατε καὶ εἴδετε ἐν ἐμοί, ταῦτα πράσσετε – which may be read in one of two ways. It is

[44] Indeed, the nearest analogy to the *Tugendkatalog* of Phil. 4:8 is *Tusc.* 5.23.67: *omnia quae pulcra, honesta, praeclara.* Paul's use of this established technique may account for the vocabulary of 4:8 which, as has often been observed, is decidedly un-Pauline.

[45] Cf. Sen., *Ad Poly.* 10.3: *quicquid nos umquam delectavit reducendum ac frequenti cogitatione pertractandum est.*

[46] For the language of "joy" in the context of the *avocatio-revocatio*, see: Sen., *Ad. Marc.* 3.4 (*laetam*); *Ad Poly.* 10.6 (*gaude . . . gaudere*); *Ep.* 99.3 (*gauderes*); Plut., *De tran. an.* 469D (χαίρειν); Ambr., *Exc. Sat.* 1.3 (*laetandum . . . est*); Jer., *Ep.* 60.7 (*gaudeas*).

[47] As it turns out, these are the things that really matter (τὰ διαφέροντα). Here Paul, like Cicero, brings together both Epicurean and Stoic consolation theory: ταῦτα λογίζεσθε (= *bona cogitare*) becomes τά διαφέροντα λογίζεσθε.

[48] In a similar way the precept of 4:4 (χαίρετε ἐν κυρίῳ πάντοτε) recalls the consolation of 3:1ff. (χαίρετε ἐν κυρίῳ). The precept of 4:6 (to pray μετὰ εὐχαριστίας) may also have in view the injunction of 2:14 (πάντα ποιεῖτε χωρὶς γογγυσμῶν), grumbling being the antithesis of thanksgiving.

possible that Paul here simply adds that virtue is to be practiced (πράσσετε) as well as contemplated (λογίζεσθε) and offers himself as an example. But it is likelier, I think, that he has something more specific in mind. The last two verbs in verse 9a (ἠκούσατε καὶ εἴδετε ἐν ἐμοί) echo 1:30 (οἷον [ἀγῶνα] εἴδετε ἐν ἐμοὶ καὶ νῦν ἀκούετε ἐν ἐμοί) where what the Philippians have seen and heard is Paul's patient endurance of suffering, including, as we have just observed, his choice to focus on what is (really) good in his circumstances and not what is (conventionally) bad (1:12–21). This suggests that 4:9a is an exhortation to follow Paul's example of managing hardship.[49] If this is the case, then what the Philippians "learned and received" (the first two verbs of verse 9a) will include such things as Paul's confidence in God's protective oversight of his mission (cf. 1:6), his belief that hardship in the ministry is a gift (1:8; 1:29) not to be grumbled at (2:13–14), and his firm conviction that suffering leads to knowing Christ (3:10) – views that give theological substance to his instruction to focus on what is good in any given situation.[50]

A postscripted thank-you note (Phil. 4:10–20)

Phil. 4:10–20 constitutes Paul's formal acknowledgment of the Philippians' gift. It is considered by many scholars to have been originally a separate document. However, there is much to tie it to the rest of the canonical letter, the argument of which it both assumes and completes.[51] We will treat it as a postscripted thank-you note,[52]

---

[49] Paul would thus be moving from precept in 4:8 to example in 4:9a. Consolatory arguments typically took this form (*praecepta* followed by *exempla*). Seneca reverses the order in *Ad Marciam*, but only after apologizing for doing so: *Scio a praeceptis incipere omnis, qui monere aliquem volunt, in exemplis desinere* (2.1). Abel, *Bauformen*, 74, 84–91, has argued that Seneca's *Ad Poly.* follows this principle exactly, chs. 1–11 being "der praecepta-Abschnitt" and chs. 14–17 "der exempla-Abschnitt"; he is followed by Kurth, *Senecas Trostschrift*, 23; cf. Johann, *Trauer und Trost*, 150–5; Atkinson, "Seneca's 'Consolatio ad Polybium,'" 867–9. See also, Cic., *Tusc.* 3.23.56; Ov., *Ex Pont.* 1.3.27, 61.

[50] Cf. Rom. 8:28; 1 Cor. 13:5.

[51] See chapter 1 above.

[52] Cf. Phil. 2:19–24 which Dibelius, *An die Philipper*, 65, interprets as "eine Art Empfehlungsbrief für Timotheus," that is nonetheless a part of the original letter; cf. Gnilka, *Philipperbrief*, 157; Collange, *Philippiens*, 103. It makes sense, if in the course of a letter Paul wants, say, to recommend Timothy or to thank the Philippians, (1) that this would form a discrete unit, and (2) that it would follow, more or less, the set form for such letters.

composed at the same time as the rest of the canonical letter, and possibly written in Paul's own hand.[53]

Phil. 4:10–20 falls naturally into three parts: (1) a report of the joy which Paul felt upon his receipt of the Philippians' gift, followed immediately by a *correctio* (οὐχ ὅτι) in which Paul affirms his indifference to external circumstances (vv. 10–13); (2) further commendation of the Philippians for their support, followed by a second *correctio* (οὐχ ὅτι) reaffirming Paul's independence of such gifts (vv. 14–17); and (3) an explicit acknowledgment of the Philippians' gift as having fully met all of Paul's needs, together with a promise that God will provide for the Philippians' own needs (vv. 18–20). It is striking that in thanking the Philippians for their gift Paul twice insists upon his own self-sufficiency (4:11–13, 17).

Paul's initial expression of appreciation in Phil. 4:10–13 may be divided into two parts: the expression of appreciation itself in verse 10, and Paul's immediate qualification of it in verses 11–13. It has often been noted that in verse 10 Paul does not explicitly thank the Philippians for their gift,[54] but reports that he "rejoiced greatly" at their continued concern for him: ἐχάρην δὲ ἐν κυρίῳ μεγάλως ὅτι ἤδη ποτὲ ἀνεθάλετε τὸ ὑπὲρ ἐμοῦ φρονεῖν, ἐφ' ᾧ καὶ ἐφρονεῖτε, ἠκαιρεῖσθε δέ.[55] This has led a number of scholars to label Phil. 4:10–20 as a kind of "dankloser Dank"[56] and to seek an explanation for this in Greco-Roman conventions of giving and receiving.[57] However, too much should not be made of this omission.[58] Paul

---

[53] For the possibility that Phil. 4:10–20 is a so-called epistolary autograph, see Harry Gamble, Jr., *The Textual History of the Letter to the Romans* (Grand Rapids: Eerdmans, 1997) 94, 145–6; Jeffrey A. D. Weima, *Neglected Endings: The Significance of the Pauline Letter Closings* (JSNTSS 101; Sheffield: JSOT Press, 1994) 123–4, who cites as comparable autographs, BGU 1.183, 2.526, 3.910; PGiss. 97; PPrinc. 71; Cic., *Ad Att.* 11.24; 12.28; 12.32. Cf. Gordon J. Bahr, "Subscriptions in the Pauline Letters," *JBL* 87 (1968) 98.

[54] Using some form of εὐχαριστῶ or some other comparable expression such as χάριν ἔχω or χάρις ὑμῖν.

[55] Cf. Sen., *De benef.* 2.32.2 and 4.40.3 on the *topos* of lacking opportunity; Berry, "Friendship Language," 109.

[56] Dibelius, *An die Philipper*, 95; Lohmeyer, *An die Philipper*, 178; Gnilka, *Philipperbrief*, 173; cf. Peterman, "'Thankless Thanks': The Epistolary and Social Convention in Philippians 4:10–20," *TynB* 42 (1991) 261–2.

[57] See the survey of scholarship in Bormann, *Philippi*, 161–205; Peterman, *Paul's Gift*, 9–15.

[58] Paul's appreciation of the Philippians' support is clearly stated in 4:10 (ἐχάρην . . . μεγάλως), and again in 4:14 (πλὴν καλῶς ἐποιήσατε συγκοινωνήσαντές μου τῇ θλίψει), as it was at the very beginning of the letter in 1:4–5 (μετὰ χαρᾶς . . . ἐπὶ τῇ κοινωνίᾳ ὑμῶν εἰς τὸ εὐαγγέλιον ἀπὸ πρώτης ἡμέρας ἄχρι τοῦ νῦν). In 4:18 Paul

here merely adapts a current epistolary idiom for the receipt of a letter[59] to his own purposes of acknowledging the Philippians' gift. He employs the same terminology to express his appreciation of the Philippians' gift earlier in 1:4–5: μετὰ χαρᾶς . . . ἐπι τῇ κοινωνίᾳ ὑμῶν εἰς τὸ εὐαγγέλιον ἀπὸ τῆς πρώτης ἡμέρας ἄχρι τοῦ νῦν.[60] At this late point in the letter he must also take into account the argument he has been making since 1:12 that material circumstances should be treated with relative indifference. Paul's choice of idiom allows him to apply his theology of joy to the problem of the gift, focusing not on the gift itself but on the Philippians and their continued care for him.[61]

Paul's concern not to contradict his earlier argument regarding external circumstances becomes readily evident in the *correctio* of 4:11–13. Having expressed his appreciation of the Philippians' gift, he immediately asserts his self-sufficiency (v. 11): οὐχ ὅτι καθ᾽ ὑστέρησιν λέγω, ἐγὼ γὰρ ἔμαθον ἐν οἷς εἰμι αὐτάρκης εἶναι. He is independent of his circumstances, whether those circumstances might be construed as positive or negative (v. 12): οἶδα καὶ ταπεινοῦσθαι, οἶδα καὶ περισσεύειν· ἐν παντὶ καὶ πᾶσιν μεμύημαι, καὶ χορτάζεσθαι καὶ πεινᾶν καὶ περισσεύειν καὶ ὑστερεῖσθαι.[62] Paul appreciates the Philippians' concern for him, but his appreci-

---

commends the gift itself: πεπλήρωμαι δεξάμενος παρὰ Ἐπαφροδίτου τὰ παρ᾽ ὑμῶν, ὀσμὴν εὐωδίας, θυσίαν δεκτήν, εὐάρεστον τῷ θεῷ. Friends could dispense with explicit expressions of thanks: cf. PMert 1.12: γράφειν δέ σοι μεγάλας εὐχαριστίας παρετέο(ν)· δεῖ γὰρ τοῖς μὴ φίλοις οὖσι διὰ λόγων εὐχαριστεῖν (cited by Berry, "Friendship Language," 108 n. 5); Peterman, "Thankless Thanks"; *idem, Paul's Gift*, 73–83.

[59] The expression "I rejoiced greatly" (variously expressed as ἐχάρην μεγάλως, ἐχάρην λίαν λίαν, or ἐχάρην πολλά) is found in contemporary letters as the response to a letter received; Koskenniemi, *Studien*, 74–6. Paul no doubt chose this expression to continue the theme of "joy" that characterizes the rest of his letter. On the possibility of choosing an epistolary idiom to reflect one's philosophical commitments, see Sen., *Ep.* 59, who winces at the "Epicurean" idiom: *magna ex epistula tua percepi voluptatem*.

[60] Here Paul also seems to substitute joy for thankfulness: εὐχαριστῶ τῷ θεῷ μου . . . μετὰ χαρᾶς τὴν δέησιν ποιούμενος. See my discussion of this text above in chapter 4. Schenk, *Die Philipperbriefe*, 43, sees ἐχάρην μεγάλως in Phil. 4:10 as semantically equivalent to εὐχαριστῶ.

[61] It is instructive to observe what Paul does and does not make the object of joy in Philippians. At various points in the letter he either rejoices in or wants to rejoice in the progress of the gospel, his own "salvation," and the Philippians' unity.

[62] For Paul's use of *peristasis* catalogues, also referred to as hardship catalogues, see Malherbe, "Hellenistic Moralists," 298–9, 236–7 n. 280; Fitzgerald, *Cracks*. Phil. 4:12 is unique in that Paul asserts in it his indifference not only to hardship but to times of abundance as well, which in the context has its most immediate reference to the Philippians' gift.

ation must not be misinterpreted as implying any wavering on his part in his the conviction that it is only the progress of the gospel (ch. 1) and the knowledge of Christ (ch. 3) that really matter. Paul's use of μεμύημαι ("I have learned [the secret]") suggests that his self-sufficiency is a kind of "secret" or μυστήριον that he has learned and not a discipline that he has acquired through practice (ἄσκησις).[63] Paul distinguishes his self-sufficiency as being from God (v. 13): πάντα ἰσχύω ἐν τῷ ἐνδυναμοῦντί με.[64]

In Phil. 4:14–17 Paul again commends the Philippians for their support (vv. 14–16) while continuing to stress his indifference to the gift itself (v. 17).[65] This time, however, the emphasis falls upon his appreciation for the Philippians and not upon his own self-sufficiency.[66] Paul's assertion of self-sufficiency in 4:11–13 could easily have offended the Philippians, as if he were saying, "Thanks for the gift, but, of course, I did not need it."[67] Indeed Seneca

---

[63] In Hellenistic philosophy (Stoicism, Epicureanism, Cynicism) self-sufficiency, while based in the knowledge afforded by the particular philosophy, was viewed as arising primarily through training and practice. Paul's choice of μεμύημαι, however, seems to locate his self-sufficiency almost exclusively in the realm of knowledge (cf. 1:9: ἐν ἐπιγνώσει καὶ πάσῃ αἰσθήσει 3:8: γνῶσις Χριστοῦ and 3:10: τοῦ γνῶναι αὐτόν).

[64] Here Paul differs radically from most Stoic authors; cf. Sevenster, *Paul and Seneca*, 111; Gnilka, *Philipperbrief*, 176. But see Berry, "Friendship Language," 115 n. 36 who cites Epict., *Diss.* 1.6.14–15, as an example of a Stoic who traced his inner strength to God; cf. more generally, Fitzgerald, *Cracks*, 70–87, 169–72, 204–5.

[65] Like Phil. 4:10–13, Phil. 4:14–17 may be divided into an expression of appreciation (vv. 14–16) that is immediately qualified (v. 17).

[66] In 4:10–13 Paul devotes one verse (v. 10) to expressing his appreciation and three verses (vv. 11–13) to asserting his self-sufficiency. In 4:14–17 this is reversed. He devotes three verses (vv. 14–16) to expressing appreciation and only one (v. 17) to qualifying it.

[67] Malherbe, "Paul's Self-Sufficiency," 135–9, has argued that Paul's assertion of self-sufficiency in Phil. 4:11 does not draw upon Stoic ideas but upon ancient friendship theory. In particular, he argues that Paul's concern in 4:11 is to clarify his friendship with the Philippians, which in the final analysis is non-utilitarian (i.e., not need-based). Malherbe's detailed exposition of the *topos* of self-sufficiency in ancient friendship theory is expert and informative. However, I am unconvinced by his exegesis of Philippians 4:10–20. Paul is not here concerned to define his relationship with the Philippians in non-utilitarian terms, but to thank the Philippians for their gift without undermining his earlier argument that one's external circumstances do not matter. It is to this end that he is constrained to assert his independence of the Philippians' gift, even though such an assertion carries with it certain problems (cf. 4:14–16). Thus Paul's assertion of self-sufficiency in 4:11, like his consolation in the letter as a whole, reflects a kind of modified Stoicism. It is perhaps significant that Malherbe's argument, if I have understood it correctly, inadvertently assumes that Paul either used Stoic terminology in 4:11 in a strictly technical sense or did not use it at all, as for instance when he writes on p. 138 that "[t]here is no Stoic introspection present here [= 4:11] despite the long exegetical tradition that has

describes just such a response at *De benef.* 2.24.2–3: "Others accept
a gift disdainfully, as one who says: I really do not need it, but
because you so much want to give it to me, I will submit my will to
yours."[68] In order to prevent such a misunderstanding, Paul
quickly reaffirms his appreciation of the Philippians' generosity
which has distinguished them since the beginning of his mission to
Macedonia and Achaia (vv. 14–16):[69]

πλὴν καλῶς ἐποιήσατε συγκοινωνήσαντές μου τῇ θλίψει.
οἴδατε δὲ καὶ ὑμεῖς, Φιλιππήσιοι, ὅτι ἐν ἀρχῇ τοῦ εὐαγγελίου, ὅτε ἐξῆλθον ἀπὸ Μακεδονίας, οὐδεμία μοι
ἐκκλησία ἐκοινώνησεν εἰς λόγον δόσεως καὶ λήμψεως εἰ
μὴ ὑμεῖς μόνοι, ὅτι καὶ ἐν Θεσσαλονίκῃ καὶ ἅπαξ καὶ δὶς
εἰς τὴν χρείαν μοι ἐπέμψατε

Even so, Paul wishes to be clear that it is not the Philippians' gift as
such that he values, but rather the spiritual benefits that will accrue
to them because of their generosity (v. 17): οὐχ ὅτι ἐπιζητῶ τὸ
δόμα, ἀλλὰ ἐπιζητῶ τὸν καρπὸν τὸν πλεονάζοντα εἰς λόγον
ὑμῶν.[70]

In Phil. 4:18–20 Paul acknowledges the Philippians' gift as
sufficient to meet his needs and promises that God himself will
meet the needs of the Philippians. Paul has thus far only spoken
obliquely of the gift,[71] first as an expression of the Philippians'
continued concern for him (τὸ ὑπὲρ ἐμοῦ φρονεῖν; 4:10), and then
as proof of their solidarity with him in suffering (συγκοινωνήσαντές μου τῇ θλίψει; 4:14). He now explicitly certifies his receipt
of the gift, which, following the idiom of the day, he praises
excessively: ἀπέχω δὲ πάντα καὶ περισσεύω· πεπλήρωμαι δεξάμενος παρὰ Ἐπαφροδίτου τὰ παρ' ὑμῶν. But even here it is not the

brought the Stoic notion into play," which requires that the lack of introspection in
4:11–13 argues decisively against a "Stoic" use of the term.
[68] *Alius accipit fastidiose, tamquam qui dicat: Non quidem mihi opus est, sed quia
tam valde vis, faciam tibi mei potestatem.* Peterman, *Paul's Gift*, 144 n. 126.
[69] Here again, however, the emphasis is not on the gift itself but on the disposition
of the Philippians who by their act of generosity have "shared" in Paul's affliction.
Cf. Phil. 1:5: ἐπὶ τῇ κοινωνίᾳ ὑμῶν εἰς τὸ εὐαγγέλιον ἀπὸ τῆς πρώτης ἡμέρας ἄχρι
τοῦ νῦν. See the comments on Phil. 4:15–16 above in chapter 2.
[70] It is typical to see in Paul's words here a claim that he is not operating from
materialistic motives. In the larger context, however, this should be read as a further
claim that he is indifferent to such things. Phil. 4:17 (οὐχ ὅτι . . .) is clearly parallel
to Phil. 4:11 (οὐχ ὅτι . . .) where Paul's point is his αὐτάρκεια (11b–13). Paul's use
of commercial language (e.g., ἐπιζητῶ τὸ δόμα in the sense of seeking payment;
λόγος as "account") has often been noted.
[71] He mentions τὸ δόμα explicitly in the *correctio* of verse 17.

gift itself that impresses Paul, but the gift in its spiritual and theological significance: ὀσμὴν εὐωδίας, θυσίαν δεκτήν, εὐάρεστον τῷ θεῷ.[72] Paul promises the Philippians that God will in turn meet their needs, reciprocating as it were on Paul's behalf: ὁ δὲ θεός μου πληρώσει πᾶσαν χρείαν ὑμῶν κατὰ τὸ πλοῦτος αὐτοῦ ἐν δόξῃ ἐν Χριστῷ Ἰησοῦ.[73]

Final greetings (Phil. 4:21–3)

Paul concludes his letter with the typical greetings (21–2) and benediction (23). He sends his greetings to each believer at Philippi (21a). He adds a greeting from "the brothers with me" (21b) and then mentions "especially those from Caesar's household" (22) as further evidence of his successes in prison. His final prayer – ἡ χάρις τοῦ κυρίου Ἰησοῦ Χριστοῦ μετὰ τοῦ πνεύματος ὑμῶν – should probably be understood in the larger context of the letter as a prayer for consolation.

[72] See the discussion in Peterman, *Paul's Gift*, 153–7.

[73] This is probably the point of *"my* God" (ὁ θεός μου) in verse 19; Lightfoot, *Philippians*, 167. Cf. Prov. 19:17 LXX: δανίζει θεῷ ὁ ἐλεῶν πτωχόν, κατὰ δὲ τὸ δόμα αὐτοῦ ἀνταποδώσει αὐτῷ (cited by Peterman, *Paul's Gift*, 155).

CONCLUSION: AN ANALYSIS OF
PHILIPPIANS

We have argued that Philippians is a letter of consolation written to answer the Philippians' discouragement over Paul's imprisonment and their own suffering for the gospel. We have identified a number of consolatory topics and arguments in the letter, and we have also identified Paul's principal consolatory strategy, adumbrated in the prayer-report of 1:9–11, that the Philippians will be able to replace their grief with joy if they will follow Paul in distinguishing between the things that matter and the things that do not. We have also found that, if the letter is thus understood, the apparent redactional break in 3:1–2 is easily resolved and Philippians reads as a unified document. We now offer, by way of conclusion, the following synopsis of the letter summarizing our interpretation.

I. Epistolary prescript (1:1–2)

II. Introductory thanksgiving period with intercessory prayer-report (1:3–11)

A. Thanksgiving proper (1:3–6): Paul thanks God for the Philippians' continued support of his mission. His imprisonment notwithstanding, he remains confident that through God's providential oversight the mission will succeed.

B. Digression (1:7–8): Paul defends his continued obvious affection for the Philippians, which has been made all the more appropriate by their partnership in the grace of suffering.

C. Intercessory prayer-report (1:9–11): Paul's prayer for the Philippians is that they might learn to discern the things that really matter (τὰ διαφέροντα). Paul here announces his principal consolatory strategy: if the Philippians will focus on the things that truly matter they will have occasion to rejoice, not to grieve.

III.   Letter body: on discerning things that matter (1:12–4:9)

A. First heading. Discerning things that matter in the gospel mission or rejoicing in the "progress" of the gospel and the "salvation" of the gospel missionary (1:12–2:30)

Summary: the first heading extends from 1:12 to 2:30 and concerns the immediate problem of Paul's imprisonment and the effects this has had on the Philippians. The Philippians have allowed themselves to be discouraged by things that do not really matter, such as Paul's imprisonment, and have failed to find encouragement in the things that do matter, such as the progress of the gospel and Paul's own fearless witness for Christ (1:12–26). Paul therefore urges the Philippians to a renewed resolve to endure suffering for the sake of the gospel (1:27–30). He furthermore exhorts them to correct certain defects that have recently manifested themselves in the congregation, defects that Paul attributes to their discouragement, offering for their imitation the example of Christ, as well as Timothy and Epaphroditus (2:1–30).

1. First consolatory argument: the distinction between what does and does not matter is applied to Paul's imprisonment. Paul's imprisonment does not matter; the progress of the gospel does. The Philippians should not be disturbed by the former and should rejoice in the latter (1:12–18a).

2. Second consolatory argument: the distinction between what does and does not matter is applied to Paul's possible execution. Paul's death does not matter; his continued bold speech does. The Philippians should not be disturbed by the former and should rejoice in the latter (1:18b–21).

3. Third consolatory argument (with ironic rebuke): Paul assures the Philippians that they will see him again. Indeed, their present failure to make progress in his absence has guaranteed it (1:22–6).

4. Correction: even before they see Paul again the Philippians should correct their present behavior. They should

no longer be disoriented by their opponents knowing that Paul too suffered and is now suffering in a similar manner (1:27–30).

5. Related exhortation: the disturbances within the congregation at Philippi are traceable in Paul's mind to their confusion over the place of suffering in the gospel ministry. Given the consolation of 1:12–30, these disturbances should now stop (2:1–30).

(a) Exhortation: The Philippians should humble themselves with respect to others, putting others first (σκο-ποῦντες τὰ ἑτέρων; 2:1–4).

(b) Example: Christ is an example of humility toward others (μορφὴν δούλου λαβών) and submissive obedience toward God (ὑπήκοος μέχρι θανάτου; 2:5–11). N.B. The example of Christ supports the exhortation that precedes it as well as that which follows it.

(c) Exhortation: the Philippians should submit to their hardships in obedience to God. Should Paul be sacrificed, they should rejoice with him in this (2:12–18).

(d) Consolation and example: Paul plans to send Timothy soon and hopes that he too will come before long. This should encourage the Philippians. The Philippians will find in Timothy a further example of Christ's humble service to others (ἐδούλευσεν), of one who cares genuinely for the things of others (τὰ περὶ ὑμῶν μερι-μνήσει; 2:19–24).

(e) Consolation and example: Paul is now sending Epaphroditus back to Philippi. Paul hopes that this too will encourage the Philippians (ἵνα ἰδόντες αὐτὸν πάλιν χαρῆτε). The Philippians will find in Epaphroditus a further example of Christ's self-sacrificing obedience (διὰ τὸ ἔργον Χριστοῦ μέχρι θανάτου ἤγγισεν; 2:25–30).

B. Second heading. Discerning the one thing that matters in the Christian life or rejoicing in the Lord (3:1–4:1)

Summary: the second heading extends from 3:1 to 4:1 and concerns a more fundamental problem. The Philippians' discouragement over perceived setbacks to the gospel mission signals a deeper problem: namely, a failure on their part to discern what matters at the level of Christian existence *per se*. Here what really matters is knowing Christ.

1. Introductory exhortation: χαίρετε ἐν κυρίῳ (3:1).

2. Warning: the Philippians should be on alert regarding those who place their confidence in the flesh (3:2–3).

3. Example: Paul radically de-values his religious accomplishments in Judaism for the sake of the "knowledge of Christ" (3:4–11).

4. Example: Paul also disregards his present accomplishments as a Christian apostle for the "upward call of God in Christ Jesus" (3:12–16).

5. Exhortation: The Philippians are to follow Paul in de-valuing worldly accomplishments. These are radically relativized by the prospect of our future transformation to be σύμμορφοι with Christ (3:17–21).

6. Concluding summary statement: the Philippians are to stand firm ἐν κυρίῳ (4:1).

C. Concluding parenesis (4:2–9)

1. Specific advice: the reconciliation of Euodia and Syntyche (4:2–3).

2. General advice on consolation: rejoice in the Lord always (4:4–5); pray with thanksgiving (4:6–7); look for the good in a given situation (4:8–9).

IV. Postscripted note of thanks (4:10–20)

Summary: Paul concludes his letter with an expression of thanks to the Philippians for their recent gift. Recalling the thanksgiving period of 1:3–11, Paul is careful to emphasize the Philippians' historic participation in the gospel. He is clear, however, that his appreciation of their gift is not to be construed as undue dependence on things that do not matter. Paul may have written this "note" in his own hand.

V. Final greetings and benediction (4:21–3)

BIBLIOGRAPHY

Reference works

Bauer, W. *A Greek–English Lexicon of the New Testament and Other Early Christian Literature*. Trans. and rev. W. F. Arndt, F. W. Gingrich, and F. W. Danker. 2nd edn. Chicago: University of Chicago Press, 1979.

Berkowitz, Luci and Karl A. Squitier, eds. *Thesaurus Linguae Graecae Canon of Greek Authors and Works*. 3rd edn. New York and Oxford: Oxford University Press, 1990.

Blass F. and A. Debrunner. *A Greek Grammar of the New Testament and Other Early Christian Literature*. Trans. and rev. R. W. Funk. Chicago: University of Chicago Press, 1961.

Cross, F. L., ed. *The Oxford Dictionary of the Christian Church*. 3rd edn. Ed. E. A. Livingstone. Oxford: Oxford University Press, 1997.

Delatte, Louis, et al., eds. *Lucius Annaeus Seneca. Opera Philosophica: Index Verborum*. 2 vols. Hildesheim; New York: George Olms, 1981.

Di Berardino, Angelo, ed. *Encyclopedia of the Early Church*. Trans. Adrian Walford, with a foreword and bibliographic amendments by W. H. Fremd. 2 vols. New York: Oxford University Press, 1992.

Flaschar, Hellmut, ed. *Grundriss der Geschichte der Philosophie. Antike*, vol. IV/1,2: *Die hellenistische Philosophie*. New edn. Basel: Schwabe, 1994.

Frede, Hermann Josef. *Vetus Latina*, vol. I/1: *Kirchenschriftsteller: Verzeichnis und Sigel*. Frieburg: Herder, 1981.

Freedman, David Noel, et al., eds. *The Anchor Bible Dictionary*. 6 vols. New York: Doubleday, 1992.

Galling, K. von, ed. *Die Religion in Geschichte und Gegenwart*. 6 vols. 3rd edn. Tübingen: Mohr (Siebeck), 1957–62.

Glare, P. G. W. *Oxford Latin Dictionary*. Oxford: Clarendon, 1982.

Hornblower, Simon and Antony Spawforth, eds. *The Oxford Classical Dictionary*. 3rd edn. Oxford: Oxford University Press, 1996.

Kittel, G., ed. *Theological Dictionary of the New Testament*. Trans. G. Bromiley. 10 vols. Grand Rapids: Eerdmans, 1964–76.

Theologisches Wörterbuch zum Neuen Testament. 10 vols. Stuttgart: Kohlhammer, 1935–79.

Klauser, T., E. Dassmann, et al., eds. *Reallexikon für Antike und Christentum*. 14 vols. Stuttgart: Hiersemann, 1950–.

Lampe, G. W. H. *A Patristic Greek Lexicon*. Oxford: Clarendon, 1961.
Lausberg, H. *Handbuch der literarischen Rhetorik*. 2 vols. 2nd edn. Munich: Hueber, 1967.
Lewis, Charlton T. and Charles Short. *A New Latin Dictionary*. New York: Harper; Oxford: Clarendon, 1892.
Liddell, H. G. and R. Scott. *A Greek-English Lexicon*. Oxford: Clarendon, 1940.
Liddell, H. G, et al., eds. *A Greek–English Lexicon. Revised Supplement*. Ed. and rev. P. G. W. Glare and A. A. Thompson. Oxford: Clarendon, 1996.
Mergeut, Hugo, ed. *Lexikon zu den philosophischen Schriften Ciceros*. 3 vols. Jena: Fischer, 1887–94. Reprint, Hildesheim: George Olms, 1961.
Moulton, J. H., W. F. Howard, and N. Turner. *A Grammar of New Testament Greek*. 4 vols. Edinburgh: T. & T. Clark, 1906–76.
Moulton, J. H. and G. Milligan. *The Vocabulary of the Greek New Testament Illustrated from the Papyri and Other Non-Literary Sources*. London: Hodder, 1930.
Wissowa, G., W. Kroll, et al., eds. *Paulys Realencyclopädie der classischen Altertumswissenschaft*. 24 vols., 19 vols., and supplement (15 vols.). Stuttgart: Metzler; Munich: Druckenmüller, 1893–1980.

Primary sources: texts, editions, translations

The Acts of the Christian Martyrs. Ed. and trans. Herbert Musurillo. Oxford: Clarendon, 1972.
Claudii Aeliani Varia historia. Ed. Mervin R. Dilts. BT. Leipzig: Teubner, 1974.
Corpus fabularum Aesopicarum. Ed. August Hausrath and Herbert Hunger. 1 vol. in 2 parts. BT. Leipzig: Teubner. I/1, 2nd edn., 1920; I/2 1959.
Aesopi fabulae. Ed. Aemilius Chambry. 2 vols. Paris: Belles Lettres, 1925, 1926.
Ägyptische Urkunden aus den königlichen Museen zu Berlin: Griechische Urkunden. Berlin: Weidmann, 1895–1937.
Alcinoos. Enseignement des doctrines de Platon. Ed. John Whittaker. Trans. Pierre Louis. Paris: Belles Lettres, 1990.
Alcinous. The Handbook of Platonism. Ed. John Dillon. Oxford: Clarendon, 1993.
Alexandri Aphrodisiensis in Aristotelis Topicorum libris octo commentaria. Ed. M. Wallies. Commentaria in Aristotelem Graeca, 2. Berlin: Reimeri, 1891.
Sancti Ambrosii Opera. Ed. C. Schenkl, et al. CSEL 32, 62, 64, 73, 78–9, 82. Vindobonae: Tempsky, 1897–.
Andronici [Rhodii] qui fertur libelli περὶ παθῶν. Pt. 1 (*De affectibus*). Ed. X. Kreuttner. Heidelberg: Winter, 1884.
Andronici Rhodii qui fertur libelli περὶ παθῶν. Pt. 2 (*De virtutibus et vitiis*). Ed. K Schuchhardt. Darmstadt: Wintert, 1883.
The Meditations of the Emperor Marcus Antonius. Ed. and trans. A. S. L. Farquharson. 2 vols. Oxford: Clarendon, 1944.

The Communings with Himself of Marcus Aurelius Antoninus, Emperor of Rome. Trans. C. R. Haines. Rev. edn. LCL Cambridge, MA: Harvard; London: Heinemann, 1930.

The Letters of Apollonius of Tyana. A Critical Text with Prolegomena, Translation and Commentary. Ed. R. J. Penella. Leiden: Brill, 1979.

The Apostolic Fathers. Ed. J. B. Lightfoot. 2 parts in 5 vols. London and New York: Macmillan, 1889–90. Reprint, Hildesheim: Olms, 1973.

The Apostolic Fathers. Trans. Kirsopp Lake. 2 vols. LCL. New York: Putnam's Sons and Macmillan, 1912–13.

Die apostolischen Väter. Ed. F. X. Funk and K. Bihlmeyer. 3rd edn. SAQ n.s. 1. Tübingen: Mohr (Siebeck), 1970.

[Aristotle]. *Rhetorica ad Alexandrum*. Trans. H. Rackham. LCL (vol. with *Aristotle. Problems II*). Cambridge, MA: Harvard; London: Heinemann, 1937.

Aristotle. Trans. H. P. Cooke, H. Tredennick, et al. 23 vols. LCL. Cambridge, MA: Harvard; London: Heinemann, 1938–60.

Athenaeus. Deipnosophistae. Trans. C. B. Gulick. 7 vols. LCL. Cambridge, MA: Harvard; London: Heinemann, 1927–41.

S. Aurelii Augustini Hipponiensis Episcopi Epistulae. Ed. A. Goldbacher. CSEL 34/1–2. Vindobonae: Tempsky, 1895–98.

Sancti Aurelii Augustini Enarrationes in Psalmos. CCSL 38–40. Turnhout: Brepols, 1956.

St. Basil. The Letters. Trans. Roy J. Deferrari. 4 vols. Cambridge, MA: Harvard; London: Heinemann, 1926.

Biblia Sacra Iuxta Vulgatam Versionem. Ed. B. Fischer, et al. 2 vols. Stuttgart: Württembergische Bibelanstalt, 1975.

Catalogue général des antiquités égyptiennes du Musée du Caire. Zenon Papyri. Ed. C. C. Edgar. 3 vols. Cairo: Impr. de l'Institute français, 1925–28.

Catalogue of the Syriac MSS. in the Convent of S. Catherine on Mount Sinai. Ed. A. S. Lewis. Studia Sinaitica 1. London: C. J. Clay, 1894, 4–16.

Catullus, Tibullus and Pervigilium Veneris. Trans. Francis W. Cornish, et al. 2nd edn. G. P. Goold. Cambridge, MA: Harvard: London: Heinemann, 1988.

Jean Chrysostome: Lettres à Olympias; vie d'Olympias. Ed. and trans. Anne-Marie Malingrey. 2nd edn. SC 13. Paris: Editions du Cerf, 1968.

Cicero. Trans. G. L. Hendrickson, H. M. Hubbell, et al. 28 vols. LCL. Cambridge, MA: Harvard; London: Heinemann, 1912–72.

[Cicero]. *Ad C. Herennium De ratione dicendi (Rhetorica ad Herennium)*. Trans. H. Caplan. LCL. Cambridge, MA: Harvard; London: Heinemann, 1954.

Clementis De praedicationibus Petri inter peregrinandum epitome. Migne, *PG* 2.57–468.

The Cynic Epistles: A Study Edition. Ed. and trans. Abraham J. Malherbe, et al. SBLSBS 12. Missoula, MT: Scholars Press, 1977.

Thasci Caecili Cypriani De mortalitate: A Commentary. Mary Louise Hannan. Catholic University of America Patristic Studies 36. Washington, D.C.: Catholic University of America, 1933.

Cyprian. Treatises. Trans. and ed. Roy J. Deferrari, et al. Fathers of the Church 36. New York: Fathers of the Church, 1958.

Sancti Cypriani Episcopi Opera. Ed. C. Moreschini. 4 vols. CCSL 3, 3A–C. Turnhout: Brepols, 1972–96.

The Letters of St. Cyprian of Carthage. Trans. G. W. Clarke. ACW 43–4, 46–7. New York: Newman, 1984–.

The Dead Sea Scrolls: Hebrew, Aramaic, and Greek Texts with English Translation, vol. I: *Rule of the Community and Related Documents.* Ed. James H. Charlesworth. Tübingen: Mohr (Siebeck); Louisville: Westminster John Knox, 1994.

Demetrii et Libanii qui feruntur ΤΥΠΟΙ ΕΠΙΣΤΟΛΙΚΟΙ *et* ΕΠΙΣΤΟΛΙΜΑΙΟΙ ΧΑΡΑΚΤΗΡΕΣ. Ed. V. Weichert. BT. Leipzig: Teubner, 1910.

Demetrius. On Style. Trans. W. R. Roberts. LCL. In Aristotle vol. XXIII, *The Poetics.* Cambridge, MA: Harvard: London: Heinemann, 1927.

Demosthenes. Trans. J. H. Vince, C. A. Vince, et al. 7 vols. LCL New York: Putnam's Sons; Cambridge, MA: Harvard; London: Heinemann, 1930–49.

Dio Cassius: Roman History. Trans. E. Cary. 9 vols. LCL. Cambridge, MA: Harvard; London: Heinemann, 1914–27.

Dio Chrysostom. Trans. J. W. Cohoon and H. L. Crosby. 5 vols. LCL. Cambridge, MA: Harvard; London: Heinemann, 1932–51.

Diodorus Siculus. Trans. C. H. Oldfather, C. L. Sherman, et al. 12 vols. LCL. New York: Putnam's Sons; Cambridge, MA: Harvard; London: Heinemann, 1933–67.

Diogenes Laertius: Lives of Eminent Philosophers. Trans. R. D. Hicks. 2 vols. LCL. Cambridge, MA: Harvard; London: Heinemann, 1925.

Elephantine-Papyri. Ed. O. Rubensohn. *Ägyptische Urkunden aus den königlichen Museen zu Berlin: Griechische Urkunden.* Sonderheft. Berlin: Weidmann, 1907.

Ennianae Poesis Reliquiae. Ed. Johann Vahlen. 2nd edn. BT. Leipzig: Teubner, 1928. Reprint, Amsterdam: Hakkert, 1967.

The Tragedies of Ennius. Ed. and trans. H. D. Jocelyn. Cambridge Classical Texts and Commentaries 10. London: Cambridge University Press, 1967.

Epicteti Dissertationes ab Arriano digestae. Ed. Heinrich Schenkl. 2nd edn. BT. Stuttgart: Teubner, 1916.

Epictetus. Trans. William A. Oldfather. LCL. 2 vols. New York: Putnam's Sons; London: Heinemann, 1926, 1928.

Epicurea. Ed. Hermann Usener. Leipzig: Teubner, 1887. Reprint, Stuttgart, 1966.

Epicurus: The Extant Remains. Ed. and trans. Cyril Bailey. Oxford: Clarendon, 1926.

Epicuro: Opere. Ed. Graziano Arrighetti. Biblioteca di cultura filosofica 41. 2nd edn. Torino: Einaudi, 1983.

The Ancient Epistolary Theorists. Trans. Abraham J. Malherbe. SBLSBS 19. Atlanta: Scholars Press, 1988. Originally in *Ohio Journal of Religious Studies* 5 (1977) 3–77.

Epistolographi Graeci. Ed. Rudolf Hercher. Bibliotheca scriptorum Graecorum. Paris: Didot, 1873.

Eusebius Werke. Achter Band. Praeparatio Evangelica. Ed. K. Mras. GCS. Berlin: Akademie-Verlag, 1956.

Favorino di Arelate. Opere: Introduzione, Testo Critico e Commento. Ed. and trans. Adelmo Barigazzi. Florence: Monnier, 1966.

Fragmenta philosophorum Graecorum. Ed. F. W. A. Mullach. 3 vols. Paris: Didot, 1860–81.

Die Fragmente der griechischen Historiker. Ed. Felix Jacoby. 3 vols. Berlin: Weidmann; Leiden: Brill, 1923–58.

Die Fragmente der Vorsokratiker. Ed. H. Diels and W. Kranz. 3 vols. 6th edn. Berlin: Weidmann, 1974–75.

The Correspondence of Marcus Cornelius Fronto. Trans. C. R. Haines. 2 vols. LCL. Cambridge, MA: Harvard; London: Heinemann, 1910–20.

Galen. On the Doctrines of Hippocrates and Plato. Third Part: Commentary and Indexes. Ed. Phillip De Lacy. Corpus Medicorum Graecorum V 4,1,2. Berlin: Akademie-Verlag, 1984.

Greek Papyri in the British Museum. Ed. F. G. Kenyon and H. I. Bell. London: British Museum, 1893–1927.

Funeral Orations by Saint Gregory Nazianzen and Saint Ambrose. Trans. Leo P. McCauley, et al. Fathers of the Church 22. New York: Fathers of the Church, 1953.

Gregorii Theologi vulgo Nazianzeni Opera quae exstant omnia. Migne, *PG* 35–7.

Gregory of Nyssa. Opera. Ed. Werner Jaeger. Berlin: Weidmann, 1921–.

Griechische Papyri im Museum des oberhessischen Geschichtsvereins zu Giessen. Ed. O. Eger, et al. Leipzig and Berlin: Teubner, 1910–12.

Himerii Declamationes et orationes cum deperditarum fragmentis. Ed. Aristides Colonna. Rome: Publica Officina Polygraphica, 1951.

Oeuvres Complètes d'Hippocrate. Ed. E. Littre. 10 vols. Paris: Baillière, 1839–61.

Homer. The Iliad. Trans. A. J. Murray. 2 vols. LCL. New York: Putnam's Sons; London: Heinemann, 1924.

Homer. The Odyssey. Trans. A. J. Murray. 2 vols. Rev. edn. Ed. George E. Dimock. LCL. Cambridge, MA and London: Harvard, 1995.

A Commentary on Horace: Odes Book I. Ed. R. G. M. Nisbet and Margaret Hubbard. Oxford: Clarendon, 1970. *Odes Book II.* Oxford: Clarendon, 1978.

Hyperidis orationes sex. Ed. C. Jensen. BT. Leipzig: Teubner, 1917.

Die Inschriften von Priene. Ed. Hiller von Gaertringen. Berlin: Georg Reimer, 1906.

Inscriptions grecques et latines de Syrie Ed. H. W. Waddington. Paris: F. Didot, 1870.

Sancti Eusebii Hieronymi De viris illustribus. Ed. E. C. Richardson. TU 14.1. Leipzig: Hinrich, 1896.

    Epistulae. Ed. Isidorus Hilberg. CSEL 54, 55, 56/1–2. Vindobonae: Österreichischen Akademie der Wissenschaften, 1996.

Josephus. Trans. H. St. Thackery, R. Marcus, and L. H. Feldman. 9 vols. LCL. Cambridge, MA: Harvard; London: Heinemann, 1956–65.

L'Empereur Julien. Oeuvres complètes. Ed. and trans. J. Bidez, Gabriel

Rochefort, and Christian Lacombrade. 4 vols. Paris: Belles Lettres, 1932–64.

L. *Caeli Firmiani Lactanti Opera omnia*. Ed. Samuel Brandt and George Laubmann. 2 vols. CSEL 19, 27. Vindobonae: Tempsky; Lipsiae: Freytag, 1890–97.

Libanii Opera. Ed. R. Foerster. 12 vols. BT. Leipzig: Teubner, 1903–27.

Titi Lucreti Cari De rerum natura libri sex. Ed. and trans. Cyril Bailey. 3 vols. Oxford: Clarendon, 1947.

Lysias. Trans. W. R. M. Lamb. LCL. Cambridge, MA: Harvard; London: Heinemann, 1930.

Martial. Epigrams. Ed. and trans. D. R. Schackleton Bailey. 3 vols. LCL Cambridge, MA and London: Harvard, 1993.

The Dissertations of Maximus of Tyre. Trans. T. Taylor. 2 vols. London: Whittingham, 1804.

Maximus Tyrius. Dissertationes. Ed. M. B. Trapp. BT. Stuttgart and Leipzig: Teubner, 1994.

Menander Rhetor. Ed. and trans. D. A. Russell and N. G. Wilson. Oxford: Clarendon, 1981.

C. Musonius Rufus. Reliquiae. Ed. Otto Hense. BT. Leipzig: Teubner, 1905. Reprint, 1990.

"Musonius Rufus. 'The Roman Socrates.'" Ed. and trans. Cora E. Lutz. *YCS* 10 (1947) 1–47.

Nemesii Emeseni De natura hominis. Ed. M Morani. BT. Leipzig: Teubner, 1987.

Novum Testamentum Graece. Ed. Barbara and Kurt Aland, et al. 27th edn. Stuttgart: Deutsche Bibelgesellschaft, 1993.

Novum Testamentum Latine. Ed. I. Wordsworth and H. I. White. Oxford: Oxford University Press, 1913–41.

The Old Testament Pseudepigrapha. Ed. J. H. Charlesworth. 2 vols. Garden City, NY: Doubleday, 1983–85.

Ovid. Metamorphoses. Trans. Frank Justus Miller. 2nd edn. LCL. Cambridge, MA: Harvard; London: Heinemann, 1921.

   The Art of Love and Other Poems. Trans. J. H. Mosley. 2nd edn. Ed. G. P. Goold. Cambridge, MA: Harvard; London: Heinemann, 1979.

   Tristia, Ex Ponto. Trans. Arthur Leslie Wheeler. 2nd edn. Ed. G. P. Goold. Cambridge, MA: Harvard; London: Heinemann, 1988.

   Sorrows of an Exile. Tristia. Trans. A. D. Melville. Intro. by E. J. Kenny. Oxford: Clarendon, 1992.

The Pseudo-Ovidian AD LIVIAM DE MORTE DRUSI (Consolatio ad Liviam, Epicedium Drusi) A Critical Text with Introduction and Commentary. Ed. Henk Schoonhoven. Groningen: Forsten, 1992.

The Oxyrhynchus Papyri. Ed. B. P. Greenfell and A. S. Hunt, et al. London: Egypt Exploration Fund, 1989–.

The Letters of St. Paulinus of Nola. Trans. P. G. Walsh. 2 vols. ACW 35–6. Westminster, MD: Newman, 1966–67.

The Poems of St. Paulinus of Nola. Trans. P. G. Walsh. ACW 40. Westminster, MD: Newman, 1975.

I carmi Paulino di Nola. Ed. and trans. Andrea Riggiero. 2 vols. Strenae Nolanae 6–7; Napoli: LER, 1996.

Philo. Trans. Francis H. Colson, George H. Whitaker, and Ralph Marcus. LCL. 12 vols. New York: G. P. Putnam's Sons; London: Heinemann, 1929–62.

"Philodemos über die Götter, Erstes Buch." Ed. H. Diels. APAW 1916, philosophisch-historische Klasse, Number 7.

"Philodemos über die Götter, Drittes Buch." Ed. H. Diels. APAW 1917, Number 4.

Philodemus Over den Dood. Ed. Taco Kuiper. Amsterdam: J. H. Paris, 1925.

Philodemi Adversus [Sophistae]. Ed. F. Sbordone. Naples: Loffredo, 1947.

The Odes of Pindar. Ed. John Sandys. 3rd edn. LCL. Cambridge, MA: Harvard; London: Heinemann, 1937. Reprint 1961.

Pindari Carmina. Ed. B. Snell and H. Maehler. 2 vols. BT. Leipzig: Teubner, 1971.

Plato. Trans. H. N. Fowler, W. R. M. Lamb, et al. 12 vols. LCL. Cambridge: Harvard: London: Heinemann, 1914–35.

The Axiochus: On Death and Immortality, A Platonic Dialogue. Ed. and trans. E. H. Blakeney. London: Muller, 1937.

Pseudo Platone Erissa (= Eryxias). Ed. Renato Laurenti. Piccola biblioteca filosofica 46; Bari: Laterza, 1969.

Pliny: Letters, Panegyricus. Trans. B. Radice. 2 vols. LCL. Cambridge, MA: Harvard: London: Heinemann, 1969.

Plutarch's Lives. Trans. B. Perrin. 11 vols. LCL. Cambridge: Harvard; London: Heinemann, 1914–26.

Plutarch's Moralia. Trans. Frank Cole Babbit, W. C. Helmbold, et al. 15 vols. LCL. Cambridge, MA: Harvard; London: Heinemann, 1927–69.

Poetae Melici Graeci. Ed. D. L. Page. Oxford, Clarendon, 1962.

Πράξεις Παύλου. *Acta Pauli nach dem Papyrus der Hamburger Staats- und Universitäts-Bibliothek.* Ed. Carl Schmidt and Wilhelm Schubart. Glückstadt and Hamburg: J. J. Augustine, 1936.

Préfaces de la Bible latine. Ed. Donatien de Bruyne. Namur: Godenne, 1920.

Propertius. Elegies. Ed. and trans. G. P. Goold. LCL. Cambridge, MA: Harvard; and London: Heinemann, 1990.

The Institutio Oratoria of Quintilian. Trans. Harold E. Butler. LCL. 4 vols. New York: Putnam's Sons; London: Heinemann, 1921–22.

Rhetores Graeci. Ed. C. Walz. 9 vols. Stuttgart and Tübingen: Cotta, 1832–36.

Sammelbuch Griechischer Urkunden aus Ägypten I, II, III. Ed. F. Preisigke. Strassburg and Berlin: Trübner, 1915–27.

Select Papyri. Ed. A. S. Hunt and E. E. Edgar. LCL. 2 vols. New York: Putnam's Sons; London: Heinemann, 1932, 1934.

The Elder Seneca: Controversiae, Suasoriae. Trans. Michael Winterbottom. 2 vols. LCL. Cambridge, MA: Harvard; London: Heinemann, 1974.

Seneca: Ad Lucilium Epistulae Morales. Trans. R. M. Gummere. 3 vols. LCL. New York: Putnam's Sons; Cambridge: Harvard; London: Heinemann, 1918–25. Rev. edn. 1943, 1953.

Seneca: Moral Essays. Trans. J. W. Basore. 3 vols. LCL. New York: Putnam's Sons; Cambridge: Harvard; London: Heinemann, 1928–35.

172   Bibliography

L. *Annaei Senecae Ad Lucilium Epistulae Morales*. Ed. L. D. Reynolds. OCT. 2 vols. Oxford: Clarendon, 1965.
Septuaginta. Ed. A. Ralphs. Stuttgart: Deutsche Bibelgesellschaft, 1935.
Sextus Empiricus. Trans. Robert G. Bury. LCL. 4 vols. New York: Putnam's Sons; London: Heinemann; Cambridge, MA: Harvard, 1933–49.
Statius. 2 vols. Trans. J. H. Mozley. LCL. Cambridge, MA: Harvard; London: Heinemann, 1928.
Greek Lyric III: Stesichorus, Ibycus, Simonides and Others. Trans. David A. Campbell. LCL. Cambridge, MA: Harvard; London: Heinemann, 1991.
Johannis Stobaei Anthologium. Ed. Curt Wachsmuth and Otto Hense. 5 vols. Berlin: Weidmann, 1884–1912. Reprint, 1958.
Stoicorum Veterum Fragmenta. Ed. Hans F. A. von Arnim. 4 vols. Leipzig: Teubner, 1905–24.
Georgius Syncellus. Chronographia. In *Corpus Scriptorum Historiae Byzantinae*. Vol. XII. Ed. W. Dindorf. Bonn: Weber, 1828.
   Ecloga Chronographica. Ed. A. A. Mosshammer. BT. Stuttgart: Teubner, 1984.
Teles (The Cynic Teacher). Ed. and trans. E. N. O'Neil. SBLTT 11. Missoula, MT: Scholars Press, 1977.
Teletis Reliquiae. Ed. Otto Hense. 2nd edn. Tübingen: Mohr (Siebeck) 1909.
Quinti Septimii Florentis Tertulliani Ad Martyres. PL 1.691–700.
The Testaments of the Twelve Patriarchs. Ed. M. de Jonge. Leiden: Brill, 1978.
Themistii Orationes. Ed. H. Schenkl, G. Downey, A. F. Norman. 3 vols. BT. Leipzig: Teubner, 1965–74.
Thucydides. Trans. Charles Forster Smith. 4 vols. LCL. Cambridge, MA: Harvard; London: Heinemann, 1919–23.
Tragicorum Graecorum Fragmenta. Ed. B. Snell and S. Radt. 4 vols. Göttingen: Vandenhoeck & Ruprecht, 1971–77.
Vetus Latina: Die Reste der altlateinischen Bibel. Ed. Hermann Josef Frede, et al. Freiburg: Herder, 1966–71.
Virgil. Trans. H. R. Faircloud. 2 vols. LCL. Cambridge, MA: Harvard; London: Heinemann, 1918. Rev. edn. 1934.
Xenophon. Trans. C. L. Brownson, O. J. Todd, et al. 7 vols. LCL. Cambridge, MA: Harvard; London: Heinemann, 1918–25.

Commentaries on Philippians

Barth, G. *Der Brief an die Philipper*. ZBK. Zurich: Theologischer Verlag, 1979.
Barth, Karl. *Erklärung des Philipperbriefes*. Munich: Kaiser, 1928. 4th edn. Munich: Kaiser, 1943.
Beare, F. W. *A Commentary on the Epistle to the Philippians*. 3rd edn. Black's New Testament Commentaries. London: A. & C. Black, 1976 [1959].
Bengel, J. A. "In Epistolam ad Philippenses." In *Gnomon Novi Testamenti*. 3rd edn., 765–82. Stuttgart: J. F. Steinkopf, 1860 [1773].

Bonnard, Pierre. *L'épître de Saint Paul aux Philippiens et l'épître aux Colossiens*. CNT, vol. 10. Neuchâtel and Paris: Delachaux et Niestlé, 1950.

Bruce, F. F. *Philippians*. GNC. San Francisco: Harper & Row, 1983.

Caird, G. B. *Paul's Letters from Prison*. Oxford: Oxford University Press, 1976.

Chrysostom, John. *In Epistolam ad Philippenses commentarius*. PG 62:177–298. ET: *Nicene and Post-Nicene Fathers*, vol. XIII, 181–255. New York: The Christian Literature Company, 1894.

Collange, Jean-François. *L'épître de Saint Paul aux Philippiens*. Neuchâtel: Delachaux et Niestlé, 1973.

de Wette, W. M. L. *Kurze Erklärung der Briefe an die Kolosser, an Philemon, an die Epheser und Philipper*. 2nd edn. Leipzig: Weidmann, 1847.

Dibelius, Martin. *An die Thessalonischer I–II; An die Philipper*. HNT 2/11. Tübingen: Mohr (Siebeck), 1937.

Ewald, P. and E. Wohlenberg. *Der Brief des Paulus an die Philipper*. Leipzig: Deichert, 1917.

Fee, Gordon D. *Paul's Letter to the Philippians*. Grand Rapids: Eerdmanns, 1995.

Fitzmyer, J. A. "The Letter to the Philippians." In *The Jerome Biblical Commentary*, edited by R. E. Brown, J. A. Fitzmyer, and R. E. Murphy, II.247–53. Englewood Cliffs, NJ: Prentice Hall, 1968.

Friedrich, Gerhard. *Der Brief an die Philipper*. 15th edn. NTD 8. Göttingen: Vandenhoeck & Ruprecht, 1965.

Gnilka, J. *Der Philipperbrief*. HTKNT 10:3. Freiburg: Herder, 1968.

Hawthorne, Gerald F. *Philippians*. Word Biblical Commentary. Waco: Word Books, 1987.

Hofmann, Johann Christian Konrad von. *Die Heilige Schrift des N. T. zusammenhängend untersucht*, vol. IV.3: Der Brief Pauli an die Philipper. 8th edn. Nördlingen: Beck, 1872.

Houlden, J. L. *Paul's Letters from Prison: Philippians, Colossians, Philemon, and Ephesians*. WPC. Philadelphia: Westminster, 1977.

Jerome. *Commentarius in Epistolam ad Philippenses*. PL 30:841–52.

Jones, Maurice. *The Epistle to the Philippians*. Westminster Commentaries. London: Methuen, 1918.

Lightfoot, J. B. *St. Paul's Epistle to the Philippians*. 4th edn. London: Macmillan, 1903.

Lohmeyer, Ernst *Der Brief an die Philipper, an die Kolosser und an Philemon*. Ed. W. Schmauch. MeyerK 9/8. Göttingen: Vandenhoeck & Ruprecht, 1928–30.

Marius Victorinus. *Marius Victorinus. Commentarii in Epistulas Pauli ad Galatas ad Philippenses ad Ephesios*. Ed. Albrecht Locher. BT. Leipzig: Teubner, 1972.

Martin, Ralph *Philippians*. NCBC. London: Marshall, Morgan & Scott, 1976; Grand Rapids: Eerdmanns, 1980.

Meyer, H. A. W. *Kritisch-exegetisches Handbuch über die Briefe Pauli an die Philipper, Kolosser und Philemon*. 4th edn. Göttingen: Vandenhoeck & Ruprecht, 1874.

Michaelis, W. *Der Brief des Paulus an die Philipper*. THNT. Leipzig: Deichert, 1935.

Müller, Ulrich B. *Der Brief des Paulus an die Philipper*. THKNT 11/1. Leipzig: Evangelische Verlagsanstalt, 1993.

O'Brien, Peter T. *The Epistle to the Philippians: A Commentary on the Greek Text*. NIGTC. Grand Rapids: Eerdmans, 1991.

Rabanus Maurus. *Enarrationum in Epistolas Beati Pauli*. PL 111.1273–112.834.

Schenk, Wolfgang. *Die Philipperbriefe des Paulus: Kommentar*. Stuttgart: Kohlhammer, 1984.

Theodore of Mopsuestia. *In Epistolam B. Pauli ad Philippenses*. In *Theodori Episcopi Mopsuesteni in Epistolas B. Pauli Commentarii: The Latin Version with the Greek Fragments*, 197–252. Edited with introduction, notes, and indices by H. B. Swete. Cambridge: At the University Press, 1880.

Theodoret. *Interpretatio Epistolae ad Philippenses*. *PG* 82:557–590.

Theophylact. *Commentarius in Epistolam ad Philippenses*. *PG* 124:1139–1204.

van Hengel, W. A. *Commentarius Perpetuus in Epistolam Pauli Ad Philippenses*. Amsterdam: Luchtmans & Müller, 1838.

Vincent, M. R. *A Critical and Exegetical Commentary on the Epistles to the Philippians and to Philemon*. ICC. Edinburgh: T. & T. Clark, 1897.

Weiss, Bernhard. *Der Philipper-Brief ausgelegt und die Geschichte seiner Auslegung kritisch dargestellt*. Berlin: Herz, 1859.

Other Pauline and related studies

Ahern, B. M. "The Fellowship of His Sufferings (Phil 3,10)." *CBQ* 22 (1960) 1–32.

Alexander, Loveday. "Hellenistic Letter-Forms and the Structure of Philippians." *JSNT* 37 (1989) 87–101.

Anger, Rudolf. *Über den Laodicenerbrief. Eine biblisch-kritische Untersuchung*. Leipzig: Gebhardt & Reisland, 1843.

Arzt, Peter. "The 'Epistolary Introductory Thanksgiving' in the Papyri and in Paul." *NovT* 36.1 (1994) 29–46.

Aspan, P. F. "Toward a New Reading of Paul's Letter to the Philippians in Light of a Kuhnian Analysis of New Testament Criticism." Ph.D. diss. Vanderbilt, 1990.

Bahr, Gordon J. "Subscriptions in the Pauline Letters." *JBL* 87 (1968) 21–47.

Bassler, Jouette M., ed. *Pauline Theology*, vol. I: *Thessalonians, Philippians, Galatians, Philemon*. Minneapolis: Augsburg Fortress, 1991.

Bauer, Walter. *Die apostolischen Väter*, vol. II: *Die Briefe des Ignatius von Antiochien und der Polykarpbrief*. HNT 18. Tübingen: Mohr (Siebeck), 1920.

Berry, Ken L. "The Function of Friendship Language in Philippians 4:10–20." In *Friendship*, edited by John T. Fitzgerald, 107–24.

Betz, Hans. D. *Galatians: A Commentary on Paul's Letter to the Churches in Galatia*. Hermeneia. Philadelphia: Fortress Press, 1979.

Bjerkelund, C. J. *Parakalô: Form, Funktion und Sinn der Parakalô-Satze in den paulinischen Briefe*. Bibliotheca Theologica Norvegica 1. Oslo: Universitetsforlaget, 1967.

Black, D. A. "The Discourse Structure of Philippians: A Study in Text Linguistics." *NovT* 37 (1995) 16–49.

Boers, Hendricus. "Form-Critical Study of Paul's Letters: I Thessalonians as a Case Study." *NTS* 22 (1976) 140–58.

Bonhöffer, Adolf F. *Epictet und die Stoa: Untersuchungen zur stoischen Philosophie*. Stuttgart: Enke, 1890.

Die Ethik des Stoikers Epictet. Stuttgart: Enke, 1894.

Epictet und das Neue Testament. Religionsgeschichtliche Versuche und Vorarbeiten 10. Giessen: Töpelmann, 1911.

Bormann, Lukas. *Philippi. Stadt und Christengemeinde zur Zeit des Paulus*. NovTSup 78. Leiden: Brill, 1995.

Bornkamm, Günther. "Der Philipperbrief als paulinische Briefsammlung." In *Neotestamentica et Patristica: Eine Freundesgabe Herrn Professor Dr. Oscar Cullmann*, 192–202. NovTsup 6. Leiden: Brill, 1962.

Paul. New York: Harper & Row, 1971.

Bruce, F. F. "St. Paul in Macedonia. 3. The Philippian Correspondence." *BJRL* 63 (1981) 260–84.

Bruston, C. "De quelques passages obscurs de l'épître aux Philippiens." *RThPh* 42 (1909) 196–228.

Bruyne, Donatien de. *Préfaces de la Bible latine*. Namur: Godenne, 1920.

Buchanan, C. O. "Epaphroditus' Sickness and the Letter to the Philippians." *EvQ* 36 (1964) 157–66.

Capper, Brian J. "Paul's Dispute with Philippi: Understanding Paul's Argument in Phil 1–2 from His Thanks in 4.10–20." *ThZ* 49 (1993) 193–214.

Chapa, Juan. "Consolatory Patterns? 1 Thes 4,13.18; 5,11." In *The Thessalonian Correspondence*, edited by Raymond F. Collins, 220–8. BETL 87; Leuven: Leuven University Press, 1990.

Cook, David. "Stephanus Le Moyne and the Dissection of Philippians." *JTS* 32 (1981) 138–42.

Culpepper, Alan. "Co-Workers In Suffering: Philippians 2:19–30." *RevExp* 72 (1980) 349–58.

Dahl, Nils A. "Euodia and Syntyche and Paul's Letter to the Philippians." In *The Social World of the First Christians: Essays in Honor of Wayne Meeks*, edited by L. Michael White and O. Larry Yarbrough, 3–15. Minneapolis: Augsburg Fortress, 1995.

Dalton, William J. "The Integrity of Philippians." *Bib* 60 (1979) 97–102.

Deissmann, Adolf. *Licht vom Osten: Das Neue Testament und die neuentdeckten Texte der hellenistisch-römischen Welt*. 4th edn. Tübingen: Mohr (Siebeck), 1923.

Dormeyer, Detlev. "The Implicit and Explicit Reader and the Genre of Philippians 3:2–4:3, 8–9: Response to the Commentary of Wolfgang Schenk." In *Semeia 48: Reader Perspectives on the New Testament*, edited by E. V. McKnight, 147–59. Atlanta: Scholars Press, 1989.

Doty, W. G. *Letters in Primitive Christianity*. Philadelphia: Fortress, 1973.

Droge, Arthur J. "*Mori Lucrum*: Paul and Ancient Theories of Suicide." *NovT* 33 (1988) 268–86.

Droge, Arthur J. and James D. Tabor. *A Noble Death: Suicide and Martyrdom among Christians and Jews in Antiquity.* San Francisco: Harper, 1992.

Ellis, E. E. "Paul and his Opponents." In *Christianity, Judaism and Other Greco-Roman Cults. Studies for Morton Smith at Sixty. Part I: New Testament,* edited by J. Neusner, 268–98. Leiden: Brill, 1975.

Engberg-Pedersen, Troels. "Stoicism in Philippians." In *Paul in His Hellenistic Context,* edited by Troels Engberg-Pedersen, 256–90. Minneapolis: Fortress, 1995.

Fascher, E. "Briefliteratur, urchristliche, formgeschichtlich." *RGG* I.1412–15 (1957).

Fitzgerald, John T. *Cracks in an Earthen Vessel: An Examination of the Catalogues of Hardships in the Corinthian Correspondence.* SBLDS 99. Atlanta: Scholars Press, 1988.

"Philippians, Epistle to the." *ABD* V.218–26 (1992).

"Philippians in the Light of Some Ancient Discussions of Friendship." In *Friendship,* edited by John T. Fitzgerald, 141–60.

Fitzgerald, John T., ed. *Friendship, Flattery, and Frankness of Speech: Studies on Friendship in the New Testament World.* NovTSup 82. Leiden, Brill, 1996.

Fitzmyer, Joseph. "New Testament Epistles." In *The Jerome Biblical Commentary,* edited by Raymond E. Brown, et al., II. 223–36. Englewood Cliffs, NJ: Prentice-Hall, 1968.

"'To Know Him and the Power of His Resurrection' (Phil 3.10)." In *Mélanges bibliques en hommage au R. P. Béda Rigaux,* edited by A. Descamps and A. de Halleux, 411–25. Gembloux: Duculot, 1970.

Flanagan, Neal. "A Note on Philippians 3:20–21." *CBQ* 18 (1956) 8–9.

Forestell, J. T. "Christian Perfection and Gnosis in Philippians 3,7–16." *CBQ* 18 (1956) 123–36.

Funk, Robert. *Language Hermeneutic and Word of God: The Problem of Language in the New Testament and Contemporary Theology.* New York: Harper & Row, 1966.

"The Apostolic Parousia: Form and Significance." In *Christian History and Interpretation: Studies Presented to John Knox,* edited by W. R. Farmer, C. D. F. Moule, and R. R. Niebuhr, 249–68. Cambridge: Cambridge University Press, 1967.

Furnish, Victor. "The Place and Purpose of Philippians III." *NTS* 10 (1963–64) 80–8.

Gamble, Harry, Jr. *The Textual History of the Letter to the Romans.* Grand Rapids: Eerdmans, 1997.

Garland, David. "The Composition and Unity of Philippians: Some Neglected Literary Factors." *NovT* 27 (1985) 141–73.

Gärtner, B. "The Pauline and the Johannine Idea of 'to know God' against the Hellenistic Background." *NTS* 14 (1967–68) 209–31.

Gnilka, Joachim. "Die antipaulinische Mission in Philippi." *BZ* 9 (1965) 258–76.

Goodspeed, Edgar J. *An Introduction to the New Testament*. Chicago: University of Chicago Press, 1937.

Problems of New Testament Translation. Chicago: University of Chicago Press, 1945.

Grayston, K. "The Opponents in Philippians 3." *ExpTim* 97 (1986) 170–2.

Griffin, Miriam. *Seneca. A Philosopher in Politics*. Oxford: Clarendon, 1976.

Gundry, R. H. *Sôma in Biblical Theology with Emphasis on Pauline Anthropology*. SNTSMS 29. Cambridge: Cambridge University Press, 1976.

Güttgemanns, Erhardt. *Der leidende Apostel und sein Herr: Studien zur paulinischen Christologie*. Göttingen: Vandenhoeck & Ruprecht, 1996.

Haenchen, Ernst. *The Acts of the Apostles: A Commentary*. 14th edn. Philadelphia: Westminster, 1971.

Harder, Günther. *Paulus und das Gebet*. NTF 1/10. Gütersloh: Bertelsmann, 1936.

Harnack, Adolf von. *Marcion: Das Evangelium vom fremden Gott*. Darmstadt: Wissenschaftliche Buchgesellschaft, 1960. Reprint of 2nd edn., 1924.

Hawthorne, Gerald. "The Imitation of Christ: Discipleship in Philippians." In *Patterns of Discipleship in the New Testament*, edited by Richard N. Longenecker, 163–79. Grand Rapids: Eerdmans, 1996.

Holladay, R. C. "Paul's Opponents in Philippians 3." *RestQ* 12 (1969) 77–90.

Holloway, Paul A. "*Bona Cogitare*: An Epicurean Consolation in Phil 4:8–9." *HTR* 91 (1998) 89–96.

"The Apocryphal *Epistle to the Laodiceans* and the Partitioning of Philippians." *HTR* 91 (1998) 321–5.

Hooker, Morna. "Philippians 2:6–11." In *Jesus und Paulus, Festschrift für Werner Georg Kümmel zum 70. Geburtstag*, 2nd edn., edited by E. E. Ellis and E. Grässer, 151–64. Göttingen: Vandenhoeck & Ruprecht, 1978.

Jaquette, James L. "Paul, Epictetus and Others on Indifference to Status." *CBQ* 56 (1994) 68–80.

"A Not-So-Noble Death: Figured Speech, Friendship and Suicide in Philippians 1:21–26." *Neot* 28 (1994) 177–92.

Discerning What Counts: The Function of the Adiaphora Topos in Paul's Letters. SBLDS 146. Atlanta: Scholars Press, 1995.

"Life and Death, *Adiaphora*, and Paul's Rhetorical Strategies." *NovT* 38 (1996) 30–54.

Jewett, Robert. "The Epistolary Thanksgiving and the Integrity of Philippians." *NovT* 12 (1970) 40–53.

"Conflicting Movements in the Early Church as Reflected in Philippians." *NovT* 12 (1970) 362–90.

Käsemann, Ernst. "Kritische Analyse von Phil. 2,5–11." *ZThK* 47 (1950) 313–60. In *idem, Exegetische Versuche und Besinnung*. Göttingen: Vandenhoeck & Ruprecht, 1960. ET "A Critical Analysis of Philippians 2:5–11." In *God and Christ: Existence and Providence*, edited by Robert Funk, 45–88. New York: Harper & Row, 1968.

Kennedy, H. A. A. "The Financial Colouring of Phil. iv, 15–18." *ExpT* 12 (1900–01) 43–4.

Kilpatrick, G. D. "ΒΛΕΠΕΤΕ in Phil 3:2." In *In Memoriam P. Kahle*, edited by M. Black and G. Fohrer, 146–8. BZAW 103; Berlin: Töpelmann, 1968.

Klijn, A. F. J. "Paul's Opponents in Philippians iii." *NovT* 7 (1965) 278–84.

Koester, Helmut. "The Purpose of the Polemic of a Pauline Fragment (Philippians III)." *NTS* 8 (1961–62) 317–32.

Koperski, V. "The Early History of the Dissection of Philippians." *JTS* 44 (1993) 599–603.

Koskenniemi, Heikki. *Studien zur Idee und Phraseologie des griechischen Briefes Bis 400 n. Chr.* Helsinki: Kirjakauppa; Wiesbaden: Harrassowitz, 1956.

Lake, Kirsopp. "Critical Problems of the Epistle to the Philippians," *The Expositor* 8/7 (1914) 481–93.

Lietzmann, Hans. *An die Römer.* 4th edn. HNT 8. Tübingen: Mohr (Siebeck), 1933.

Lightfoot, J. B. *St. Paul's Epistle to the Colossians and to Philemon.* London: Macmillan, 1892.

Lincoln, Andrew T. *Paradise Now and Not Yet.* SNTSMS 43. Cambridge: Cambridge University Press, 1981.

Lohmeyer, Ernst. *Kyrios Jesus: Eine Untersuchung zu Phil. 2,5–11.* 2nd edn. Heidelberg: Carl Winter, 1961.

Lohse, Eduard. *Colossians and Philemon: A Commentary on the Epistles to the Colossians and Philemon*, translated by William R. Poehlman and Robert J. Karris, edited by Helmut Koester. Hermeneia. Philadelphia: Fortress, 1971.

Luter, A. B. and M. V. Lee, "Philippians as Chiasmus: Key to the Structure, Unity and Theme Questions." *NTS* 41 (1995) 89–101.

Mackay, B. S. "Further Thoughts on Philippians." *NTS* 7 (1961) 161–70.

Malherbe, Abraham J. "Exhortation in I Thessalonians." *NovT* 25 (1983) 254–6. Reprinted in *idem, Paul and the Popular Philosophers*, 49–66. Minneapolis: Fortress, 1989.

Paul and the Thessalonians, Philadelphia: Fortress, 1987.

"Hellenistic Moralists and the New Testament." *ANRW* II.26.1.267–333 (1992).

"Paul's Self-Sufficiency (Philippians 4:11)." In *Friendship*, edited by John T. Fitzgerald, 125–39.

"Conversion to Paul's Gospel." In *The Early Church in Its Context: Essays in Honor of Everett Ferguson*, edited by Abraham J. Malherbe, Frederick W. Norris, and James W. Thompson, 230–44. NovTSup 90. Leiden: Brill, 1998.

Marshall, Peter. *Enmity at Corinth: Social Conventions in Paul's Relationship with the Corinthians.* WUNT 2/23. Tübingen: Mohr (Siebeck), 1987.

Martin, Ralph. *Carmen Christi: Philippians ii.5–11 in Recent Interpretation and in the Setting of Early Christian Worship.* SNTSMS 4. Cambridge: Cambridge University Press, 1967. Rev. edn., Grand Rapids: Eerdmans, 1983.

Marxsen, W. *Introduction to the New Testament: An Approach to Its Problems*. Trans. G. Buswell. Oxford: Blackwell, 1968.

Meeks, Wayne A. "The Man from Heaven in Philippians." In *The Future of Early Christianity: Essays in Honor of Helmut Koester*, edited by Birger A. Pearson, 329–36. Minneapolis: Fortress, 1991.

Metzger, Bruce. *The Canon of the New Testament*. Oxford: Clarendon, 1987.

Michaelis, W. πάθημα. *TDNT* V.932 (1967).

Müller-Bardoff, J. "Zur Frage der literarischen Einheit des Philipperbriefes." *WZJena* 7 (1957–58) 591–604.

Mullins, Terence Y. "Disclosure: A Literary Form in the New Testament." *NovT* 7 (1964) 44–50.

"Formulas in the New Testament Epistles." *JBL* 91 (1972) 386–8.

"Visit Talk in New Testament Letters." *CBQ* 35 (1973) 350–8.

Niebuhr, Reinhold. *An Interpretation of Christian Ethics*. San Francisco: Harper & Row, 1963.

O'Brien, Peter T. "Thanksgiving and the Gospel in Paul." *NTS* 21 (1974) 144–55.

Introductory Thanksgivings in the Letters of Paul. NovTSup 49. Leiden: Brill, 1977.

Otto, Randall. "'If Possible I May Attain the Resurrection from the Dead' (Philippians 3:11)." *CBQ* 57 (1995) 324–40.

Perkins, Pheme. "Philippians: Theology for the Heavenly Politeuma." In *Pauline Theology*, vol. I, edited by Jouette M. Bassler, 89–104.

Peterlin, Davorin. *Paul's Letter to the Philippians in Light of the Disunity in the Church*. NovTSup 79. Leiden: Brill, 1995.

Peterman, Gerald W. "'Thankless Thanks': The Epistolary and Social Convention in Philippians 4:10–20." *TynB* 42 (1991) 261–70.

Paul's Gift from Philippi: Conventions of Gift-Exchange and Christian Giving. SNTSMS 92. Cambridge: Cambridge University Press, 1997.

Pfitzner, Victor C. *Paul and the Agon Motif. Traditional Athletic Imagery in the Pauline Letters*. NovTSup 16; Leiden: Brill, 1967.

Pilhofer, Peter. *Philippi*, vol. I: *Die erste christliche Gemeinde Europas*. WUNT 87. Tübingen: Mohr (Siebeck), 1995.

Pink, Karl. "Die pseudo-paulinischen Briefe II." *Bib* 6 (1925) 179–200.

Pollard, T. E. "The Integrity of Philippians." *NTS* 13 (1967) 56–66.

Rahtjen, B. D. "The Three Letters of Paul to the Philippians." *NTS* (1959–60) 167–73.

Reed, Jeffrey T. "Are Paul's Thanksgivings 'Epistolary'?" *JSNT* 61 (1996) 87–99.

Reumann, John H. P. "Philippians 3:20–21 – A Hymnic Fragment? *NTS* 30 (1984) 593–609.

"Philippians, Especially Chapter 4, as a 'Letter of Friendship': Observations on a Checkered History of Scholarship." In *Friendship*, edited by Fitzgerald, 83–106.

Robinson, James M. "The Historicality of Biblical Language." In *The Old Testament and Christian Faith*, edited by Bernhard W. Anderson, 124–58. New York: Harper & Row, 1963.

"Die Hodajot-Formel in Gebet und Hymnus des Frühchristentums." In

Apophoreta: Festschrift für Ernst Haenchen, edited by W. Eltester and F. H. Kettler, 194–235. BZNW 30. Berlin: Töpelmann, 1964.

Rolland, P. "La structure littéraire et l'unité de l'épître aux Philippiens." *RevSR* 64 (1990) 213–16.

Roller, Otto. *Das Formular der paulinischen Briefe.* BWANT 4/6. Stuttgart: Kohlhammer, 1933.

Russell, D. A. "Letters to Lucilius." In *Seneca*, edited by C. D. N. Costa, 70–95. London: Routledge, 1974.

Russell, R. "Pauline Letter Structure in Philippians." *JETS* 25 (1982) 295–306.

Ste Croix, G. E. M. de and A. N. Sherwin-White, "Why Were the Early Christians Persecuted? – An Amendment." *Past and Present* 27 (1964) 23–33.

Sampley, J. Paul. *Pauline Partnership in Christ.* Philadelphia: Fortress, 1980.

   Walking Between the Times: Paul's Moral Reasoning. Minneapolis: Fortress, 1991.

Sanders, E. P. "Paul on the Law, His Opponents, and the Jewish People." In *Anti-Judaism in Early Christianity*, vol. I: *Paul and the Gospels*, edited by Peter Richardson and David Granskou, 75–90. Studies in Judaism and Christianity 2; Waterloo, Ontario: Wilfrid Launer University, 1986.

Sanders, Jack T. "The Transition from Opening Epistolary Thanksgiving to Body in the Letters of the Pauline Corpus." *JBL* 81 (1962) 348–62.

Schmithals, Walter. "Die Irrlehrer des Philipperbriefes," *ZTK* 54 (1957) 297–341. Revised version in *Paulus und die Gnostiker*, 47–87. TF 35. Hamburg-Bergstedt: Herbert Reich, 1965. ET, "The False Teachers of the Epistle to the Philippians." In *idem, Paul and the Gnostics*, 65–122. Nashville: Abingdon, 1972.

Schneemelcher, Wilhelm. "The Epistle to the Laodiceans." *NTApoc* II.42–6 (1992).

Schubert, Paul. *Form and Function of the Pauline Thanksgivings.* BZNW 20. Berlin: Töpelmann, 1939.

Sellew, Philipp. "*Laodiceans* and the Philippians Fragments Hypothesis." *HTR* 87 (1994) 17–28.

   "*Laodiceans* and Philippians Revisited: A Response to Paul Holloway." *HTR* 91 (1998) 327–9.

Sevenster, J.N. *Paul and Seneca.* Trans. H. Meyer. NovTSup 4; Leiden: Brill, 1961.

Siber, Peter. *Mit Christus leben: Eine Studie zur paulinischen Auferstehungshoffnung.* ATANT 61; Zurich: Theologischer Verlag, 1971.

Souter, A. *The Text and Canon of the New Testament.* Revised by C. S. C. Williams. London: Duckworth, 1954.

Spicq, C. *Agapè dans le Nouveau Testament.* 3 vols. Paris: Gabalda, 1959.

Stowers, Stanley. *Letter Writing in Greco-Roman Antiquity.* Philadelphia: Westminster, 1986.

   "Friends and Enemies in the Politics of Heaven: Reading Theology in Philippians." In *Pauline Theology*, vol. I, edited by Jouette M. Bassler, 105–21.

Steen, Henry A. "Les clichés épistolaires dans les lettres sur papyrus grècques." *C&M* I.119–76 (1938).

Tannehill, Robert C. *Dying and Rising with Christ: A Study in Pauline Theology*. BZNW 32; Berlin: Töpelmann, 1967.

Walter, Nicholas. "Die Philipper und das Leiden: Aus den Anfängen einer heidenchristlichen Gemeinde." In *Die Kirche des Anfangs: Festschrift für Heinz Schürmann zum 65. Geburtstag*, edited by Rudolf Schnackenburg et al., 417–33. Leipzig: St. Benno, 1977.

Wansink, Craig S. *Chained in Christ: The Experience and Rhetoric of Paul's Imprisonments*. JSNTSup 130. Sheffield: Sheffield Academic Press, 1996.

Watson, Duane F. "A Rhetorical Analysis of Philippians and the Implications for the Unity Question." *NovT* 30 (1988) 57–88.

Weima, Jeffrey A. D. *Neglected Endings: The Significance of the Pauline Letter Closings*. JSNTSS 101. Sheffield: JSOT Press, 1994.

Wendland, Paul. *Die urchristlichen Literaturformen*. HNT 1/3. Tübingen: Mohr (Siebeck), 1912.

Wettstein, Johann Jakob. *Novum Testamentum*. 2 vols. Amsterdam: Dommerian, 1752. Facsimile edn., Graz: Akademische Duuck-U. Verlangsanstalt, 1962.

White, John L. "Introductory Formulae in the Body of the Pauline Letter." *JBL* 90 (1971) 91–7.

Light from Ancient Letters. FFNT. Philadelphia: Fortress, 1986.

White, L. Michael. "Morality between Two Worlds: A Paradigm of Friendship in Philippians." In *Greeks, Romans, and Christians: Essays in Honor of Abraham J. Malherbe*, edited by D. L. Balch, E. Ferguson, and W. A. Meeks. 201–15. Minneapolis: Fortress, 1990.

Wick, Peter. *Der Philipperbrief: Der formale Aufbau des Briefs als Schlüssel zum Verständnis seines Inhalts*. BWANT 7/15 (= 135). Stuttgart: Kohlhammer, 1994.

Wilder, Amos. *The Language of the Gospel: Early Christian Rhetoric*. New York: Harper & Row, 1964.

Wiles, Gordon P. *Paul's Intercessory Prayers*. SNTSMS 24. Cambridge: Cambridge University Press, 1974.

Zahn, Theodor. *Introduction to the New Testament*. Trans. from the 3rd German edn. 3 vols. New York: Scribners, 1909.

Ancient consolation and related topics

Abel, Karlhans. *Bauformen in Senecas Dialogen. Fünf Strukturanalysen: dial. 6, 11, 12, 1 und 2*. Bibliothek der klassischen Altertumswissenschaften. N.F., 2. Reihe, Bd 18. Heidelberg: Winter, 1967.

Alexiou, M. *The Ritual Lament in Greek Tradition*. Cambridge: Cambridge University Press, 1974.

Atkinson, J. E. "Seneca's 'Consolatio ad Polybium.'" *ANRW* II.32.2.860–84 (1985).

Beyenka, M. M. *Consolation in Saint Augustine*. Catholic University of America Patristic Studies, 83. Washington, D.C.: Catholic University of America, 1950.

"Saint Augustine and the *Consolatio Mortis*." *CBull* 29 (1953) 25–8.

Buresch, Carl. "Consolationum a Graecis Romanisque scriptarum historia critica." *Leipziger Studien zur classischen Philologie* 9 (1886) 1–170.

Chapa, Juan. *Letters of Condolence in Greek Papyri.* Papyrologica Florentina 29; Florence: Gonnelli, 1998.

Dillon, John M. *The Middle Platonists: A Study in Platonism, 80 B.C. to A.D. 220.* London: Duckworth, 1977.

"*Metriopatheia* and *Apatheia*: Some Reflections on a Controversy in Later Greek Ethics." In *Essays in Ancient Philosophy II*, edited by John P. Anton and Anthony Preus, 508–17. Albany: SUNY, 1983.

Duval, Y.-M. "Formes profanes et formes bibliques dans les oraisons funèbres de saint Ambroise." In *Christianisme et formes littéraires de l'Antiquité tardive en occident*, edited by Alan Cameron and Manfred Fuhrman, 292–301. Foundation Hardt, Entretiens, 23; Geneva: Foundation Hardt, 1977.

Esteve-Forriol, José. *Die Trauer- und Trostgedichte in der römischen Literatur.* Munich: Schubert, 1962.

Evaristus, Mary. *The Consolations of Death in Ancient Greek Literature.* Washington: Catholic University Press, 1917.

Favez, Charles. *L. Annaei Senecae Dialogorum liber XII Ad Helviam matrem de consolatione, texte latin publié avec une introduction et un commentaire explicatif.* Lausanne and Paris: Payot, 1918.

"Le sentiment dans les consolations de Sénèque." *Mélanges Paul Thomas: recueil de mémoires concernant la philologie classique dédié à Paul Thomas*, 262–70. Bruges: Sainte Catherine, 1930.

La consolation latine chrétienne. Paris: J. Vrin, 1937.

"Les Epistulae 92, 259 et 263 de S. Augustin." *MH* I.65–8 (1944).

Fern, Mary E. *The Latin* Consolatio Mortis *as a Literary Type.* Saint Louis, MO; University of Saint Louis, 1941.

Forschner, Maximilian. *Die stoische Ethik: Über den Zusammenhang von Natur-, Sprach- und Moralphilosophie im altstoischen System.* Stuttgart: Klett-Cotta, 1981.

Frede, Michael. "The Stoic Doctrine of the Affections of the Soul." In *The Norms of Nature*, edited by Malcolm Schofield and Gisela Striker, 93–110.

Furley, David. "Nothing to us?" In *The Norms of Nature*, edited by Malcolm Schofield and Gisela Striker, 75–91.

Garland, R. *The Greek Way of Death.* London: Duckworth, 1985.

Gercke, Alfred. "De Consolationibus." *Tirocinium philologum sodalium Regii Seminarii Bonnensis*, 28–70. Berlin: Weidmann, 1883.

Giesecke, Alfred. *De philosophorum veterum quae de exilium spectant sententiis.* Leipzig: Teubner, 1891.

Gosling J. C. B. and C. C. W. Taylor, *The Greeks on Pleasure.* Oxford: Clarendon, 1982.

Grasmück, E. L. *Exilium: Untersuchungen zur Verbannung in der Antike.* Paderborn: Scöhningh, 1978.

Gregg, Robert. C. *Consolation Philosophy: Greek and Christian Paideia in Basil and the Two Gregories.* Patristic Monograph Series 3. Cambridge MA: Philadelphia Patristic Foundation, 1975.

Griessmair, E. *Das Motiv der Mors Immatura in den griechischen metrischen Grabinschriften*. Innsbruck: Universitätsverlag, 1966.

Grollios, Constantine. Τέχνη ἀλυπίας. κονοί τόποι τοῦ Πρὸς Πολύβιον τοῦ Σενέκα καὶ πηγαὶ αὐτῶν. Ἑλληνικά, παράρτημα 10. Thessaloniki; Athens: Christou & Son, 1956.

Seneca's Ad Marciam: Tradition and Originality. Athens: Christou, 1956.

Guignet, Marcel. *Les procédés épistolaires de Saint Grégoire de Nazianze*. Paris: Picard, 1911.

Guttilla, G. "Tematica cristiana e pagana nell'evoluzione finale della *consolatio* di san Girolamo." *ALCP* 17–18 (1980–81) 87–152.

"La fase iniziale della *consolatio* latina cristiana." *ALCP* 21–2 (1984–85) 108–215.

Hani, J. "*La consolation antique*." *REA* 75 (1973) 103–110.

Häsler, Berthold. *Favorin über die Verbannung*. Bottrop i.W.: Postberg, 1935.

Hosenfelder, M. "Epicurus: Hedonist malgré lui." In *The Norms of Nature: Studies in Hellenistic Ethics*, edited by M. Schofield and G. Striker, 245–63.

Hultin, N. "The Rhetoric of Consolation: Studies in the Development of the 'Consolatio Mortis.'" Ph.D. diss. Johns Hopkins, 1965.

Inwood, Brad. *Ethics and Human Action in Early Stoicism*. Oxford: Clarendon, 1985.

Irwin, T. H. "Conceptions of Happiness." In *The Norms of Nature*, edited by Malcolm Schofield and Gisela Striker, 205–44.

Johann, H. T. *Trauer und Trost: Eine quellen- und strukturanalytische Untersuchung der philosophischen Trostschriften über den Tod*. Studia et Testimonia Antiqua 5. Munich: Fink, 1968.

Kassel, Rudolf. *Untersuchungen zur griechischen und römischen Konsolationsliteratur*. Zetemata 18. Munich: Beck, 1958.

Kayser, F. *De Crantore academico dissertatio*. Heidelberg, 1841.

Kelly, J. N. D. *Golden Mouth: The Story of John Chrysostom: Ascetic, Preacher, Bishop*. Ithaca, NY: Cornell, 1995.

Kierdorf, Wilhelm. *Laudatio Funebris: Interpretation und Untersuchungen zur Entwicklung der römischen Leichenrede*. Beiträge zur klassischen Philologie 106. Meisenheim am Glan: Hain, 1980.

Kuiper, K. "De Crantoris fragmentis moralibus." *Mnemosyne* 29 (1901) 341–62.

Kumaniecki, K. "A propos de la 'Consolatio' perdue de Cicéron." *AFLA* 46 (1969) 369–402.

Kurth, Thomas. *Senecas Trostschrift an Polybius. Dialogue 11: Ein Kommentar*. Beiträge zur Altertumskunde 59. Stuttgart: Teubner, 1994.

Lattimore, Richmond. *Themes in Greek and Latin Epitaphs*. Illinois Studies in Language and Literature 28.1–2. Urbana: University of Illinois, 1942.

Lesses, Glenn. "Virtue and the Goods of Fortune in Stoic Moral Theory." *Oxford Studies in Ancient Philosophy* 7 (1989) 95–128.

Lier, B. "Topica carminum sepulcralium Latinorum." *Philologus* 62 (1903) 445–77, 563–603; 63 (1904) 54–65.

Logemann, J. C. "De defunctorum virtut. in carm. sepulcr. lat. laudatis." Ph.D. diss., Amsterdam, Rotterdam, 1916.

Long, Anthony A. and David N. Sedley, *The Hellenistic Philosophers*. 2 vols. Cambridge: Cambridge University Press, 1987.

Loraux, N. *L'invention d'Athènes: histoire de l'oraison funèbre dans la "cité classique."* Civilisations et sociétés 65. Paris: Mouton, 1981.

Lutz, Cora. "Musonius Rufus: The Roman Socrates." *YCS* 10 (1947).

Malunowiczówna, Leokadia. "Les éléments stoïciens dans la consolation grecque chrétienne." In *Studia Patristica, 13. Papers presented to the Sixth International Conference on Patristic Studies held in Oxford 1971, Part 2*, edited by E. A. Livingstone, 35–45. TU 116. Berlin: Akademie-Verlag, 1975.

Manning, C. E. "The Consolatory Tradition and Seneca's Attitude to the Emotions." *G&R* 21 (1974) 71–81.

On Seneca's "Ad Marciam." Mnemosyne Supplement 69. Leiden: Brill, 1981.

Meinel, Peter. *Seneca über seine Verbannung. Trostschrift an die Mutter Helvia.* Bonn: Habelt, 1972.

Mitchell, Jane F. "Consolatory Letters in Basil and Gregory Nazianzen." *Hermes* 96 (1968) 299–318.

Moles, J. L. "The Career and Conversion of Dio Chrysostom." *JHS* (1978) 79–100.

Montefiore, C. G. *Ancient Jewish and Greek Encouragement and Consolation.* Preface by S. D. Temkin. Bridgeport, Connecticut: Hartmore House, 1971.

Nisbet, R. G. M. and M. Hubbard, *A Commentary on Horace: Odes, Book I.* Oxford: Clarendon, 1970.

Polhenz, Max. "Das Dritte und Vierte Buch der Tusculanen." *Hermes* 41 (1906) 321–55.

Pohlenz, Max. "De Posidonii libris περὶ παθῶν." *Jahrb. für class. Philol.* Suppl. 24 (1989) 537–633.

Purdie, Albert B., ed. *Some Observations on Latin Verse Inscriptions.* London: Christophers, 1935.

Rabbow, Paul. *Seelenführung: Methodik der Exerzitien in der Antike.* Munich, Kösel-Verlag, 1954.

Rist, John M. "Pleasure: 360–300 B.C." *Phoenix* 28 (1974) 167–79.

Robinson, T. M. *Plato's Psychology.* PhoenSup 8. Toronto: University of Toronto, 1970.

Sandbach, F. H. *The Stoics.* New York: Norton, 1975.

Savon, H. "Une consolation imitée de Sénèque et de saint Cyprian (Pseudo-Jérôme, epistula 5 ad amicum aegrotum)." *RecAug* 14 (1979) 153–90.

Schaeffer, W. "Argumenta consolatoria: quae apud veteres Graecorum scriptores inveniuntur." Ph.D. diss., Göttingen, 1921 (*non vidi*).

Schmitz, Otto and Gustav Stählin. παρακαλέω, παράκλησις. *TDNT* V.788–93 (1967).

Schofield, Malcolm and Gisela Striker. *The Norms of Nature: Studies in Hellenistic Ethics.* Cambridge: Cambridge University Press, 1977.

Scourfield, J. H. D. *Consoling Heliodorus. A Commentary on Jerome*

"Letter 60." Oxford and New York: Clarendon Press and Oxford University Press, 1993.

Steinmetz, Peter. "Die Stoa." In *Grundriss der Geschichte der Philosophie*, vol. IV/2: *Die Philosophie der Antike: Die hellenistische Philosophie*, edited by Hellmut Flashar, 495–716. Basel: Schwabe, 1994.

Stork, Traudel. *Nil igitur mors est ad nos: Der Schlussteil des dritten Lukrezbuches und sein Verhältnis zur Konsolationsliteratur*. Bonn: Rudolf Habelt, 1970.

Tolman, Judson. *A Study of the Sepulchral Inscriptions in Buecheler's Carmina Epigraphica Latina*. Chicago: University of Chicago Press, 1910.

van der Horst, Pieter W. *Ancient Jewish Epitaphs: An Introductory Survey of a Millennium of Jewish Funerary Epigraphy (300 BCE–700CE)*. Contributions to Biblical Exegesis and Theology 2. Kampen: Kok Pharos, 1991.

van Geytenbeck, A. C. *Musonius Rufus and the Greek Diatribe*, rev. edn. Translated by B. L. Hijmans. Assen: Van Gorcum, 1962.

van Heusde, Andreas C. *Diatribe in locum philosophiae moralis qui est de consolatione apud Graecos*. Utrecht, 1840.

Vérilhac, A.-M. Παῖδες ἄωροι. *Poésie funébaire*, 2 vols. Athens: Athens' Academy Press, 1978–82.

Wallach, Barbara Price. *Lucretius and the Diatribe against the Fear of Death: De Rerum Natura III 830–1094*. Leiden: Brill, 1976.

Rhetoric and the "rhetorical situation"

Biesecker, Barbara A. "Rethinking the Rhetorical Situation from within the Thematic of *Différance*." *Philosophy and Rhetoric* 22 (1989) 110–30.

Bitzer, Lloyd. "The Rhetorical Situation." *Philosophy and Rhetoric* 1 (1968) 1–14. Reprinted in *Philosophy and Rhetoric*, Supplementary Issue (1992) 1–14.

"Functional Communication: A Situational Perspective." In *Rhetoric in Transition: Studies in the Nature and Uses of Rhetoric*, edited by Eugene White, 21–38. University Park and London: Pennsylvania State University, 1980.

Brinton, Alan. "Situation in the Theory of Rhetoric." *Philosophy and Rhetoric* 14 (1981) 234–48.

Burke, Kenneth. *Permanence and Change*. New York: Bobbs-Merrill, 1965.

Conley, T. "Philo's Use of *Topoi*." In *Two Treatises of Philo of Alexandria: A Commentary on De Gigantibus and Quod Deus Sit Immutabilis*, edited by David Winston and John Dillon, 171–8. Brown Judaic Studies 25; Chico, CA: Scholars Press, 1983.

Consigny, Scott. "Rhetoric and Its Situations." *Philosophy and Rhetoric* 7 (1974) 175–86.

Edelman, Murray. *Politics as Symbolic Action*. Chicago: Markham Publishing Co., 1977.

Gitay, Yehoshua. "Reflections on the Study of the Prophetic Discourse: The Question of Isaiah 1:1–20." *VT* 23 (1983) 206–21.

Grimaldi, William M. A. "The Aristotelian *Topics*." *Traditio* 14 (1958) 1–16. Reprinted in *Aristotle: The Classical Heritage of Rhetoric*, edited by Keith V. Erickson, 176–93. Metuchen, NJ: Scarecrow, 1974.

Hall Jamieson, Kathleen M. "Generic Constraints and the Rhetorical Situation." *Philosophy and Rhetoric* 6 (1973) 162–70.

Kennedy, George. *New Testament Interpretation through Rhetorical Criticism*. Chapel Hill: University of North Carolina Press, 1984.

Kirby, John T. "The Rhetorical Situations of Revelation 1–3." *NTS* 34 (1988) 197–207.

Larson, Richard L. "Lloyd Bitzer's 'Rhetorical Situation' and the Classification of Discourse: Problems and Implications." *Philosophy and Rhetoric* 3 (1970) 165–8.

McKeon, Richard. "Creativity and the Commonplace." *Philosophy and Rhetoric* 6 (1973) 199–210.

Martin, Joseph. *Antike Rhetorik*. Handbuch der Altertumswissenschaft 2.3. Munich: Beck, 1974.

Miller, Arthur B. "Rhetorical Exigence." *Philosophy and Rhetoric* 5 (1972) 111–18.

Ochs, Donovan J. "Aristotle's Concept of Formal Topics." *Speech Monographs* 36 (1969) 419–25.

Patton, J. H. "Causation and Creativity in Rhetorical Situations: Distinctions and Implications." *QJS* 65 (1979) 36–55.

Perelman Chaim and L. Olbrechts-Tyteca. *The New Rhetoric: A Treatise on Argumentation*. Translated by John Wilkinson and Purcel Weaver. Notre Dame and London: University of Notre Dame, 1969.

Pogoloff, Stephen Mark. "Isocrates and Contemporary Hermeneutics." In *Persuasive Artistry: Studies in New Testament Rhetoric in Honor of George A. Kennedy*, edited by Duane F. Watson, 338–62. JSNTSS 50. Sheffield: JSOT Press, 1991.

Logos and Sophia: The Rhetorical Situation of I Corinthians. SBLDS 134. Atlanta: Scholars Press, 1992.

Pomeroy, Ralph. "Fitness of Response in Bitzer's Concept of Rhetorical Discourse." *Georgia Speech Communication Journal* 4 (1972) 42–71.

Schoon-Janßen, Johannes. *Umstrittene "Apologien" in den Paulusbriefen: Studien zur rhetorischen Situation des 1. Thessalonischerbriefes, des Galaterbriefes und des Philipperbriefes*. GTA 45. Göttingen: Vandenhoeck & Ruprecht, 1991.

Schüssler-Fiorenza, Elizabeth. "Rhetorical Situation and Historical Reconstruction in I Corinthians." *NTS* 33 (1987) 386–403.

Snyman, Andreas H. "Style and the Rhetorical Situation of Romans 8.31–39." *NTS* 34 (1988) 218–31.

Stamps, Dennis L. "Rethinking the Rhetorical Situation: The Entextualization of the Situation in the New Testament Epistles." In *Rhetoric and the New Testament: Essays from the 1992 Heidelberg Conference*, edited by Stanley E. Porter and Thomas H. Olbricht, 193–210. JSNTSS 90. Sheffield: JSOT Press, 1993.

Thurén, Lauri. *The Rhetorical Strategy of 1 Peter*. Åbo: Åbo Akademis Förlag, 1990.

Tomkins, P. K., J. H. Patton, and L. F. Bitzer, "Tomkins on Patton and Bitzer; Patton on Tompkins; Bitzer on Tomkins (and Patton)." *QJS* 66 (1980) 85–93.

Vatz, Richard. "The Myth of the Rhetorical Situation." *Philosophy and Rhetoric* 6 (1973) 154–61.

Watson, Duane F. "A Rhetorical Analysis of Philippians and Its Implications for the Unity Question." *NovT* 30 (1988) 57–88.

Wichelns, Herbert A. "Some Differences between Literary Criticism and Rhetorical Criticism." In *Historical Studies of Rhetoric and Rhetoricians*, edited by Raymond F. Howes, 217–24. Ithaca, New York: Cornell University Press, 1961.

Wilkerson, K. E. "On Evaluating Theories of Rhetoric." *Philosophy and Rhetoric* 3 (1970) 82–96.

Wuellner, Wilhelm. "Where is Rhetorical Criticism Taking Us?" *CBQ* 49 (1987) 448–63.

INDEX OF MODERN AUTHORS

INDEX OF PASSAGES CITED

194   *Index of passages cited*